Mistaken Identity

Mistaken Identity

THE SUPREME COURT AND THE POLITICS OF MINORITY REPRESENTATION

Keith J. Bybee

PRINCETON UNIVERSITY PRESS

PRINCETON, NEW JERSEY

Library of Congress Cataloging-in-Publication Data

Bybee, Keith J., 1965–
Mistaken identity : the Supreme Court and the politics
of minority representation / Keith J. Bybee
p.   cm.
Includes bibliographical references and index.
1. Minorities — Suffrage — United States.   2. Proportional
representation — United States.   3. United States. Voting Rights Act
of 1965.   4. Representative government and representation — United
States.   5. Election districts — United States.   6. Political
questions and judicial power — United States.   I. Title.
KF4893.B93   1998
ISBN 0-691-01729-8 (cloth : alk. paper)
342.73'053 — dc21   97-51799   CIP

This book has been composed in Sabon

Princeton University Press books are printed on acid-free paper
and meet the guidelines for permanence and durability of the
Committee on Production Guidelines for Book Longevity of the
Council on Library Resources

http://pup.princeton.edu

Printed in the United States of America

1   2   3   4   5   6   7   8   9   10

TO MY PARENTS

Contents

Acknowledgments

THIS BOOK began as a dissertation at University of California, San Diego. The central members of my dissertation committee, Harry Hirsch, Tracy Strong, and Alan Houston, each provided me with invaluable guidance. Harry Hirsch played an especially important role in directing my work. His criticism was always crisp and to the point. (Early on, I gave him a two-part thesis proposal, which he characterized in three words: "impossible and derivative.") Harry backed his high standards with unwavering support, constantly encouraging me to hone my analysis and refine my arguments. I also developed my work by presenting papers at meetings of the American Political Science Association and the Western Political Science Association. I thank these audiences and in particular John Brigham and Mark Rush, who both read my work with care. None of this intellectual encouragement would have meant very much without the broader support of my fellow graduate students in the seminar room and on the soccer field. For their friendship from the very beginning, I thank Chris Nevitt, Lisa Reynolds, Frank Sposito, and Jennifer Wooddell.

At Harvard, I undertook the task of transforming my dissertation into a book. Along the way, I learned a great deal from conversations with Sam Beer, Peter Berkowitz, Jill Frank, Arthur Maass, Steve Macedo, Paul Peterson, and Michael Sandel. I also profited from discussions in the Law and Courts Study Group, organized by Shep Melnick, and from the comments of Melissa Williams, who read an early version of the entire manuscript. I received truly excellent research assistance from Ted Brader, Kim Pattillo, Aaron Rosenberg, and Phoebe Taubman. Finally, I was given critical insight into the deliberative process by the members of the Great Books Club: Matt Dickinson, Michael Hagen, Michael Jones-Correa, and Brad Palmquist.

At Princeton University Press, I have benefited from the efficiency and good humor of Malcolm Litchfield. The two reviews of my manuscript, by Jennifer Hochschild and an anonymous reader, were thoughtful, detailed, and highly constructive. In the end, this book may not live up to their recommendations, but it nonetheless has been improved by their efforts.

Throughout the whole of this project, my parents, my brothers Bruce

ACKNOWLEDGMENTS

and Greg, and my sister Lisa have given me a strong foundation on which to stand. I sometimes wondered whether I would ever finish this book; my family never entertained any such doubts. My wife Jennifer has recently joined this chorus of support, adding her voice to those who have done so much to maintain my sense of perspective. Thank you for sustaining me. I could not have done it alone.

Mistaken Identity

Introduction

[I]t is the reason, alone, of the public, that ought to control and regulate the government.
James Madison, 1788

[I]n our political system it is not at all easy to have a public discussion of voting rights, at least in the context of race. Sometimes it seems as if judgments about race are analogous to theological convictions. They are not movable. . . . The whole area is pervaded by accusations, mischaracterizations and strange dichotomies.
Cass Sunstein, 1994

FOR SEVERAL WEEKS in the spring of 1993, national news coverage was dominated by the controversy surrounding Lani Guinier. Nominated by President Clinton to head the Justice Department's Civil Rights Division, Guinier drew strong criticism for her writings on the Voting Rights Act of 1965. Conservatives claimed that Guinier held "breathtakingly radical" views that, if realized, would reconfigure our entire scheme of representative government. In particular, critics portrayed Guinier as a "quota queen" who wished to institute a "racial spoils system," directly assigning legislative seats to minorities under the guise of ensuring fair representation. Guinier's supporters denounced conservative claims as distortions and defended her views as well within the mainstream of voting-rights enforcement. President Clinton initially downplayed fears of Guinier's radical impact on voting-rights policy: "I expect the policy to be made by the United States Congress. And I expect the Justice Department to carry out that policy." Later, in the face of mounting opposition, Clinton changed his position, withdrawing Guinier's nomination on the grounds that her views on minority representation did not agree with his own.[1]

[1] Guinier's critics focused largely on Guinier 1991a and 1991b. But see also Guinier 1992a, 1992b, 1993a, 1993b, and 1994. My account of Guinier's nomination is drawn from the *Los Angeles Times*, 22 May 1993, p. A1; 3 June 1993, pp. A1, A10; 4 June 1993, pp. A1, A32, A33; 22 May 1993, p. A12; and 4 June 1993, p. A1.

The Guinier episode led many to draw lessons about the inability of the Clinton administration to read the political winds. As with his early nominations for attorney general, Clinton demonstrated a penchant for self-inflicted wounds by selecting an individual unacceptable to opposition politicians. But the Guinier controversy calls attention to more than the failings of the president's appointment process. The hue and cry surrounding Guinier reveal a high-stakes politics of representation. Setting aside for the moment the question of whether Guinier was fairly treated, the welter of conservative charges suggest that many political actors take the issue of fair minority representation to be quite important. The degree of political hyperbole in such claims should not, of course, be underestimated. Still, the fact is that academic analyses of minority representation echo the seriousness of conservative fears. As the authors of a comprehensive book on the subject conclude, the current politics of minority representation raises problems that are so "broad and fundamental as to require rethinking our entire system of representation."[2]

How can we begin to make sense of this controversial politics of minority representation? In attempting to defuse the debate over Guinier, President Clinton located the responsibility for resolving voting-rights questions in Congress. One could argue that the configuration of congressional politics must be grasped before the politics of minority representation can be understood. Congress does indeed appear to provide a reasonable starting place for analysis. The issues of minority representation crystallized with the passage of the Voting Rights Act of 1965. Moreover, during the past thirty years, Congress has amended the act on four occasions, importantly altering debates over the meaning of fair minority representation each time.[3]

Congress has not, however, been the sole locus of significant decision making in this area. Nor did the participants in the Guinier controversy take Congress to be the only relevant player. Guinier's hotly contested writings were, after all, works of advocacy designed to influence *judicial* interpretations of the Voting Rights Act. Her efforts to shape judicial reasoning placed Guinier on a well-worn path: much of the politics of

---

[2] Grofman, Handley, and Niemi 1992, p. 110.

[3] The congressional re-enactments and extensions have also implicated a number of political actors worth studying. In this vein, one could point not only to the civil rights groups that have often stimulated congressional action, but also to the Justice Department, which has acted as the administrative organ responsible for enforcing congressional policy.

4

minority representation has been contested in the courtroom and developed by judges.[4] The worry about Guinier was not simply that, as a member of the Justice Department, she would flout current congressional policy. Critics also feared that she would successfully sway judicial decision making, persuading the Supreme Court to enforce a particular reading of a complex, open-textured statute. While Congress may set the broad outlines of policy, the Guinier incident indicated that the judiciary itself may make a crucial difference in how the politics of minority representation is conceptualized and practiced.

The importance of judicial action was conveniently underscored a few weeks after the withdrawal of Guinier's nomination, as the Supreme Court set new limits for legislative districting in *Shaw v. Reno* (1993).[5] In this case, the Court considered a North Carolina congressional district drawn pursuant to the Voting Rights Act. The district followed the I-85 corridor for nearly 160 miles, connecting disparate African-American neighborhoods. At points, the district was no wider than I-85 itself, prompting one state legislator to remark, "If you drove down the interstate with both car doors open, you'd kill most of the people in the district."[6] It was also from this district that Melvin Watt, the first black member of Congress from North Carolina since Reconstruction, was elected.

Shaw was a close decision, with a five-member majority ruling that race-conscious redistricting could violate the Constitution. More specifically, the majority concluded that stringing together geographically separated members of the same race into a single district approached "political apartheid."[7] The majority viewed such districting as a state-sponsored assertion that all members of a racial group thought alike and had the same political interests. These harms of racial stereotyping were compounded by the pernicious message segregated districts sent to elected officials, encouraging them to represent the dominant racial group in their district rather than their constituency as a whole.

The Court did not rule that the district at issue in *Shaw* actually inflicted the harms of "political apartheid." But *Shaw* did establish a framework in which the congressional districts designed to enhance minority representation could be contested. Following the 1990 census, the number of congressional districts in which African Americans were

[4] Grofman, Handley, and Niemi 1992, pp. 25–27.
[5] *Shaw v. Reno*, 509 U.S. 630 (1993).
[6] Ibid. at 636.
[7] Ibid. at 647.

a majority jumped from seventeen to thirty-two. The number of congressional districts in which Latinos were a majority increased from nine to nineteen.[8] In the wake of *Shaw*, voters around the country filed suits against many of these majority-minority districts.[9] The Court ruled on one such suit in *Miller v. Johnson* (1995).[10] The five-member majority in *Miller* fleshed out the general reasoning of *Shaw*, arguing that the harms of political apartheid were incurred whenever race was used as the "predominant factor" in legislative districting.[11] On this ground, the Court struck down a 260-mile-long congressional district in Georgia—a district that had compiled a majority of African Americans by grouping together black neighborhoods of urban Atlanta with the poor black populace of the Georgia coast.

Coming at a time when pundits increasingly blame majority-minority districts for harming Democratic candidates, *Miller* helped ensure that the Court's handling of minority representation would remain in the headlines.[12] The Court's profile was heightened by *Miller*'s apparent loose ends. Writing for the *Miller* majority, Justice Anthony Kennedy touched on the larger question of the Voting Rights Act's constitutionality but managed to skirt the issue by blaming the Justice Department for erroneously trying to maximize the number of majority-minority districts.[13] Moreover, Justice Sandra Day O'Connor filed a cautious concurrence to the majority opinion, indicating that she understood Justice Kennedy to establish a "demanding" standard that would subject only "extreme" instances of racial gerrymandering to meaningful judicial review.[14] O'Connor's equivocation blurred the message of *Miller*, leading one commentator to note that the case was best understood as a "5-to-5 decision."[15] The sense of indeterminacy persisted even as the

---

[8] Peterson 1995, p. 11. There were also marked increases in the number of majority-minority districts at the state legislative level. See Bositis 1994, pp. 54–59.

[9] *New York Times*, 9 Mar. 1994, p. A8.

[10] *Miller v. Johnson*, 115 S.Ct. 2475 (1995).

[11] Ibid. at 2488.

[12] The claim is that majority-minority districts help Republican candidates by lumping large numbers of loyal Democratic voters together. On the growing debate over the partisan consequences of racial districting, see Hill 1995; Bullock 1995; Engstrom 1995; Kelly 1995; Swain 1995; Pildes, Raskin, and Swain 1996; Rosen 1996; and NAACP 1994. See also *New York Times*, 7 Dec. 1994, p. A23; 10 Dec. 1994, p. A8, and 1 Jan. 1995, p. A9.

[13] *Miller* at 2491–94.

[14] Ibid. at 2497.

[15] See *New York Times* 14 July 1995, p. A1. O'Connor's equivocation in *Miller* was consistent with her claim in *Shaw* that minority representation raised some of "the most complex and sensitive issues" in the Court's recent history. See *Shaw* at 633.

Court used the *Miller* rationale to strike down additional majority-minority districts. Overturning three majority-minority districts in Texas, members of the Court produced *six* separate opinions, including two by O'Connor in which she announced the judgment of the Court and then concurred with herself.[16]

Thus, whatever the ultimate fate of racial districting is to be, events ranging from the aborted Guinier nomination to the most recent decisions demonstrate that the Supreme Court will be a focal point of policy-making and conflict. What is at stake in the Court's actions? How should judicial involvement in the politics of minority representation be understood? In the future, what direction should the Court pursue?

This book provides an answer to these questions. I begin with a historical review of the Voting Rights Act and its amendments, focusing on the Court's role in the development and enforcement of the act (chapter one). This history reveals an important dynamic: as the act has been repeatedly reaffirmed over the past thirty years, it has garnered ever-greater criticism and controversy. I argue that levels of disagreement have escalated as the Voting Rights Act has moved away from simpler questions of political access toward more complicated questions of political membership and representation. It is because the central issue has become *how* minorities should count, rather than *whether* they should count at all, that the act has become the target of increasingly contentious debate.

To understand the politics of the Voting Rights Act, one must understand the issues at stake in the struggle for meaningful political membership. To this end, I develop an analytical framework in which the Court's participation in politics of minority representation can be situated (chapter two). I argue that questions of political identity are always at the heart of debates over representation; this is so because claims about how representational institutions ought to be designed always hinge on prior conceptions of who is to be represented in the first place. Representational debates thus draw on competing notions of who "the people" are and turn on questions of how self-government ought to be achieved. The politics of minority representation, no less than other representational conflicts, engenders contests over fundamental political identities and basic governmental aims. Engaged in the politics of minority representation, the Supreme Court helps ascertain what the basic structure of the political community ought to be.

Indeed, I argue that the constitutive role of the Court extends even

[16] *Bush v. Vera*, 116 S.Ct. 1941 (1996).

further. Involvement in the politics of minority representation confronts the Court with the challenge of articulating the foundations of its own political authority. Since the earliest days of the republic, claims of judicial power have been derived from the Court's capacity to speak on behalf of the people as a whole. As a result, when the Court responds to questions of minority representation, it not only selects a notion of "the people" around which representational institutions may be organized but also chooses a conception of "the people" on which its own action may be premised. The Court does not stand outside the representational conflicts it adjudicates; the meaning of fair representation as well as the extent of judicial power rest on understandings of political identity.

At minimum, the intersection between fair representation and Court power suggests that judicial interpretations of the Voting Rights Act depend on assertions about who "the people" are. The centrality of political identity has not always been appreciated. Examining the public debate over the act, I demonstrate that ideological positions have been animated by sharply divided conceptions of "the people," which many commentators have either misapprehended or simply neglected (chapter three). Without acknowledging the conceptual depth of existing disagreements, attempts to advance the debate over minority representation are bound to fail.

Beyond suggesting that claims of identity should be recognized, the interdependence of fair representation and judicial power also indicates how notions of identity ought to be *used*. If our government is to remain democratic—if it is to engender rule by the sovereign people rather than to foster rule by an unaccountable judiciary—then the Court must not rely on conceptions of "the people" that prevent the citizenry from finally speaking for themselves. I use this standard to gauge the debate over the Voting Rights Act as it has developed on the bench. During the 1960s and 1970s, members of the Court adopted a diversity of approaches to minority representation, organizing their views around conceptions of popular vigilance, abstract individualism, legislative learning, and interest group competition (chapter four). I argue that each of these approaches is problematic, for each sustains an understanding of judicial authority that ultimately fails to preserve the capacity of the people to speak for themselves.

In the last twenty years, the Court has abandoned its original diversity of views, settling on a dichotomous treatment of minority representation polarized around "individualist" and "group" notions of political identity (chapter five). The individualist and group views have fractured the Court, just as conflicting versions of political identity have splintered the broader ideological debate. Although the individualist and group camps each offer some valuable insights, I argue that both finally stumble over a mistaken account of political identity, which impairs the prospects for popular sovereignty (chapter six). In particular, I argue that both views have an important feature in common: each takes political identity to be something formed prior to and apart from politics itself. The shared belief that political identity is "prepolitical" has hardened the lines of opposition, creating a zero-sum debate that has foreclosed valuable democratic options. In short, by predicating judicial authority on essentialized conceptions of identity, the Court has truncated the range of political possibilities, ultimately leaving the people unable to control the grounds on which the political community is constructed.

Given these circumstances, I suggest that the emphasis on fixed, prepolitical notions of political identity should be left behind for a more flexible, politically informed rendering of "the people." More specifically, I argue that the Court should develop its earlier views of legislative learning, focusing on how understandings of political identity are forged *within* the process of political deliberation. Rather than policing claims about immobile identities, the Court should work to preserve the conditions that allow elected representatives to learn. The adjudication of representational controversies would thus remain sensitive to the concerns of democratic sovereignty, ultimately permitting the people to speak for themselves even as the Court speaks on their behalf.

Of course, by reorienting the jurisprudence of minority representation toward a theory of political deliberation, members of the Court cannot hope to resolve all disagreements over the Voting Rights Act. To expect such consensus is to ignore the complex struggle over political membership that has long characterized the politics of minority representation. Even among those who favor severe limits on the pursuit of fair minority representation, there is an acknowledgment that the issue will always be a center of controversy.[17] Still, if the turn toward political deliberation will not solve all the puzzles of minority representation, it will provide a new set of terms in which such puzzles can be framed. New terms allow for a new conception of minority representation, free from the problematic claims and strange dichotomies which currently plague

---

[17] Thernstrom 1987, p. 244.

public discussion. And, in the end, it is with the hope of advancing public discussion that this book is written.

More than 150 years ago, Alexis de Tocqueville wrote that "there is hardly a political question in the United States which does not sooner or later turn into a judicial one."[18] While many have agreed with Tocqueville's observation, agreement on how judicial action ought to be studied has been less common. In the field of political science, scholarship has emphasized the political origins of judicial decision making, treating judicial activity as the continuation of ordinary policymaking by other means. Such "political jurisprudence" views decisions in terms of political attitudes and, in doing so, typically pays little attention to the structure of judicial reasoning.[19]

In this book, my concern is less with the *origins* of judicial decision making than with the *meaning* of the principles articulated in those decisions.[20] Although I provide a general overview of leading cases, I also devote several chapters to a close examination of judicial reasoning, carefully evaluating the arguments justices use to support their conclusions. I take these arguments to be worthy of close study because I see judicial reasoning as a particular way of making sense, a technique of using analogies and metaphors to render issues so that they are suitable for judgment.[21] I view the law, in other words, as a resource for engaging in particular forms of thought and debate. Working with the law, judges construct arguments that operate like narratives—naming relevant characters and conditions, enumerating events, and investing these events with significance. Judges use legal discourse to frame "a set

---

[18] Tocqueville 1966, p. 270.

[19] The classic work of political jurisprudence is Shapiro 1964 (see also Shapiro 1981 and 1988; and Murphy 1964). Political jurisprudence draws on legal realism (Kalman 1986; Purcell 1973; and Horwitz 1992) and rejects the notion that judges are capable of arriving at singularly correct answers (cf. S. Barber 1989 and Dworkin 1977 with Shapiro 1983 and 1989). For a discussion of political jurisprudence as the conventional wisdom of political science, see Brigham 1987 (cf. Stumpf 1983; O'Brien 1983). For a strong, recent statement of political jurisprudence, see Segal and Spaeth 1993.

[20] For broad arguments in favor of studying judicial meaning, see Constable 1994; Gillman 1993; and Melnick 1994.

[21] White 1984 and 1985. See also Brigham 1978; Carter 1985; Geertz 1983; and Scheppele 1988 and 1990. The classic work describing the analogical structure of judicial reasoning is Levi 1949 (see also Minow 1987a; Fuller 1967, pp. 55, 65, 87–89, 115, 134–35; and, more generally, Lakoff and Johnson 1980; Quinn and Holland 1987; and Quinn 1991).

of questions that reciprocally define and depend upon a world of thought and action," creating "a set of roles and voices by which meanings will be established and shared."[22] Judicial opinions thus constitute a distinct "culture of argument" that defines issues and various ways to approach them.[23] My aim is to assess the culture of argument established in a specific context, focusing on how conceptions of political identity have been used to support different views of fair minority representation and judicial authority.[24]

Of course, in investigating the meaning of judicial arguments, I am not claiming that political preferences play no role in judicial decision making. Legal outcomes are clearly sensitive to membership change; as conservative politicians control more judicial appointments, judicial decisions become more conservative. But the terms in which judges frame legal controversies are also important. Indeed, the form of judicial argument, as a particular mode of envisioning the issues in question, often makes a crucial difference to the outcome.[25] The evaluation of judicial reasoning is necessary not only to understand a decision, but also to begin to see how decision making might be made more reasonable. It is to this evaluation that I now turn.

[22] White 1985, p. 71.

[23] Ibid., pp. 28–35. This approach differs from other approaches claiming that a broad "legal consciousness" or "community of understanding" influences entire cohorts of judges for distinct historical periods (See Kennedy 1980; Klare 1978; Mensch 1982; Garvey 1971; and Tushnet 1989). As a method of case analysis, legal consciousness studies tend to understate the importance of conflicts that do occur on the bench (see Smith 1988b). Within the context of a given legal order, judges still confront important choices.

[24] For studies of political identity in other judicial contexts, see Noonan 1976, pp. 3–64; Horwitz 1985; and O'Neill 1981.

[25] This proposition has received a good deal of empirical verification. See Segal 1984; Baum 1988 and 1992b; George and Epstein 1992; Lloyd 1995; H. W. Perry 1991; and, especially, Epstein and Kobylka 1992.

The Voting Rights Act and the Struggle for Meaningful Political Membership

MEMBERSHIP within a political community is an issue of prime importance. As Michael Walzer has noted, individuals without membership "are cut off from the communal provision of security and welfare. Even those aspects of security and welfare that are, like public health, collectively distributed are not guaranteed to non-members: for they have no guaranteed place in the collectivity and are always liable to expulsion. Statelessness is a condition of infinite danger."[1]

Important as it is, achieving membership within a political community is not necessarily the same thing as achieving *equal* membership. Throughout our own history, the official rhetoric of equal political membership among Americans has frequently been belied by extensive discrimination. In fact, such contradictions between political rhetoric and reality were a hallmark of the nation's formation.[2] The egalitarian claims of the Declaration of Independence were repeated and ratified by colonies that practiced slavery. In a similar spirit, the Constitution itself, a document that sought to secure the "blessings of liberty," sheltered the slave trade and assigned slaves a stunted political status.[3] Once slavery had been abolished, African Americans were still systematically denied the full range of rights guaranteed to others. At best, African Americans enjoyed what Justice Benjamin Curtis called "naked citizenship"—a nominal status with few of the privileges and immunities granted to white male members of the American polity.[4]

Over time, this flourishing of exclusionary politics under the umbrella of inclusionary principles infused the possession of rights with special meaning. Naked citizens longed to be clothed for more than just rea-

[1] Walzer 1983, pp. 31–32.

[2] Many figures were, of course, aware of these contradictions at the time (see Bailyn 1967, pp. 230–46). For documentation of inegalitarianism in the American political tradition, see Smith 1988a, 1989; and Kettner 1978.

[3] Art. I, sec. 2 and sec. 9. For discussions of the three-fifths clause, see Lynd 1967; and Diamond 1989.

[4] Justice Benjamin Curtis, dissenting, *Dred Scott v. Sandford*, 60 U.S. 393, 584 (1857).

sons of self-protection. Representing more than just the capacity to defend one's interests, citizenship rights became signs of social standing and membership: to have rights was to be truly included, to count. The connotations of social belonging were most clearly connected with the right to vote. Indeed, among those prohibited from voting, the social status that accompanied the ballot often eclipsed the political use that could be made of it. As Judith Shklar once observed: "It was the denial of the suffrage to large groups of Americans that made the right to vote such a mark of social standing. To be refused the right was to be almost a slave, but once one possessed the right, it conferred no other personal advantages. Not the exercise, only the right, signified deeply."[5]

The status of suffrage as a symbol of belonging is indeed a special feature of the American political tradition. Yet, in taking the right to vote to be a sign of membership, it is important to realize that the meaning of membership can be contested. Scholars such as Shklar tend to recount the struggle of "out" groups such as African Americans to get "in" without devoting much attention to what counts as inclusion in the first place.[6] Of course, the decision to leave the complexities of membership unexplored may seem reasonable under some circumstances. When a group is strictly prevented from registering or entering the voting booth, for example, the difference between members and nonmembers seems clear. The question of what counts as inclusion is answered by the egregious denial of access. Definitions of equal standing are to be found simply in the repeal of laws that grant the right to vote to some and not to others.

Nonetheless, the very "obviousness" of exclusion can mislead, suggesting that membership always has a single, clear meaning. In principle, political membership is never a matter of simply being "in" or "out" — once formally included, one can still be discriminated against in a number of different ways. Moreover, once the most obvious forms of discrimination and exclusion are displaced, the meaning of genuine inclusion may itself become the main object of dispute.

Such a possibility is not merely hypothetical. The development of the Voting Rights Act of 1965 demonstrates that after excluded groups began to win basic suffrage rights, the struggle for inclusion did not dissipate. Instead, the focus of political action shifted away from the goal of

[5] Shklar 1991, p. 27. See also Foner 1988.

[6] See Barber 1993 for a complementary view of Shklar's limitations. See Tushnet 1988 for a more general argument that controversies over the meaning of racial equality did not stop once minority rights had been written into the Constitution.

gaining standing to that of achieving *meaningful* standing; members of minority groups no longer wished simply to vote but to be *seriously heard*. Thus, the history of the Voting Rights Act reveals that understandings of membership are essentially contested rather than unitary — illustrating, in other words, that the politics of representation is organized around the issue of *how* minorities should count, rather than whether they should count at all.[7] It is this struggle for meaningful membership that must grasped if the contentious politics of minority representation is to be understood.

THE ROAD TO THE VOTING RIGHTS ACT

To see why the simple dichotomy between membership and nonmembership is too crude to explain the controversy over minority voting rights, one must begin with the exclusionary history that led to the passage of the Voting Rights Act in the first place. After the close of the Civil War, the ratification of the Thirteenth, Fourteenth, and Fifteenth Amendments to the Constitution promised African Americans civil and political rights equal to those enjoyed by whites.[8] The Civil War amendments bolstered the efforts of military governments installed by the victorious North in the 1860s. By 1868 these military governments had registered more than seven hundred thousand blacks throughout the former Confederacy.[9] Congress quickly countered the white resistance that greeted black enfranchisement, relying on authority of the Civil War Amendments to pass three Enforcement Acts in the early 1870s.

Congressional efforts to ensure political rights for African Americans failed.[10] In part, this failure stemmed from the political terrorism of white supremacist groups such as the Ku Klux Klan. During eight months in 1868, for instance, more than one thousand people were

[7] I shall have more to say about the idea of essentially contested concepts in chapter two.

[8] The Thirteenth Amendment ended slavery. The Fourteenth Amendment contained sections providing, among other things, (i) for national citizenship and (ii) that no state shall "deny to any person within its jurisdiction the equal protection of the laws." The Fifteenth Amendment provided that the "right of citizens of the United States to vote shall not be denied or abridged by the United States or any State on account of race, color, or previous condition of servitude."

[9] Grofman, Handley, and Niemi 1992, p. 5; Kousser 1992, p. 140.

[10] The political exclusion of African Americans was not immediately accomplished. Blacks continued to vote and to form some political alliances with conservative whites into the 1880s. See Woodward 1974, pp. 31–65.

killed in Louisiana as a result of political violence.[11] Where blacks could not be kept from the polls by terrorism, ballot box stuffing and other forms of political fraud shored up white power. The twin tactics of violence and fraud did, of course, have their limits. Aggressive repression on a large scale not only tended to breed an unstable environment potentially dangerous for property owners but also provided grounds on which blacks could appeal for Northern intervention.[12]

Local lawmakers across the South soon discovered that structural discrimination could sustain black disenfranchisement without the risks of violence or fraud. Various devices of structural discrimination were designed to make it difficult for blacks to qualify for the franchise as well as to reduce the efficacy of any black votes actually cast. Among the most important forms of structural discrimination were registration barriers (such as the poll tax, grandfather clauses, and literacy tests); white primaries (to reduce blacks to the role of ratifying white-approved candidates); gerrymandering (to concentrate blacks into few districts); annexation (to alter the composition of the electorate); at-large voting (to submerge minority populations); and the redesign of governing bodies (to reduce, for example, the total number of elected offices).[13]

The state and local campaign of structural discrimination was ultimately facilitated by federal retrenchment. In 1894 a Democratically controlled Congress repealed substantial portions of earlier enforcement legislation.[14] Congressional action was preceded as well as followed by Supreme Court rulings weakening the enforcement acts and directly condoning structural discrimination in southern states.[15] By the turn of the century, then, African Americans were largely shut out of southern politics. Individual blacks did manage to remove some barriers to political participation through litigation, persuading the Supreme Court to strike down grandfather clauses in 1915 and the white primary in 1944.[16] But such isolated acts of intervention left the Southern system of minor-

---

[11] Kousser 1992, pp. 141–42.

[12] Ibid., pp. 142–45.

[13] Kousser (1984) has counted sixteen such forms of structural discrimination.

[14] Grofman, Handley, and Niemi 1992, p. 9.

[15] *United States v. Reese*, 92 U.S. 214 (1876), and *United States v. Cruikshank*, 92 U.S. 542 (1876), gutted the enforcement acts of 1870 and 1872. *Williams v. Mississippi*, 170 U.S. 213 (1898), upheld suffrage restrictions in Mississippi, while *Giles v. Harris*, 189 U.S. 475 (1903), and *Giles v. Teasley*, 193 U.S. 146 (1904), did the same for Alabama.

[16] *Guinn v. United States*, 238 U.S. 397 (1915); *Smith v. Allwright*, 321 U.S. 649 (1944). See Elliot 1974, pp. 55–88, for an account of black voting rights litigation from 1868 to 1962.

15

ity disenfranchisement largely intact.[17] As migration after World War II increased the importance of the African American vote in the North, the federal government passed three civil-rights acts in 1957, 1960, and 1964 designed in part to enfranchise blacks through federally sponsored litigation. While more frequent than private suits, government litigation also proved to be a slow, expensive, and only partially successful strategy. From 1952 to late 1964, the number of blacks registered to vote in the South actually doubled, but registration levels remained low in absolute numbers, with less than a quarter of eligible blacks on the voting rolls in the Deep South.[18]

THE VOTING RIGHTS ACT

The long history of discrimination and exclusion presented civil-rights reformers of the 1960s with a clear goal: African Americans wanted access to the voting booth. Large protests against black disenfranchisement, centered in Selma, Alabama, and organized by Martin Luther King, Jr., catapulted the question of minority voting rights to the front of the political agenda in early 1965.[19] As violent white reactions rocked Selma, President Lyndon Johnson asked his attorney general to prepare the "goddamnedest toughest" voting-rights bill possible.[20] The resulting bill contemplated an unprecedented extension of federal authority into local political practices. In Congress southerners claimed that federal enforcement of voting rights was an unconstitutional distortion of federalism. Northerners of both parties countered that the Fifteenth Amendment gave Congress ample authority to enact remedial legislation.[21] The advocates of change proved stronger, and Congress ultimately passed the voting rights bill by a large bipartisan margin, split along regional lines.[22] On August 6, 1965, the Voting Rights Act became law.

[17] Grofman, Handley, and Niemi 1992, pp. 10–12.

[18] U.S. Commission on Civil Rights, 1965, pp. 8–10; Davidson 1992, p. 13. In November of 1964, Mississippi showed a black registration rate of only 6.7 percent.

[19] U.S. Commission on Civil Rights, 1965, pp. 10–12; Davidson 1992, pp. 14–17.

[20] Davidson 1992, p. 17. In addition to genuine concern for minority voting rights, LBJ clearly had some incentive to fill Democratic ranks thinned by white flight.

[21] Parker 1990, pp. 189–91. Of course, criticism of the act was not completely limited to questions of federalism in 1965 or in following years. On the legislative debates in 1965, 1970, 1975, and 1982, see Thernstrom 1987. For a sense of the debates surrounding the latest set of amendments in 1992, see U.S. House of Representatives 1992.

[22] See Kousser 1992 for a comparison between congressional voting patterns in 1965 and those following the Civil War.

The Voting Rights Act placed a battery of federal enforcement mechanisms behind the effort to ensure minority political access. The permanent sections of the act codified the Fifteenth Amendment, provided penalties for the act's violation, and empowered the attorney general to litigate for (i) the suspension of literacy tests, (ii) the appointment of federal examiners to oversee voter registration, and (iii) the retention of court jurisdiction to review proposed changes in voting procedures before localities could enforce them.[23]

The core of the act, however, was to be found in its temporary sections, which placed the burdens of litigation and administrative appeal on selected state and local jurisdictions rather than on the federal government or aggrieved individuals.[24] Section 4 banned literacy tests outright for five years in any political subdivision where such a test was in force, and where less than 50 percent of the eligible population was registered to vote on November 1, 1964, or less than 50 percent of the eligible population voted in the 1964 presidential election. This triggering formula "covered" six southern states entirely and part of a seventh.[25] These states and subdivisions could "bail out" of coverage upon demonstrating to the D.C. District Court that they had not used literacy tests in a racially discriminatory fashion for the past five years. Section 5 required covered subdivisions to submit any changes in voting practices to the Justice Department for "preclearance," allowing the attorney general to determine whether such changes would deny or abridge the right to vote on account of race or color. As an alternative, Section 5 also permitted covered subdivisions to seek preclearance from the D.C. District Court. Sections 6 through 8 gave the attorney general discretionary authority to install federal examiners and poll watchers in covered subdivisions, ensuring that qualified individuals could actually register and vote. Finally, Section 9 set forth the

[23] Sections 2, 3, 11, and 12. Section 4(e) enfranchised Puerto Ricans illiterate in English who could prove they had completed six years of school in Puerto Rico. Section 10 instructed the attorney general to contest the constitutionality of the poll tax in local and state elections. The Voting Rights Act as passed by Congress and its subsequent amendments can be found in *United States Statutes At Large*, 79 Stat. 437, 84 Stat. 314, 89 Stat. 400, 96 Stat. 131, and 106 Stat. 921. The entire act as amended through 1982 is reprinted in Grofman and Davidson 1992, pp. 319–38.

[24] This placement of burdens made the act unique among federal civil-rights legislation (Days 1992, p. 53).

[25] The states were Alabama, Georgia, Louisiana, Mississippi, South Carolina, Virginia, and portions of North Carolina. Alaska as well as parts of Arizona, Hawaii, and Idaho were also initially culled, but they managed to free themselves from coverage under the bailout procedures specified in Section 4.

procedures by which covered subdivisions could contest federally compiled registration lists.

In the years immediately following the passage of the act, more than 1 million African Americans were registered to vote in the seven covered states, nearly doubling the number of minority registrants in the South.[26] It is important to note that in these early years the increased registration levels were not due primarily to actions taken pursuant to the act. Both the exercise of preclearance powers and the use of federal examiners were sparing throughout the late 1960s.[27] Instead, the act's suspension of literacy tests coupled with the *threat* of active federal intervention created an environment in which private civil-rights organizations could effectively register voters.[28]

The early success of the act threw light on the important barriers to minority registration and voting that remained. African Americans seeking basic political access were still hampered by restrictive registration hours and hostile officials. Moreover, the registration levels of language minorities such as Latinos and Native Americans were depressed across the nation, reflecting the exclusionary effects of literacy tests and English-only ballots outside the South.[29] In light of these problems, the Voting Rights Act was amended twice in the 1970s. In 1970 Congress renewed the temporary provisions of the act for five more years, banning literacy tests nationwide until 1975, altering the triggering formula of Section 4 to cover regions outside the South, and toughening bailout procedures by requiring covered subdivisions to show they had not employed a discriminatory test in the past ten years.[30] In 1975 the act's temporary provisions were again renewed, this time for seven years, extending coverage to language minorities, increasing bailout requirements to seventeen years, and generally au-

---

[26] U.S. Commission on Civil Rights 1975, pp. 40–43. White registration also surged during this period, keeping white registration ahead of black registration throughout the 1960s (Davidson and Grofman 1994, pp. 365–67, 369–72).

[27] U.S. Commission on Civil Rights 1975, pp. 25, 33. Yet, in the majority black districts actually visited by federal examiners, significant (although perhaps temporary) increases in black registration did occur (Davidson and Grofman 1994, pp. 367–69).

[28] U.S. Commission on Civil Rights 1975, p. 44.

[29] Ibid., pp. 69–203.

[30] The 1970 amendments covered, among other regions, parts of Wyoming, Connecticut, New Hampshire, Maine, and New York City. They also established uniform residency requirements for participation in presidential elections and extended the right to vote in all elections to eighteen-year-olds. The age qualifications for state elections were struck down in *Oregon v. Mitchell*, 400 U.S. 112 (1970).

thorizing aggrieved individuals as well as the attorney general to sue subdivisions.[31]

As the Voting Rights Act grew more comprehensive and permanent over the course of the 1970s, the nature of politics surrounding the act began to change. Like the original legislation, the amended act perpetuated an environment of potential penalties and administrative interventions that facilitated the efforts of private groups to register voters. The character of voting-rights politics altered, however, as the various provisions of the act began to be used affirmatively. More specifically, the fight for basic political *access* continued under the act's extensions, but the center of voting rights enforcement gradually gravitated toward issues of *meaningful inclusion* as the once quiescent preclearance provisions gained in importance.

It was the Supreme Court that first raised such complicated issues in its 1969 decision *Allen v. State Board of Elections*.[32] At issue in *Allen* was whether Mississippi's switch from district to at-large elections in county supervisor races was subject to preclearance under Section 5 of the Voting Rights Act. This question forced the Court to focus on a problem beyond the denial of political access—for while the shift to at-large elections did not strictly prevent anyone from voting, it arguably "diluted" the voting power of the black minority by placing it among a politically hostile white majority.[33] Writing for the Court, Chief Justice

[31] The 1975 amendments extended the notion of discriminatory "test or device" to include the provision of voting materials only in English where more than 5 percent of the eligible voters were members of a language minority group (defined as American Indians, Asian Americans, Alaskan natives, or people of Spanish heritage). Where such conditions obtained and where (i) less than 50 percent of the subdivision's eligible voters were registered as of November 1, 1972, or (ii) less than 50 percent of such persons voted in the 1972 presidential election, the subdivision was covered and subject to Section 5. Thus, the entire states of Alaska, Arizona, and Texas became covered as well as parts of California, Colorado, Florida, and South Dakota. Outside such newly covered areas, where the numerical threshold of language minorities obtained and the literacy rate for that group was below the national average, the 1975 amendments required multilingual voting materials to be provided for the next ten years. The 1975 amendments also codified the Twenty-sixth Amendment to the Constitution and banned literacy tests permanently.

[32] *Allen v. State Board of Elections*, 393 U.S. 544 (1969). The Court had previously upheld Sections 4 and 5 of the act as constitutional in *South Carolina v. Katzenbach*, 383 U.S. 301 (1966). In general, voting rights litigation has been the most successful of any civil-rights litigation (Caldeira 1992, p. 245).

[33] See Davidson 1984, p. 4, for a more formal definition of vote dilution. *Allen* was not the first case in which the Court encountered the notion of diluted votes. Among other cases, *Gomillion v. Lightfoot*, 364 U.S. 339 (1960), was an important precursor. In chapter four, I discuss *Allen* and its antecedents in greater detail.

Earl Warren embraced the notion of vote dilution, broadly interpreting Section 5 so that the federal government could review even the most minor changes in election law.

The judicial acceptance of vote dilution amounted to a realization that equal access to the ballot did not ensure equally effective votes. In this way, the Court began to push past the "first generation" problem of securing minority ballot access toward the "second generation" problem of securing meaningful political participation.[34] On the heels of the broad ruling in *Allen*, the number of electoral changes submitted to the Justice Department for preclearance rose significantly.[35] The rush of preclearance requests put the federal government in the business of ascertaining the point at which the political inclusion of minorities was sufficiently fair. Throughout this period, it was the Supreme Court that attempted to set standards for determining when an electoral scheme subject to preclearance could be said to result in fair minority representation.[36]

The most controversial and complex questions of representation did not, however, surface in the context of Section 5 preclearance. Debate and policy in this area remained constrained for a variety of reasons. Although Section 5 gave the federal government broad powers of review, the practice of preclearance remained restricted to a small portion of the country. Moreover, preclearance within the covered areas proved to be somewhat less than airtight, with the subdivisions themselves being relied upon to report electoral changes and to comply with the attorney general's decisions.[37] Perhaps more importantly, the Supreme Court assigned Section 5 a limited depth to match its limited scope. In *Beer v. United States* (1976), the Court held that preclearance findings of vote dilution depended on whether new electoral laws actually lowered the pre-existing status of minority voters.[38] This notion of "nonretrogression" provided a simple standard against which electoral alterations in covered subdivisions could be measured. But while non-

---

[34] The generational classification is from Guinier 1991a, but its substance is echoed throughout the entire voting rights literature. See, for example, Shapiro 1985, p. 232.

[35] More than thirty thousand changes were submitted from 1975 to 1980 (U.S. Commission on Civil Rights 1981, p. 66).

[36] See, for example, *Georgia v. United States*, 411 U.S. 526 (1973), and *City of Richmond* (Va.) *v. United States*, 422 U.S. 358 (1975).

[37] Jones 1985; Days 1992, pp. 58–65. Private parties were permitted to sue covered subdivisions for failing to submit changes pursuant to *Allen*.

[38] *Beer v. United States*, 425 U.S. 130 (1976).

retrogression did much to prevent the installation of new dilutionary devices, it also did little to address the discriminatory impact of voting rules and procedures already in place.[39] The enforcement of Section 5 largely reduced the general issues of vote dilution to the prevention of backsliding, effectively circumscribing broader questions of fair representation.[40]

Questions that were not raised in the context of Section 5 were confronted directly in the context of the Constitution itself. As early as 1971, in *Whitcomb v. Chavis*, the Supreme Court considered the claim that an Indiana multimember district unconstitutionally diluted the vote of poor blacks.[41] The proportion of elected representatives from the minority ghetto fell well below the percentage of the district's population made up by ghetto residents. Examining the political structures and practices in the district, the Court nonetheless held that (i) the at-large election scheme was not purposely designed to discriminate against blacks and (ii) blacks were not in fact denied an equal opportunity to participate in the nomination or election of candidates. Those who claimed to be part of an unfairly treated racial minority were actually disaffected members of a Democratic party that consistently lost. As Justice White concluded for the majority, "the voting power of ghetto residents may have been 'canceled out' . . . but this seems a mere euphemism for political defeat at the polls."[42]

Two years later the Court found in *White v. Regester* an instance where the claim of unfair representation was not euphemistic.[43] Considering obstacles in the political process, low numbers of black and Latino representatives, the lack of elected officials' responsiveness, and the history of racial discrimination, the Court argued that several multimember districts in Texas unconstitutionally removed minorities from the political system. In contrast to *Whitcomb v. Chavis*, the "totality of circumstances" in Texas suggested minorities were not political losers

---

[39] See *City of Lockhart v. United States*, 460 U.S. 125 (1983). See also Grofman, Handley, and Niemi 1992, p. 29; Davidson and Grofman 1994, p. 33; O'Rourke 1992, pp. 93–95. Recall that many such devices of structural discrimination were installed after the end of Reconstruction.

[40] Compare Thernstrom (1987, pp. 138–55, 170–71), who argues that the baseline used for nonretrogression tests has been manipulated in the past to address existing schemes of vote dilution.

[41] *Whitcomb v. Chavis*, 403 U.S. 124 (1971).

[42] Ibid. at 153.

[43] *White v. Regester*, 412 U.S. 755 (1973).

so much as they were political pariahs.[44] Minorities possessed the vote yet were without political voice; armed with the franchise, they remained unable to elect officials of their choice and, thus, were taken to be unfairly represented. Again writing for the Court, Justice White accepted the lower court remedy of breaking up the multimember districts into single member districts — districts drawn to ensure the election of some minority-preferred candidates and "to bring the [minority] community into the full stream of political life."[45]

Together *Whitcomb v. Chavis* and *White v. Regester* approached the question of vote dilution by looking squarely at the issue of meaningful political inclusion. The fact that there were a disproportionate number of minority officeholders did not itself decide the issue, for fair representation was not synonymous with proportional representation.[46] Faced with claims of minority vote dilution, the Court focused on the processes of political competition, attempting to ascertain the degree to which these processes constituted minorities either as disappointed competitors or as victims of discrimination. Unlike Section 5, such an inquiry did not simply seek to prevent the erosion of some preexisting minority status; instead, the quality of minority representation itself was taken up as a subject of investigation. Only if minority groups possessed a certain presence in the political community would representation be deemed legitimate or authentic, immune to judicial restructuring.

THE RESULTS TEST AND THE ESTABLISHMENT OF MEMBERSHIP ISSUES

The debate over the representation of minority groups was joined in a number of lower court cases throughout the 1970s until the Supreme Court cut conversation short in 1980.[47] In *Mobile v. Bolden*, the Court held that unconstitutional minority vote dilution obtained only where

[44] The list of factors that comprised the "totality of circumstances" was organized in the lower court decision *Zimmer v. McKeithen*, 485 F.2d 1297 (5th cir. 1973).

[45] Ibid. at 769. The drawing of safe minority districts became the standard remedy where vote dilution was found (Abrams 1988, p. 470n).

[46] *Whitcomb v. Chavis* at 160.

[47] Davidson 1992, pp. 37–38. Twenty-three lower court cases were decided within the "totality of circumstances" framework — nineteen of these cases were decided in the Fifth Circuit alone (U.S. Senate 1982a, p. 32). By another count, at least forty such cases were litigated in covered subdivisions from 1973 to 1980 (Davidson and Grofman 1994, p. 28).

electoral rules were designed with a racially discriminatory purpose.[48] Unless elected officials specifically sought to exclude a minority group, all citizens were taken to be equal political competitors regardless of the actual effects any voting rule might have. The showing of intentional discrimination was, as majority author Justice Potter Stewart recognized, quite difficult.[49] The paucity of records (in many cases) and the availability of race-neutral "good government" justifications (in all cases) meant that the search for discriminatory intent in the design of political institutions was likely to be fruitless. Just as the interpretation of Section 5 in *Beer* curtailed questions of fair representation by stressing nonretrogression, *Bolden* foreclosed discussion of minority political membership and representational authenticity by emphasizing intent. The debate over how the political community ought to be organized thus ended with a validation of the status quo.

Bolden set the stage for the 1982 amendments to the Voting Rights Act.[50] With debate centering on the question of whether the "intent standard" articulated in *Bolden* ought to be upheld or rejected, Congress renewed the coverage and preclearance provisions of the act for another twenty-five years.[51] In its extension of the act, Congress explicitly rejected the intent standard, amending Section 2 to prohibit any test or procedure that "results in the denial or abridgment" of the minority right to vote. The difficulty of proving discriminatory intent was only one reason for Congress's endorsement of the "results standard." The primary reason was that the problem of intent deflected attention from the core issues of minority power. As the report of the Senate Judiciary Committee stated, "if an electoral system operates today to exclude blacks or Hispanics from a fair chance to participate, then the matter of what motives were in an official's mind 100 years ago is of the most limited relevance."[52] While discriminatory intent would remain neces-

---

[48] *Mobile v. Bolden*, 446 U.S. 55 (1980).

[49] Ibid. at 70.

[50] For an account of the goals of the civil rights lobby in the 1982 amendment process, see Pertschuk 1986, pp. 148–80, and Caldeira 1992.

[51] 1997 was set as a date for reconsideration of this renewal. With these amendments, Section 5 covered nine entire states and parts of thirteen others. Moreover, bailout was arguably made more difficult, with covered jurisdictions being required to comply with all preclearance rules over the past ten years as well as to take affirmative steps to incorporate minorities (See U.S. Senate 1982a, pp. 43–62; 1982b, pp. 52–59). In addition, provisions requiring multilingual ballots in noncovered subdivisions were extended until 1992. Handicapped and illiterate voters were also given greater protection.

[52] U.S. Senate 1982a, p. 36.

sary to demonstrate *unconstitutional* minority vote dilution (for *Bolden*'s interpretation of the Constitution was untouched by congressional revisions), the amended Section 2 linked *statutory* claims to discriminatory results.[53] As was the case in the pre-*Bolden* line of constitutional decisions, questions concerning minority presence in the political community were once again to be the primary focus of voting rights enforcement.

In the language of the amended Section 2 itself, the goal was to determine if any citizens had "less opportunity than other members of the electorate to participate in the political process and to elect representatives of their choice."[54] Although the extent to which minorities had been elected was an important factor to consider, the amended act expressly denied that equal political opportunity was solely a matter of proportional minority representation. Instead, the determination of whether minorities were (i) victims of discrimination without a viable political voice or (ii) political losers who could still be assumed to possess political influence was meant to hinge on a whole variety of factors. Enumerated in the report of the Senate Judiciary Committee, the relevant factors are worth stating in detail.[55]

1. The extent to which any history of official discrimination has touched the right of members of minority groups to vote or otherwise participate in the political process.

---

[53] Shortly after the 1982 amendments became law, the Court substantially retracted *Bolden* without actually dropping the language of intent at the constitutional level in *Rogers v. Lodge*, 458 U.S. 613 (1982).

[54] The text of the amended Section 2 reads as follows: "Sec. 2. (a) No voting qualification or prerequisite to voting or standard, practice, or procedure shall be imposed or applied by any State or political subdivision in a manner which results in a denial or abridgment of the right of any citizen of the United States to vote on account of race or color . . . as provided in subsection (b). (b) A violation of subsection (a) is established if, based on the totality of circumstances, it is shown that the political processes leading to nomination or election in the State or political subdivision are not equally open to participation by members of a class of citizens protected by subsection (a) in that its members have less opportunity than other members of the electorate to participate in the political process and to elect representatives of their choice. The extent to which members of a protected class have been elected to office in the State or political subdivision is one circumstance which may be considered: *Provided*, That nothing in this section establishes a right to have members of a protected class elected in numbers equal to their proportion in the population." See Grofman and Davidson 1992, p. 319.

[55] The following list is a summary. For the actual language of the Senate report, see U.S. Senate 1982a, pp. 28–29.

2. The extent to which voting in elections is racially polarized.

3. The extent to which unusually large voting districts, majority vote requirements or other voting practices are used which may enhance the opportunity to discriminate against a minority group.

4. Whether there is a candidate slating process and whether minorities have been excluded from that process.

5. The extent to which minority groups bear the effects of discrimination in such areas as education, employment, and health, which hinder their ability to participate effectively in the political process.

6. Whether political campaigns have been characterized by overt or subtle racial appeals.

7. The extent to which members of minority groups have been elected to public office.

8. "Additional factors" which may be of probative value are: (i) whether there is a significant lack of responsiveness on the behalf of elected officials to the particularistic needs of minority groups; and (ii) whether the policy underlying the use of voting practices or requirements has only a tenuous justification.

The Judiciary Committee refused to rank these factors in any order of importance, concluding that courts should rely on their "overall judgment" in their analysis of minority participation.[56]

The Supreme Court determined what the "overall judgment" of at-large elections should turn on in *Thornburg v. Gingles* (1986).[57] In this case, Justice William Brennan reasoned that minority groups could not successfully claim to be harmed by an at-large, multimember electoral system unless they possessed the potential to elect representatives of their choice under an alternative single-member district arrangement. Therefore, an at-large electoral system diluted votes only where a minority group was (i) politically cohesive, (ii) sufficiently large and geographically compact to form a majority in a single-member district, and (iii) opposed by a white-majority voting bloc often enough that the minority-preferred candidate usually lost. Where the three prongs of this vote dilution test could be met, the Court approved the drawing of single-member districts with sufficient numbers of minorities to ensure the election of minority-preferred candidates.

With the streamlining of Section 2 in *Gingles*, the number of voting

---

[56] Indeed, the committee indicated that in some cases other unenumerated factors may be relevant (Ibid., p. 29).

[57] *Thornburg v. Gingles*, 478 U.S. 30 (1986).

dilution cases nearly doubled.[58] The sharp increase in litigation occurred even though the *Gingles* ruling only concerned a single kind of Section 2 application. Since Section 2 was neither restricted to a portion of the country nor to changes in electoral procedures, it stood as the main statutory bulwark against all voting-rights discrimination. The long reach of Section 2 also touched areas already covered by other provisions of the act. In 1987 the Justice Department officially incorporated Section 2 standards into Section 5 preclearance requirements, thereby holding covered subdivisions accountable to the same results-oriented scrutiny as the rest of the country.[59]

Perhaps the most critical consequence of Section 2's ascendancy was that it forcefully brought issues of membership and inclusion to the surface of Voting Rights Act politics. Battles over political access that characterized the early years of the act gave way to debates over the political presence of minorities. The identification and resolution of certain problems (such as the *Gingles* approach to vote dilution in at-large elections) did little to narrow the scope of debate. As more at-large districts were successfully challenged, attention turned toward the kind of political opportunity permitted by other electoral procedures, raising a number of broad questions about race, political membership, and authentic representation.[60] At what point did minorities enjoy equal political opportunity? Should majority-minority single-member districts be drawn wherever possible, even if this involves connecting widely separated pockets of minority population? More generally, should the *Gingles* criteria be taken to set the final limits of fair representation? Ultimately, should fair representation require proportional systems that guarantee power sharing at electoral and legislative levels?

As it had done in cases from *Allen* to *Gingles*, the Supreme Court provided the arena in which answers to these questions could begin to be formulated. For instance, in the 1991 decision *Chisom v. Roemer*, the Court expanded the protections of the Voting Rights Act to include

---

[58] McDonald 1992, p. 71. Moreover, the *Gingles* standard made private suits (as opposed to Justice Department suits) more feasible. As a result, a vast bulk of litigation under the amended Section 2 has been initiated by private minority plaintiffs (Davidson and Grofman 1994, p. 385).

[59] Davidson 1992, p. 40. For changes submitted and objections tendered under Section 5 from 1965–88, see Parker 1990, p. 183. Grofman, Handley, and Niemi (1992, p. 31, n.6) claim the incorporation of Section 2 began unofficially as early as 1986.

[60] See generally, Grofman, Handley, and Niemi 1992, pp. 109–28, and Abrams 1988, pp. 507–20.

judicial elections.[61] Writing for the majority, Justice John Paul Stevens ruled that Section 2 encompassed the opportunity to elect *any* candidate standing for popular election. The varying duties assigned to different elected officials did not mean that some elections were exempt from meeting Section 2 requirements. The election of all officials, including judges as well as legislators, would be held to standards that ensured minorities a fair share of input and influence. The Court's solicitude for minority choice in *Chisom* did not necessarily translate into support for minority control of the policymaking apparatus. In *Presley v. Etowah County Commission* (1992), Justice Anthony Kennedy held that changes in the structure of political authority (in this case, transferring budgetary control from a newly elected black official to a majority white council) need not be precleared under Section 5 as they bore no relationship to the substance of voting power.[62]

Although *Presley* left open the question of whether Section 2 could be used to contest the design of institutional structures, the Court imposed additional limits on the pursuit of minority representation in *Shaw v. Reno* (1993).[63] The *Shaw* Court concluded that districting schemes that separated voters on the basis of race, without sufficient justification, were unconstitutional. According to Justice Sandra Day O'Connor, the stringing together of geographically separated members of the same race into one "extremely irregular" district approached "political apartheid."[64] The extent to which this conclusion invalidated the majority-minority districts already drawn throughout the country initially remained unclear. But in *Miller v. Johnson* (1995), the Court rejected efforts by the Department of Justice to maximize the number of majority-minority districts during Section 5 preclearance.[65] Wherever race was used as the "predominant factor" in legislative redistricting, the process was held to be presumptively unconstitutional.[66] The Court continued to strike against race-conscious redistricting in the wake of *Miller*, not only pruning majority-minority districts in Texas, Georgia, and North Carolina, but also invalidating the Justice Department practice of incorporating Section 2 standards into Section 5 preclearance requirements.[67]

---

[61] *Chisom v. Roemer*, 111 S.Ct. 2354 (1991).

[62] *Presley v. Etowah County Commission*, 502 U.S. 491 (1992).

[63] *Shaw v. Reno*, 509 U.S. 630 (1993).

[64] Ibid. at 642, 647.

[65] *Miller v. Johnson*, 115 S.Ct. 2475 (1995).

[66] Ibid. at 2488.

[67] *Bush v. Vera*, 116 S.Ct. 1941 (1996); *Shaw v. Hunt*, 116 S.Ct. 1894 (1996); *Abrams*

As the Court curbed the pursuit of minority representation, Congress amended the Voting Rights Act again in 1992, following the trend of previous congressional revisions by strengthening its provisions. This round of amendments primarily concerned the distribution of multilingual ballots in noncovered jurisdictions.[68] Congress not only extended the provision of multilingual ballots for fifteen additional years (giving this portion of the act the same expiration date as the other temporary sections) but also lowered the population threshold for issuing such ballots to minority-language groups. As a result of these changes, a number of cities were forced to provide non-English ballots, including Los Angeles, where ballots in six languages were required.

On balance, what has been the effect of such congressional and judicial tinkering? The impact of reforms like majority-minority districts has varied according to local political conditions.[69] Nonetheless, the act has paid minorities some clear dividends. Across the entire South (including the states originally covered by the act), registration among voting-age African Americans increased from 43.3 percent to roughly 63.7 percent between 1964 and 1988. During a similar period, the number of black elected officials in the seven originally covered states alone rose from fewer than one hundred to almost thirty-three hundred; nationwide, figures rose from fewer than two hundred to more than seven thousand. Directly comparable registration figures for Latinos are not available, but in the six states with the largest Latino populations, the number of Latino elected officials nearly tripled between 1973 and 1990.[70] Moreover, in the six-year period from 1984 to 1990 alone, the number of Latino officials elected nationwide increased from 3,063 to nearly five thousand.[71]

The success suggested by these figures can be somewhat misleading. Improved as they may be, the registration and voting rates of minorities still remain well below that of whites.[72] In no state do African Ameri-

---

v. *Johnson*, 65 U.S.L.W. 4478 (1997); and *Reno v. Bossier Parish School*, 117 S.Ct. 1491 (1997).

[68] See footnotes 31 and 51 for background on multilingual ballots.

[69] Cameron, Epstein, and O'Halloran 1996; and Canon, Schousen, and Sellers 1996.

[70] Davidson 1992, p. 43; McDonald 1992, p. 73. The statement here concerns population as a whole and not simply voting-age population. Since Latino populations can feature a significant proportion of noncitizens, the gross statistic is more reliable.

[71] Fraga and Anhalt 1993, p. 9.

[72] Over the past few decades, levels of registration and voting have decreased for all voters. The rate of decline has been lower for blacks and Latinos than it has been for

cans or Latinos hold elected office at levels equal to that of whites. Relative to their share of the electorate, whites everywhere enjoy over-representation, while minorities are universally under-represented.[73] It is true that the escalation in minority office holding has placed some people of color in the highest echelons of power. Fourteen African Americans and six Latinos were elected to Congress in 1992, and almost all won in districts that had been drawn under the terms of the Voting Rights Act. Indeed, the increase of African Americans in the House during 1992 was the largest absolute increase in black representatives ever in a single year.[74] Yet, recent judicial decisions promise to shrink the number of minorities in Congress. Moreover, the advances in minority representation have not been equally distributed among different offices. The large majority of African American and Latino officials occupy positions in municipal government and on school boards.[75] Thus, minorities have achieved the greatest gains at the lowest levels of government, where the fiscal resources continue to dwindle and demands from an increasingly poor electorate continue to rise.[76]

Whether these figures translate into the equal political opportunity mandated by the Voting Rights Act is, of course, the larger question that the Supreme Court has confronted piecemeal in cases like *Shaw* and *Miller*. Unfortunately, this larger question has no simple answer, for the days when the line between political inclusion and exclusion could be drawn without controversy are long past. The minority struggle for equal membership has developed into a struggle over the meaning of political membership itself. To place the politics of minority representation in the proper perspective, a more comprehensive understanding of this struggle for meaningful membership must be developed.

---

whites, but the latter still register and vote at a higher level than the former (ibid., pp. 3–6). Moreover, the act does virtually nothing to respond to the special issues of noncitizenship and geographic dispersion, which depress Latino participation (Cain and Miller 1996).

[73] Fraga and Anhalt 1993, pp. 11–13.

[74] Engstrom 1995, p. 24.

[75] Fraga and Anhalt 1993, pp. 8–10.

[76] Judd and Swanstrom 1994, pp. 107–76. In addition, the increases in minority representation have been largely restricted to bigger cities and towns. Many smaller towns (especially in the South) still elect very few people of color (Davidson and Grofman 1994, pp. 314–16, 386).

The Supreme Court and Representation: Building an Analytical Framework

THE CONTROVERSIES surrounding the Voting Rights Act have grown sharper as the act has become more entangled in questions of meaningful political membership. As the politics of minority voting rights has moved away from issues of formal access toward issues of fair representation, the locus of debate has shifted away from efforts to secure suffrage and toward efforts to secure a significant political voice. While Congress has played an important role in the act's evolution, it is the Supreme Court that has critically influenced the way in which minority voting rights have been framed and understood. From the introduction of "vote dilution" in *Allen v. State Board of Elections* (1969) to the discussion of "political apartheid" in *Shaw v. Reno* (1993), the Supreme Court has articulated standards of representation for the adjudication of minority claims. Even when Congress amended the act in 1982 to counter the reasoning of *Mobile v. Bolden* (1980), it was the Court that subsequently interpreted and applied the congressional amendments in *Thornburg v. Gingles* (1986).

The trajectory of the act's development suggests two questions, one general and the other particular. First, how should we evaluate the politics of representation in which the struggle for meaningful membership has unfolded? Second, and more specifically, how should we evaluate the Supreme Court's participation in this politics of representation? The answers to these two questions will provide the basis for understanding the contentious voting-rights debate of the last three decades.

To anticipate, I will argue that political identity is central to the study of minority representation. In part, this is true because *any* debate over representation depends on political identity, with competing views turning on different notions of what people and which interests are to be represented. Understandings of political identity are also important because the Supreme Court usually justifies its own power in terms of its capacity to represent the people as a whole. When adjudicating issues of representation, the Court not only chooses between rival conceptions of "the people" at stake in public debate, but it also selects a conception of "the people" on whose behalf the Court shall speak. I will rely on these interlocking claims (i.e., that any politics of representation is predicated on contending views of "the people" and that the Court gives itself political authority commensurate with "the people" it claims to represent) to indicate how political identity matters in the politics of minority representation as well as to suggest which versions of political identity might serve this politics best.

UNDERSTANDING THE POLITICS OF REPRESENTATION

The study of representation should start with a definition of terms or, what amounts to the same thing, a discussion of Hanna Pitkin's seminal work *The Concept of Representation*. Pitkin's book is one of the most frequently cited texts in political science. Yet, even so, her text is not often read — or, to state the point more accurately, her book is not often read as presenting an argument so much as it is used as an encyclopedic resource, a compendium of all the possible uses of representation. My discussion of representation thus begins by recapitulating (and recovering) the argument at the heart of Pitkin's work.

According to Pitkin, the word *representation* means to make present in some sense that which is itself not present literally or fully. Therefore, as Pitkin notes, representation is a matter of "*re-presentation*, a making present again."[1] Political representation, the "making present" of the people in the authoritative decisions of their government, can be conceived of in a number of ways. Political representation may be viewed as purely formal, with all those who are merely "authorized" to act on the behalf of the people being labeled representatives.[2] Or such representation may be defined as a matter of "standing for" the people, with only those who descriptively or symbolically resemble the people being designated as representatives.[3] Finally, political representation may be seen as a matter of "substantively acting for" the people, with only those whose actions are in some way guided by their constituents being deemed representatives.[4]

[1] Pitkin 1967, p. 8, emphasis original.

[2] Ibid., pp. 14–59. In this view, a directly elected legislator is as representative as a bureaucrat.

[3] Ibid., pp. 60–111.

[4] Ibid., pp. 112–67.

Each of these views of political representation is, of course, open to some interpretation.[5] All these views together, along with their various interpretations, form a complex matrix of conceptual resources that can be used to fashion a political community. In other words, political representation provides a means for generating a common political framework, a way of adjudicating disputes and developing consensus. "One of the most important features of representative government," Pitkin writes, "is its capacity for resolving the conflicting claims of the parts, on the basis of their common interest in the welfare of the whole."[6] Theories of representation are thus used to establish the foundations of a shared democratic politics, to enact the promise of *e pluribus unum*.

Since representation can be interpreted in a wide range of ways, the *kind* of political community to be forged via representative government is itself open to debate. The result is that representational debates are always anchored in disputes over the nature of the political community. As Pitkin concludes in her analysis of political theory, "the position a writer adopts within the limits set by the concept of representation will depend on his *metapolitics*—his broad conception of human nature, human society, and political life. His views on representation will not be arbitrarily chosen, but embedded in and dependent on the pattern of his political thought."[7] The rendering of representation a theorist gives depends on the political purposes she seeks to serve. As a consequence, no version of representation is final or all-inclusive; each treatment of political representation incorporates its own sense of what people and which interests are to count.[8]

What Pitkin finds to be true in political theory, holds as well in concrete political practice. At stake in actual representational controversies—conflicts over how the people ought to be made politically pre-

---

[5] For example, political representation as "substantively acting for" the people may be read narrowly as requiring the representative to act strictly on constituent instructions (the pure delegate) or read broadly to allow the representative a good deal of independence (the pure trustee). See ibid., pp. 144–67.

[6] Ibid., p. 217.

[7] Ibid., p. 167, emphasis added.

[8] Thus, Pitkin's claim has much in common with the notion of "essentially contested concepts" coined by W. B. Gallie and developed by William Connolly. See Connolly 1983. An emphasis on the contestability of representation permits Pitkin to outflank critics. Writers that stress one view of representation, or that seek to dissolve tension between several views, do not prove Pitkin wrong so much as they provide a particular rendering of representation consistent with Pitkin's general argument. See Schwartz 1988 for one such attempt to read representation through the lens of civic republicanism.

sent—are "metapolitical" visions of whom the people are, what their interests look like, and how their politics ought to be conducted. The basic terms of representational debates are thus invested with their own emphases and exclusions, comprising a distinct discourse that frames political thought and action.[9] Political actors engaged in such a discourse of representation appeal to a limited set of assumptions and commitments, producing specific understandings of what counts as meaningful or important in the debate. Any given politics of representation, then, engenders a discrete repertoire of strategies for making sense of the political community. To identify and evaluate this repertoire is to understand the politics of representation.

Stated in this way, Pitkin's argument is somewhat abstract. The analytical leverage provided by her framework is nonetheless quite powerful. To see this, consider the example of James Madison. Like many Americans of his time, Madison was deeply concerned with political representation. The issue of representation not only motivated the first break between Britain and the colonies but also remained a key factor until the ratification of the Constitution more than a decade later.[10] Such a prolonged concern with the theory and practice of representation deeply marked American politics, differentiating it at base from the politics of other nations. Indeed, while some scholars have stressed the broad distinction between Europe's feudal past and America's liberal tradition, eighteenth-century Americans frequently focused their own claims of American exceptionalism more narrowly on representation.[11] As Madison observed, "the difference most relied on between the American and other republics consists in the principle of representation, which is the pivot on which the former move, and which is supposed to have been unknown to the latter."[12]

As a leading participant in early American politics, Madison defended his own account of representation—a defense that can be understood

[9] See Connolly 1983, pp. 1–44, 179–247; and Strong 1990, pp. 1–38, 72–109. I am not endorsing here the stronger approach to political discourse, which renders intellectual history in terms of broad "political paradigms" governing thought and action over the course of centuries. See Pocock 1971, chap. 1; 1975; and 1985, chap. 1. I make no claims to have identified such a paradigm.

[10] Bailyn 1967, pp. 160–75; Wood 1969, pp. 162–96, 593–615; Reid 1989, pp. 4–5.

[11] Hartz 1955; Tocqueville 1966.

[12] Hamilton, Madison, and Jay 1961, No. 63, p. 386. To be precise, Madison actually conceded the existence of representation in the ancient world, but he claimed that American government was unique because it entirely removed the people from all positions of direct legislative power.

as turning on "metapolitical" assumptions.[13] Madison began with the claim that rational political deliberation was the goal of the Constitution: "[I]t is the reason, alone, of the public, that ought to control and regulate the government. The passions ought to be controlled and regulated by the government."[14] For Madison, public passion posed the primary threat to stable self-government. Interactions between liberty, self-love, and an unequal distribution of property ensured that democratic society would always be riven with factional conflict. A government that relied upon the popular will risked rule by factional passion, fostering rages for "wicked" projects such as debtor relief.[15] At the extreme, the turbulent history of direct democracies revealed the destructiveness of public passion where the people and the government were coterminous. "Had every Athenian been a Socrates," Madison argued, "every Athenian assembly would still have been a mob."[16]

Fearing a politics of passion, Madison cast representation as a means for distancing the people from the government. Excluding the people from direct decision making altogether, representation created the possibility of a more rational politics. The electoral structure established by the Constitution permitted the majority to defeat "sinister" minority views and encouraged the selection of those individuals who knew the "true interest of their country."[17] Where elections failed to "refine" or "enlarge" public views, the conditions upon which public reason prevailed could nonetheless be achieved.[18] Separating political institutions from the people, representation allowed the republic to be expanded greatly, embracing a multiplicity of factional interests under the jurisdiction of a single government. In the large, diverse republic, Madison thought it unlikely that a majority of citizens bent on invading minority rights could coalesce and carry out its plans. Where passion was unable to convulse the community, the concerted action of a majority would

---

[13] See Reid 1989, pp. 21, 68–70, for a sense of the metapolitical assumptions at work in the earlier conflict between the American colonists and Britain.

[14] Hamilton, Madison, and Jay 1961, No. 49, p. 317. My interpretation of Madison's thought is informed by Pitkin 1967, pp. 190–98; Beer 1993; Sunstein 1993, pp. 17–39; and Bessette 1994, pp. 6–39.

[15] Ibid., No. 10, p. 84.

[16] Ibid., No. 55, p. 342.

[17] Ibid., No. 10, pp. 80, 82.

[18] Ibid., p. 82.

almost of necessity have to depend upon principles of "justice and the general good."[19]

In addition to cultivating social equilibrium, representation helped mute passion within government itself. Madison reasoned that a legislative assembly left on its own would simply reproduce the factional divisions of the multitude without facing similar obstacles to collective action.[20] The design of the Constitution addressed this problem of legislative tyranny by charging government officers with different duties and electing them by different means. The division of power among the government's branches, allowing each to check and balance the other, loosened the grip of passion on representatives, reconfiguring the private interest of each into a "sentinel" over the rights of all.[21]

I shall have more to say about the substance of Madison's representational views in the coming chapters. For now, however, the value of Madison is largely analytical. Madison's reliance on conceptions of popular passion and public reason concretely illustrates Pitkin's abstract claim: the Madisonian account of representation is embedded within and draws its meaning from a broader "metapolitical" vision of who the people are and how their politics ought to be organized. Pitkin's approach thus helps to expose the conceptual depths of Madison's position, indicating how his defense of particular representational institutions rests on a distinct political theory. Beyond furnishing a better understanding of Madison, the identification of metapolitical premises also provides a basis for comparative evaluation, calling attention to the conceptual dimensions along which competing theories of representation ought to be measured.[22] In this vein, the application of Pitkin's metapolitical analysis suggests a contemporary extension. Keeping the

[19] Ibid., No. 51, p. 325.

[20] Ibid., No. 48, p. 309.

[21] Ibid., No. 51, p. 322. The balancing among "representative" institutions included the judiciary (see ibid., No. 78, and Wood 1969, pp. 453–63, 547–53). I discuss below the implications of treating the judiciary as being in some sense representative.

[22] The Antifederalists, for example, rejected Madison's claims about public passion. On the contrary, they emphasized the political danger of aristocratic corruption (see Kenyon 1966). A comparison between theories of passion and corruption could be developed historically. (The Antifederalist argument was prefigured by Whig political theories and later echoed by Progressives of the 1920s — see Wood 1969, pp. 515–16; Beard 1949, and Nedelsky 1990a.) It could also be developed normatively (by seeking notions of representation better than those linked to passion or corruption — see Nedelsky 1990a, pp. 224ff, and 1990b for an attempt to do so with notions of property).

Madisonian example in view, one could examine the current politics of minority representation for (i) metapolitical conceptions of "the people" and their interests; (ii) the visions of the political community generated in terms of such metapolitical conceptions; and (iii) the emphases, omissions, and bias built into these visions of the political community. At the end of such an examination, alternative renderings of minority representation, free from the constraints of the existing discourse, could be described and discussed.

But before these tasks can begin — before a better understanding of the politics of minority representation can be reached — the significance of conducting representational politics in the judicial arena must be considered. The question set forth at the outset of this chapter must again be posed and addressed directly: What kind of problem does the politics of representation denote for the Supreme Court?

UNDERSTANDING JUDICIAL INVOLVEMENT IN THE POLITICS OF REPRESENTATION

> Even if he is mediocre there are a lot of mediocre judges and people and lawyers. They are entitled to a little representation, aren't they, and a little chance?
> *(Senator Hruska defending the unsuccessful nomination of Judge G. Harrold Carswell to the Supreme Court in 1970)*

To get a proper sense of the relationship between the judiciary and representational politics, it is important to understand that among the branches of American government the Supreme Court is a unique representative body. Appointed by the president and confirmed by the Senate, Supreme Court justices are constitutionally permitted to hold office "during good behavior," a phrase that has in practice allowed most justices to serve on the Court for life.[23] Effective life tenure frees justices from the restraints of direct electoral accountability, creating a Court that can review and interpret legislation from an independent perspective.[24] In this sense, the Court might be said to be unrepresentative by

[23] Art. III, sec. 1.

[24] Although some scholars have denied that the Court has significant independence (Dahl 1957; Rosenberg 1992), the balance of evidence suggests otherwise. The Court may

design. Yet, if judicial independence distances the Court from the mass constituencies that underwrite and oversee representative government, the aim of such independence is *not* that the Court will forego the task of representing altogether. Instead, judicial independence permits the Court to represent the interests of the people as a whole.

Of course, if the Court is to represent the people as a whole, it must first be possible to think of the entire people as a coherent political actor capable of having interests. The claim that the entire people could express a political will emerged during the initial years of the republic. Many of the earliest state constitutions had been written by state legislatures, but in the 1780s states began to rely on constitutional conventions to write their political charters.[25] Constitutional conventions provided an institutional context in which the political will of the people could be asserted independently from that of the legislature. State constitutions consequently represented something more than ordinary legislation; they were dictates of the whole people that not only provided the framework for ordinary legislation, but also remained unaltered unless changed by the people themselves. Framed and ratified by convention, the United States Constitution could be similarly viewed as a product of the whole people, making it unique among national charters. As Alexis de Tocqueville noted, "The American Constitution is not considered immutable, as in France; it cannot be changed by the ordinary authorities of society as in England. It is a thing apart; it represents the will of the whole people and binds the legislators as well as plain citizens, but it can be changed by the will of the people in accordance with established forms in anticipated eventualities."[26]

This is not to say that the entire people literally participated in the production of the Constitution. In fact, only a small proportion of eligible Americans were involved in the ratification process.[27] The use of constitutional conventions nonetheless opened a new political possibility. The identification of the Constitution with the will of the people created an opportunity for political actors to claim to speak for the people by interpreting the constitutional text. Throughout our history

---

not unilaterally determine policy (McCloskey 1960; Rosenberg 1991; M. Shapiro 1981), but it nonetheless has an important degree of influence beyond direct legislative control (Baum 1992a; Abraham 1993; B. Perry 1991; Lasser 1988; Segal and Spaeth 1993).

[25] Wood 1969, pp. 306–43. This method of constitution writing was even more frequently used throughout the nineteenth century (Rodgers 1987).

[26] Tocqueville 1966, p. 101.

[27] Berkowitz 1993.

the Supreme Court has been the institution which has most consistently exploited this opportunity.[28] Early assessments of the Supreme Court reveal that the capacity to represent "the people" was initially put forth as the central justification for judicial power. Defending the Constitution during the New York ratification debates, Alexander Hamilton fit the Court into the representative scheme articulated by Madison. Hamilton argued that the Court's independence from the legislature not only prevented the "pestilential breath of faction" from poisoning the "fountain of justice" but also allowed the Court to police legislative activity in the name of the people.[29] The Constitution was, according to Hamilton, an expression of the popular will; judicial enforcement of the Constitution against the legislature simply kept the servant obedient to the master. Hamilton thus claimed that the judicial review of legislation did not "suppose a superiority of the judicial to the legislative power. It only suppose[d] that the power of the people [was] superior to both."[30] Indeed, as a spokesman of the people, the Court might even go so far as to represent the people as a whole against the majority, guarding the Constitution from popular "ill humors" that "occasion dangerous innovations in the government, and serious oppressions of the minor party in the community."[31] As with the other institutions established by the Constitution, it was the Court's distance from the passionate populace that gave the judiciary a representative political voice.

Much like Hamilton, Chief Justice John Marshall also thought the proper understanding of the Court's authority hinged on its role as the people's representative. Marshall saw the Constitution as an act of the

---

[28] Compare Fishkin 1991. It is, of course, possible to think of courts in general as nonrepresentative. The whole natural-law tradition grounds legal authority in universal codes of justice and does not rely on courts somehow being representative of the people. See D'Entreves 1970. In the American context, it is important to note two things. First, claims concerning the Constitution's supremacy have always been rooted in appeals to the document's origins in the whole people. Even during the founding, assertions that the Constitution was an expression of natural or eternal justice never provided the sole grounds for the view that the Constitution is "higher law." See Corwin 1928, pp. 151–52. Second, while attempts to situate Supreme Court decision making within moral theory currently abound in constitutional scholarship, they generally preserve judicial connections to the people by seeking to identify moral theories that are themselves expressive of the American public's values and aspirations. See, for example, Dworkin 1977; and Smith 1985.

[29] Hamilton, Madison, and Jay 1961, No. 81, p. 484; No. 78, pp. 465–66.

[30] Ibid., No. 78, pp. 467–68.

[31] Ibid., p. 469.

entire people assembled, making the United States government in form and substance "emphatically and truly a government of the people."[32] Marshall contended that such a popularly forged charter could only be rendered in broad outline.

> A constitution, to contain an accurate detail of all the subdivisions of which its great powers will admit, and of all the means by which they may be carried into execution, would partake of the prolixity of a legal code, and could scarcely be embraced by the human mind. It would probably never be understood by the public. Its nature, therefore, requires, that only its great outlines should be marked, its important objects designated, and the minor ingredients which compose those objects be deduced from the nature of the objects themselves.[33]

Marshall argued further that the people could not supply the interpretative extensions their Constitution required. Having constructed a political order, the constitutional authors withdrew from the public stage and left behind a new set of governmental institutions. According to Marshall, only the judiciary among the newly created institutions could legitimately and finally "say what the law is."[34] Thus, the Supreme Court bore the responsibility for interpreting the supreme law codified in the Constitution, acting as the only authoritative representative of the (entire) sovereign people.

In the arguments of Hamilton and Marshall, judicial representativeness emerged as a straightforward political fact. In truth, however, invocations of "the people" were fraught with ambiguity and conflict. Although the Constitution presented itself as a work of "We the People," the identity of the people was not disclosed within the document. During the early decades of the republic, this lacuna raised a particular question of definition: When the Constitution spoke of "the people," did it view them as a single national community or as an assemblage of states?[35] Unlike Hamilton and Marshall, many political actors viewed the Constitution as a pact among the various states, effectively denying that a national people could be the font of constitutional authority.[36]

---

[32] *McCulloch v. Maryland*, 17 U.S. 316, 405 (1819). For an extended analysis of the role "the people" play in *McCulloch*, see White 1984, chap. 9. On Marshall's thought more generally, see Stimson 1990.

[33] *McCulloch* at 407.

[34] *Marbury v. Madison*, 5 U.S. 137, 177 (1803).

[35] Moore 1996.

[36] The state-centric view was thrown into doubt by the Civil War (Newmyer 1988; Beer

With conflicting conceptions of "the people" in play, claims about judicial power could be easily multiplied in incompatible directions — a situation that would only be exacerbated as additional conceptions beyond the nation/state dichotomy were introduced.

The indeterminacies of "the people" understandably encouraged some jurists to take a dim view of the term. Alexander Bickel, for example, saw the word *people* as a "mystic abstraction" used by both Hamilton and Marshall to obscure the hard fact that the Court's political interventions are undemocratic.[37] "[C]oherent, stable — and *morally supportable* — government is possible only on the basis of consent," Bickel wrote, "[and] the secret of consent is the sense of common venture fostered by institutions that reflect and represent us and that we can call to account."[38] An electorally unaccountable, politically activist Court inevitably frustrated this "sense of common venture," disabling self-government even as it claimed to be enacting the people's will.

Bickel correctly noted that appeals to "the people" did not restrain the Court in the same manner that popular elections disciplined legislators. Yet Bickel was wrong to suggest that judicial references to "the people" were simply mystical or misleading. After all, Bickel himself assigned the Court an important representative function. He argued that the long-range interests of the nation were not likely to be well represented by legislators concerned with immediate results. The independence and training of Supreme Court justices permitted them to "appeal to men's better natures, to call forth their aspirations, which may have been forgotten in the moment's hue and cry."[39] Thus, Bickel did not reject claims about the Court's representativeness. On the contrary, he tried to circumscribe the political authority derived from such claims by decrying their antidemocratic implications.[40] In the end, the difference between Hamilton and Marshall, on the one hand, and Bickel, on the other, was not that the former invoked a "mystic" notion

---

1993), but it has survived as a viable component of American political discourse. See *U.S. Term Limits v. Thornton*, 514 U.S. 779 (1995).

[37] Bickel, 1962, pp. 16–17.

[38] Ibid., p. 20, emphasis original.

[39] Ibid., p. 26.

[40] In later works, Bickel's sense of the Court's legitimate limits, as well as of the dangers of violating such limits, grew stronger. See Bickel 1975. Bickel's pattern of argument — recognizing the Court as a representative of the people while limiting the range of political authority that can be said to flow from such representation — is shared by conservatives such as Robert Bork and Raoul Berger. See Perry 1982, pp. 61–69.

of the people but that the former and the latter disagreed on what counted as a legitimate understanding of "the people" in the first place.

The surprising commonality between Bickel, Marshall, and Hamilton is instructive because it underscores the singularity of the Supreme Court's representativeness. The Court is a representative institution — not in the sense that justices are directly accountable to electoral constituencies but in the sense that the Court usually justifies its political authority in terms of its capacity to speak for the people as a whole. In other words, judicial representation is not a matter of *political agency* (responding to the demands of a preexisting constituency) so much as it is a matter of *political entrepreneurship* (organizing or creating the constituency on whose behalf the Court shall speak). From the perspective of Pitkin's analysis, one would expect the Court's political entrepreneurship to entail controversy and debate. Pitkin argued that representational debates turn on competing conceptions of political identity — disputants disagree about representation because they possess different understandings of what people ought to be represented in the first place. The Supreme Court is certainly unusual because its claims to authority are linked to its own understanding of "the people" on whose behalf it deliberates. Yet the judicial interest in formulating a view of political identity hardly frees the Court from the ambiguities and limits that characterize representational politics. Members of the Court are no more likely than anyone else to arrive at a single conception of "the people" free of all biases and exclusions. As a consequence, no version of judicial representation will be final or beyond debate; each treatment of the Court's authority will incorporate its own sense of what people and which interests are to count.

To say that the claim of judicial representativeness is inherently controversial, however, is not to say that in every instance all such claims are equally valid. The absence of one final or universal theory of representation does not make it impossible to distinguish better theories from worse ones. The value of any given representational theory depends on the context in which it operates and the purposes it seeks to serve. Accounts of representation may be more or less appropriate for local circumstances, more or less suited for specific institutional settings and political environments. While complete consensus on ultimate questions may prove elusive, one can still hope to refine the terms of debate.[41]

What standard can be used to evaluate judicial claims of represen-

[41] See Geertz 1973, p. 29.

tativeness? Or, to put this question another way, what theories of representation are appropriate for an institution like the Supreme Court? I have argued that the Court exercises its power through political entrepreneurship, articulating a specific understanding of "the people" on whose behalf the Court then acts. If this process is to be consistent with democratic rule — if it is to engender government by the sovereign people rather than to erect government by an unaccountable judiciary — then the Court's political entrepreneurship must be exercised so that it can be reviewed and ultimately controlled by the people and their electoral representatives. In a word, the Court must not speak for the people in a way that prevents the people from finally speaking for themselves. This requirement takes on particular significance when the Court adjudicates cases concerning political representation. Like all legal controversies, disputes over the meaning of fair representation provide the Court with an opportunity to recast the parameters of its own authority. Even so, representational litigation (including litigation over minority representation) is uniquely important because it directly affects the electoral rules that dictate the terms of political power. The politics of representation thus places the judiciary in a critical position: in judging between different representational theories, members of the Court not only select a form of political community that they believe ought to obtain but they also reconfigure the institutional environment and, in doing so, directly determine the sort of political community that will obtain. In such a context, where the Court simultaneously chooses the terms on which itself and the people exercise power, it is essential that judicial actions taken on behalf of the people ultimately preserve the people's capacity to act for themselves.

As a threshold matter, this requirement prohibits the Court from unilaterally excluding individuals from the political community. Assertions of judicial authority that extinguish the political existence of some groups clearly leave the whole people unable to speak for themselves. *Dred Scott v. Sandford* (1857), in which the Court ruled that African Americans were not part of "We the People," is an infamous example of such a violation.[42] Short of outright exclusion, the Court can also fail to satisfy its representative requirement by not making its political entrepreneurship public. By refusing to justify or take responsibility for its selected conception of "the people," the Court obscures the grounds on which its claims of authority can be evaluated. Without a public expla-

---

[42] *Dred Scott v. Sandford*, 60 U.S. 393 (1857).

nation of how the judiciary performs its representational tasks, the citizenry lack a principled basis on which to assess and ultimately direct the Court's political role. In this sense, then, one could say that Alexander Bickel had it backward: mystification does not occur when the Court invokes notions of "the people" so much as when it fails to explain how such notions are used to sustain judicial power.

The view of judicial representativeness I have described allows Court power to be justified in a wide range of ways. Even so, it is important to keep in mind that the criteria governing judicial representativeness are not completely plastic and they do rule out some approaches. Indeed, when judged against the criteria I have elaborated, several leading accounts of judicial representativeness prove to be inadequate.

Bruce Ackerman, for example, explains judicial authority by arguing that the Supreme Court *directly* represents "We the People."[43] According to Ackerman, the short-term interests of normal American politics occasionally give way to "constitutional politics," in which an engaged citizenry renders judgments about fundamental political principles. The Court preserves these extraordinary judgments against the fleeting decisions of more ordinary times, acting as "an on-going representative of a mobilized People during the lengthy periods of apathy, ignorance, and selfishness that mark the collective life of the private citizenry of a liberal republic."[44]

Ackerman elaborates his argument with an immense amount of historical detail, but his model of judicial action remains that of the Court responding to the people's commands. This portrait of the Court as a political agent is highly problematic, not only because there is no reliable mechanism for informing the Court when its constituency has spoken but also because it disregards the Court's entrepreneurial activity.[45] These twin difficulties undermine Ackerman's discussion from the outset. He attempts to portray the original Constitution as the literal expression of the people's will, even though constitutional ratification actually involved only a small fraction of eligible Americans. The fact of low participation is, to say the least, inhospitable to the practice of political agency. Without the full mobilization and engagement of the people, the Court-as-political-agent can have no authority for there exists no constituency to mandate action in the first place. Wishing to

[43] Ackerman 1991.

[44] Ibid., p. 265.

[45] These problems similarly plague scholars who argue that the Court's political agency is exercised on behalf of less extraordinary majorities (see Abrams 1993).

maintain a significant degree of judicial power, Ackerman is forced to choose between his view of political agency and an accurate description of constitutional ratification. He chooses the former, insisting that the whole people literally authored the Constitution.[46] In straying from the facts of ratification, Ackerman also deflects attention away from the way in which the judiciary actually relied on the people. As I have noted, the absence of complete participation hardly foreclosed the possibility of political entrepreneurship. The use of ratifying conventions permitted *the claim* that the Constitution was the work of the entire people and, in doing so, allowed the Court to rationalize its own authority in like terms. Such an entrepreneurial maneuver raises questions of accountability, for judicial action is not strictly initiated by a popular constituency. Yet, the fact that any given instance of entrepreneurship may be questionable and worthy of public disapprobation is no reason to deny its existence. Indeed, the refusal to recognize the Court's entrepreneurship undermines the public capacity to understand and ultimately to restrain judicial power.

Although his approach is in some ways superior to Ackerman's, John Hart Ely also underplays the Court's political entrepreneurship.[47] Ely believes that the Court should act in the name of all citizens, preserving the integrity of the political process by preventing those with power from neglecting those without it. Unlike Ackerman, Ely does not claim that "a mobilized People" can literally direct judicial action. Instead, he argues that the Court itself should draw a vision of representative government from the constitutional text. Ely's mistake is to insist that the Court can derive only one possible understanding of "the people," their interests, and the institutions designed to represent them.

To see this, consider Ely's celebration of the reapportionment revolution.[48] In 1962, faced with state legislatures that had failed to reapportion themselves for more than sixty years, the Supreme Court declared that large population disparities across legislative districts were unconstitutional.[49] Over the course of the next three decades, the Court applied an equal-population standard ("one person, one vote") to all levels of government, ensuring that members of the same legislative

---

[46] See Berkowitz 1993.

[47] Ely 1980.

[48] The literature on reapportionment is enormous. See, for example, M. Shapiro 1964 and 1985; Dixon 1968; Polsby 1971; Elliot 1974; Levinson 1985; Lowenstein and Steinberg 1985; McCubbins and Schwartz 1988; Tribe 1988; and Maveety 1991.

[49] *Baker v. Carr*, 369 U.S. 186 (1962).

body would each be responsible to roughly the same number of constituents.[50] Ely views the one-person–one-vote rule as a constitutionally decreed reinforcement of the representative system. Placing particular emphasis on the most recent constitutional amendments, he argues that there is a "strengthening constitutional commitment to the proposition that all qualified citizens are to play a role in the making of public decisions" — a commitment that amounts to a "general ideal . . . of at least rough equality in terms of one's influence on governmental choices."[51] According to Ely, this ideal of equal influence is instantiated by the one-person–one-vote guarantee of numerical equality.

The difficulty with his conclusion is that there are actually many different ways of conceptualizing equal influence.[52] Even if one accepts Ely's reading of the Constitution as definitive, it is entirely reasonable to treat numerical equality as a floor rather than as a ceiling. At the time of the reapportionment revolution, a number of justices and a chorus of scholars reasoned in precisely this vein, calling for recognition of the ways in which *group* membership also shaped the effective representation of individuals.[53] Their argument was that even where the rule of equal population prevailed, legislators might still deny distinct political voices by submerging them within districts controlled by a dominant group.

Ely fails to investigate the significance of group attachments, treating equal population as *the* constitutional means of equalizing political influence at the electoral stage. In doing so, he misunderstands the impli-

---

[50] The one-person–one-vote rule was applied with varying degrees of rigor at state and national levels of government. For the judicial decisions developing this rule, see *Gray v. Sanders*, 372 U.S. 368 (1963); *Wesberry v. Sanders*, 376 U.S. 1 (1964); and *Reynolds v. Sims*, 377 U.S. 533 (1964).

[51] Ely 1980, p. 123.

[52] See, generally, Wolin 1989, pp. 120–36; and Wolin 1993.

[53] See Justice Stewart's dissent in *Lucas v. Forty-fourth General Assembly of Colorado*, 377 U.S. 713, 744–65 (1964); M. Shapiro 1964, pp. 216–52, and 1985; Dixon 1968, pp. 3–23, 46–56, and 1971; Bickel 1971; Elliot 1974, pp. 237–74; and Maveety 1991, pp.19–38 (As I discuss in chapter 5, Justice Stewart would later embrace a form of individualism in *Mobile v. Bolden*, 446 U.S. 55 [1980]). During the reapportionment revolution, the Court did in fact explore group-based arguments in decisions concerning minority representation (see chapter four). It's worth noting that group-based arguments still surface in the one-person–one-vote context (see *Board of Estimate v. Morris*, 489 U.S. 688 [1989]; and Gelfand and Allbritton 1989). Note also that the judicial interest in group-oriented approaches has been extended to political as well as racial groups. See *Gaffney v. Cummings*, 412 U.S. 735 (1973); *Davis v. Bandemer*, 478 U.S. 109 (1986); and Grofman 1990.

cations of reapportionment that were stated so clearly by Justice Felix Frankfurter. Dissenting from the Court's initial decision to evaluate representational schemes, Justice Frankfurter argued that controversial theoretical choices were implicit in legislative apportionment:

> What, then, is this question of legislative apportionment? Appellants invoke the right to vote and to have their votes counted. But they are permitted to vote and their votes are counted. They go to the polls, they cast their ballots, they send their representatives to the state councils. Their complaint is simply that the representatives are not sufficiently numerous or powerful—in short, that [the state] has adopted a basis of representation with which they are dissatisfied. Talk of "debasement" or "dilution" is circular talk. One cannot speak of "debasement" or "dilution" of the value of a vote until there is first defined a standard of reference as to what a vote should be worth. What is actually asked of the Court in this case is to choose among competing bases of representation—ultimately, really, between competing theories of political philosophy—in order to establish an appropriate frame of government . . . for all the States of the Union.[54]

The adjudication of reapportionment plans requires the Court to intervene among competing conceptions of "the people" and to determine how the political community ought to be structured. Contrary to Ely, "one person, one vote" can only be a *part* of this debate over the warp and woof of representation. Judicial representativeness may be elaborated in a way that supports numerical equality across districts, but it is not the only way (or necessarily the best way) in which the Court's entrepreneurship can be exercised.

James Boyd White offers an account of judicial representativeness that avoids some pitfalls of Ely's approach. White assigns the Court responsibility for representing a whole variety of popular identities and interests in its decisions.[55] His insistence that multiple perspectives be recognized—an insistence that he calls a standard of "many-voicedness"—is consistent with a broader argument about judicial legitimacy.[56] When any court decides in favor of one disputant, state authority is

---

[54] *Baker v. Carr* at 299–300, citations omitted. Frankfurter believed the Court could not handle such choices. Hence his claim made sixteen years prior to *Baker*: "Courts ought not to enter this political thicket [i.e., legislative apportionment]." See *Colegrove v. Green*, 328 U.S. 549, 556 (1946), and my discussion of this case in chapter 4.

[55] White 1973; 1984; 1985; and 1990.

[56] White 1985, p. 124.

placed behind the prevailing party. The result is a problem of legitimacy, which can be solved only if the defeated party can be persuaded to accept the judge's decision. Among other things, courts have long relied on mechanisms of consent to secure the compliance of losing litigants.[57] White's standard of "many-voicedness" is an effort to elicit the consent that all courts seek. Calling for inclusive opinions, he suggests how the Supreme Court might represent the interests of the entire people, thereby enhancing consent and bolstering judicial legitimacy. Unlike Ely, White does not claim there is a fixed understanding of "the people" on whose behalf the Court ought to speak. On the contrary, he argues for the elimination of judicial strategies that prevent alternative conceptions of "the people" from rising to the surface. Rigid appeals to plain meaning or original intent should be disavowed, for example, because they preclude the "simultaneous recognition of contrasting positions" and, thus, fail to represent the interests of the people and win their consent.[58]

The problem with White's position is that his demand for "many-voicedness" fails to confront fundamental controversies of representational politics. White understands the need for a flexible style of judicial representation, permitting the Court to speak for the people without impairing their capacity to speak for themselves. Yet White fails to apprehend the essential contestability of the concepts on which all theories of representation are based.[59] In articulating a theory of how the Court ought to represent, White takes a position on controversial terrain. His appeal to many-voicedness is itself a move in a politics of representation concerned with the basis of judicial power. Of course, participation in such a politics by no means invalidates his effort; as I have argued, to offer any theory of representation is always to offer a contestable way of making sense out of the political community. The point is that the political nature of representation must be recognized. No version of representation is all-inclusive, for each version incorporates its own sense of what people and which interests are to count. While the standard of many-voicedness is more capacious than the standard of "one person, one vote," *both* standards are embedded within their own discrete visions of the political community. Thus, it is not enough simply to demand equal respect for different voices, for the substance of re-

---

[57] See also M. Shapiro 1981, pp. 1–64.

[58] White 1984, p. 267; 1985, pp. 116, 134, 241; and 1990, pp. 113–59. See also Carter 1985, pp. 143, 146, 150, 164, 178.

[59] For a complementary critique, see Fish 1994, pp. 172–75.

spect will depend on the kind of equality posited and the type of polity pursued. White's mistake is to fail to identify and defend such baseline choices.

The example of critical race theory provides an illustration. Critical race theorists share White's goals of equal recognition and many-voicedness.[60] But critical race theorists contend that such goals can be achieved only by valuing the victim's account of racial harm *above* that of a First Amendment absolutist or of anyone else. To recognize some, others must be substantially or completely ignored.[61] The fact that critical race theorists can coherently advocate a hierarchy of "stories" on the basis of White's premises is telling. It suggests that the quest for judicial inclusiveness is less a matter of simply hearing all litigants than of hearing each litigant in the appropriate way. Critical race theorists derive their understanding of what's appropriate from a series of claims about the depth of American racism.[62] To argue against them, one must contest the claims on which their understanding rests. To respond, as White does, simply with the assertion that judicial argument ought to strive for many-voicedness is to miss the point.

THE ANALYTICAL SIGNIFICANCE OF POLITICAL IDENTITY AND JUDICIAL REPRESENTATIVENESS

There are additional accounts of judicial representativeness that might be discussed, but my aim in this chapter has been to outline an analytical framework rather than to review a scholarly literature.[63] To this end, I have argued that conceptions of political identity are central to the politics of representation. I began with the claim that representational theories rest on metapolitical assumptions concerning who "the people" are, what their interests look like, and how their politics ought to be conducted. On this basis, I have suggested that different theories of rep-

[60] See, e.g., Matsuda 1993; Delgado 1993 and 1989; and Massaro 1989.

[61] Compare Minow 1987a, p. 92: "Even when we understand them, some voices will lose."

[62] See Lawrence et. al. 1993, pp. 6–7.

[63] See Dworkin 1977, pp. 131–49 (arguing that, given the narrow self-interest of elected legislators, only an independent court can represent the constitutional interests of all people); Hirsch 1992, pp. 90–116 (arguing that only the Court can represent important "social facts" derived from broad consensus among the people); and Sunstein 1984, 1988, and 1990 (arguing that the Court subverts "naked preferences" of the legislature by insisting that politicians pursue the public good).

resentation express distinct ways of making sense out of the political community, providing different means of negotiating conflict and developing consensus. Unless such conflicting visions of political community are distinguished and compared, competing theories of representation cannot be adequately understood.

I have argued that when the Supreme Court participates in the politics of representation, the role of political identity becomes at once more significant and better defined. This is so because the Court is a representative institution — not in the sense that justices are directly accountable to electoral constituencies, but in the sense that the Court usually justifies its political authority in terms of its capacity to speak for the people as a whole. Judicial representation is a matter of political entrepreneurship, creating the constituency on whose behalf the judiciary shall speak rather than strictly responding to the demands of a preexisting constituency. As a result, one can say that the meaning of fair representation and the extent of judicial power *both* rest on understandings of "the people." Adjudicating disputes over voting rules and electoral districts, the Court generates different justifications for its own authority as it endorses different conceptions of who "the people" are and how they ought to be represented. The judicial discourse of representation is therefore comprised by conflicting visions of the political community as well as by conflicting visions of the Court's role within these alternative political communities.

Taken together, these factors suggest a standard for gauging judicial intervention: if our government is to remain democratic, then the Court must not speak for the people in a way that prevents the people from finally speaking for themselves. At minimum, this standard prohibits the Court from unilaterally excluding groups from its understanding of "the people." Such actions diminish the citizenry and literally leave the whole people incapable of evaluating and controlling judicial power. The Court may also violate this standard by failing to explain the notion of "the people" on which it relies. Where the basic fact of political entrepreneurship is denied (as in the case of Ackerman) or where the contestability of representational claims is misconstrued (as with Ely and White), the Court obscures the basis on which it exercises authority and, thereby, insulates itself from informed evaluation.

All of this suggests that when assessing judicial participation in the politics of minority representation, one should consider (i) what notions of political identity are at stake and (ii) whether judicial reliance on such notions ultimately preserves the capacity of the people to speak for themselves. To pursue these two prongs of analysis is not to presume some unattainable ideal of theoretical rigor. Supreme Court justices have no special talents or advantages that permit them to articulate a single, all-inclusive interpretation of the ever-contestable concept of representation. Moreover, the Court is necessarily sensitive to the peculiarities of any given dispute. Fleshing out legal standards on a case-by-case basis, members of the Court allow matters of emphasis and degree to shift in response to specific contexts. Such a process works against large-scale a priori theorizing, but it does permit the Court to reach decisions without having to resolve all controversies in a single stroke — an advantage that produces, as Edward Levi noted, "the *only* kind of system which will work when people do not agree completely."[64] Yet, even though justices are not professional political theorists, judging often involves theoretical issues. When intervening in the politics of minority representation, the Supreme Court inevitably confronts competing notions of political identity. The following chapters evaluate this confrontation.

[64] Levi 1949, p. 104, emphasis added. See also Sunstein 1996.

Sound and Fury: Identifying the Role of Political Identity in the Public Debate

THE CHALLENGE of any Court-led politics of representation is to raise conceptions of political identity to the surface, bringing critical attention to bear on how the judiciary fashions the political community as it shapes its own political power.

The first step toward meeting this analytical challenge requires an examination of the public debate over the adjudication of minority representation under the Voting Rights Act of 1965. Three basic positions have prevailed in the debate, distinguished largely by their different views on whether the Voting Rights Act should be rolled back, pushed forward, or simply maintained. Given these differences in orientation, these ideological responses to the act can be called conservative, progressive, and centrist.[1] The conflicting claims of conservatives and progressives set the outer limits of debate, making discussion of minority representation a sharply contested and exceedingly polarized affair. In such a context of mutually exclusive assertions, the centrist attempt to strike a reasonable balance appears immediately appealing.

Yet the middle position articulated by centrists does not hold. The centrist effort to defuse the conflict between conservatives and progressives is incomplete and conceptually shallow. Failing to acknowledge the centrality of political identity in representational disputes, centrist commentators miss the conceptual depth of existing disagreements, offering a defense of the act incommensurate with the criticisms that assail it. The debate over minority representation simply cannot be advanced without taking seriously the ways in which conservatives and progressives talk past or misunderstand one another. An analysis of

---

[1] Davidson 1992, has called these three camps *narrow constructionists, expansive constructionists*, and *stand-patters*. These labels are cumbersome. Largely for purposes of exposition, I use the terms *conservative, progressive*, and *centrist*. To avoid confusion, it is important to remember that I define the various responses in terms of their specific orientation to the act—thus, my distinctions cannot be said to correspond perfectly to the divisions between Republicans and Democrats.

centrism and its shortcomings paves the way for the direct examination of Supreme Court decisions in the next two chapters.

CONSERVATIVES AND PROGRESSIVES

The conservative view, set forth by Abigail Thernstrom and others, argues that the Voting Rights Act has been used to grant minorities quotas of political power.[2] While conservatives acknowledge the original need to end the political exclusion of southern blacks, they assert that the nationwide inquiry into vote dilution has significantly distorted American politics. Once minorities can register and vote freely, their voting strength cannot be said to be more "diluted" than that of any other political participants — winners or losers. To speak of vote dilution or meaningful representation is to deflect the Voting Rights Act away from the question of equal political opportunity. Instead, as Thernstrom writes, the central question becomes: "How much special protection from white competition are blacks entitled to?"[3]

Conservatives argue that the transformation of the Voting Rights Act into an affirmative-action program has been collectively driven by intimidation, opportunism, and confusion.[4] As early as the 1975 amendments, conservatives claim, civil-rights lobbyists gained control of Democratic legislators, making support for the act into a litmus test for liberal credentials. A vote against the extension of the act was consequently taken as a vote for political exclusion and racial discrimination. Such framing locked Democrats into backing any and all efforts to enhance minority voting rights, effectively holding congressional majorities hostage to the civil-rights agenda. Conservatives contend that Republican legislators pursued the carrot of racial gerrymandering while avoiding the stick of civil-rights pressure.[5] Packing large numbers of minorities into majority-minority districts, Voting Rights Act remedies effectively bolstered Republican fortunes by preventing the minority (largely Democratic) population from obtaining influence in additional

---

[2] Thernstrom 1987. For related strains of conservatism, see Alexander 1989; O'Rourke 1992; Skerry 1993; Butler 1985; Graham 1992; Lane 1991; and Swain 1992; 1993.

[3] Thernstrom 1987, p. 5.

[4] Ibid., pp. 31–42, 79–136, 222–44. See also O'Rourke 1992; Graham 1992; and Lane 1991.

[5] In fact, Republican senators themselves claimed that civil-rights intimidation tainted deliberations over the 1982 amendments (see U.S. Senate 1982a, pp. 210–13).

districts. In this way, the "happy coincidence" between safe minority seats and efficient Republican districts wedded the interests of minority incumbents and Republican candidates; lost in the bargain, however, were the real interests of rank-and-file minorities.[6]

Finally, conservatives claim that the confusion of the courts in general (and of the Supreme Court in particular) has pushed the follies of Congress to their apogee. Erroneously believing that political pathologies can be cured simply with the application of the right rules, legal professionals have hijacked the Voting Rights Act, using it as a vehicle to circumvent the usual electoral mechanisms and clear a path for affirmative action. Thus, judicial proceedings, rather than democratic ones, have been used to determine how the people and their government ought to be connected. As Timothy O'Rourke writes, "the meaning of voting rights has come to have more to do with rights than with voting. . . . political equality has come to focus on equality more than on politics, [and] the democratic process has given way to judicially decreed results."[7]

The net result of the elite failure to deliberate seriously about the Voting Rights Act is that public awareness of representational policy has been usually low. In the words of Thernstrom, the Voting Rights Act has been "a controversial policy that has somehow stirred no controversy."[8] Nonetheless the consequences of conducting politics by racially sensitive legal rules are multiple and malign: (i) stereotypes of helpless minority victims are reinforced; (ii) minority officials preside over racially gerrymandered "rotten boroughs" and have little incentive to respond to the actual interests of their constituents; and (iii) the likelihood of racial balkanization is increased as society suffers under a federally sanctioned politics of race.[9]

The conservative account of the Voting Rights Act is opposed at virtually every turn by a group of progressives led by Lani Guinier, among others.[10] Progressives see the Voting Rights Act as guaranteeing equal opportunity to participate in a broadly conceived political process.[11]

---

[6] Thernstrom 1987, p. 234.

[7] O'Rourke 1992, p. 113.

[8] Thernstrom 1987, p. 233.

[9] Ibid., pp. 242–44; Skerry 1993, pp. 330–41; Swain 1993, pp. 47–73.

[10] Guinier 1991a; 1991b; 1992a; 1992b; 1993a; 1993b, and 1994. For related strains of progressivism, see Abrams 1988; 1993; Jones 1985; Karlan 1989; 1991; and 1993; Parker 1990; Hacker 1992; Still 1991; Blacksher 1993; and Young 1990.

[11] Guinier 1991a, pp. 1081–1101; Jones 1985; Karlan 1989, pp. 183–85; and Abrams 1988, pp. 451–53.

Thus, the act was designed to remedy the denial of minority choice *throughout* the political process — a denial that was manifest not only in the exclusion of minorities from the voting booth but also in the paucity of minority legislators and the failure of public policy to serve minority interests. In this view, the creation of majority-minority districts is a significant step toward the goal of protecting minority political choice, but it stops well short of guaranteeing that minority groups have their interests represented and actually satisfied a fair proportion of the time.

For progressives, then, to focus solely on the equal opportunity to elect officials is to guarantee that minorities receive only token representation in legislatures subject to white majority control. Conservative talk of "special protection" or "affirmative action" simply misses the point: an advantaged white majority enjoys a disproportionate amount of political power. From this perspective, it is not a matter of securing a special set-aside for minorities; instead, it is a question of ensuring equally meaningful participation for all voters, minority and nonminority alike. This aim can be achieved in part by the court-ordered deployment of modified at-large voting rules or of racially competitive "influence" districts, two mechanisms which ensure that even small, disbursed minority groups remain significant players in the electoral game.[12] Yet electoral reform alone will not suffice. As Guinier argues, "political equality requires both a standard for evaluating legislative influence and explicit mechanisms for overcoming inequality within the governing policymaking body."[13] Where minority legislators are opposed by a hostile white majority, a progressive standard of full participation can only be met by assigning minority vetoes or by requiring supermajorities for legislative decisions.

Given the progressive view, the question to ask of the Voting Rights Act is not "How has its enforcement spun out of control?" but rather "Why has its development stalled short of achieving its goal?"[14] Pro-

[12] Guinier 1991b, pp. 1461–76; Karlan 1989, pp. 226, 232; Still 1991; Abrams 1988, pp. 504–7, 519, 523, 525. Abrams (1988, pp. 488–501) and Fraga (1992) argue further that given the transformative potential of political participation, a change in electoral rules alone may be sufficient to achieve racial collaboration. (See Schwartz 1988, pp. 12–13, 129–32, for the stronger claim that district elections allow the same experience of transformative participation enjoyed by the ancient Greeks.) A focus on the realities of racial exclusion generally leads other progressives to reject such a strong civic republican or communitarian stance.

[13] Guinier 1992a, p. 288.

[14] Thernstrom's account of the act's development is attacked directly by Karlan and

gressives find the beginnings of an answer to this question in the exigencies of litigation. At a basic level, progressives claim that the process of litigating the act has pushed voting-rights law toward simple, easily administrable standards. Looking for a core value around which lawsuits could be organized, litigators have taken levels of minority electoral success to be the key indicator of equal political opportunity. Thus, the complex issue of fair minority representation has gradually been reduced to a few bits of numerical data.[15] While this simplifying strategy has worked to root out some forms of vote dilution, less readily quantifiable issues of representation and policy responsiveness have been dropped out of the legal calculus.

If only the pressures of litigation had been responsible for the act's stunted development, however, the protection of voting rights could easily be advanced by better measures of equal political opportunity — measures that progressives claim to have identified in their discussions of equitable legislative decision making. It is the additional pressure of racism, many progressives contend, that has kept minority power from seriously challenging white political control. In the face of proposals that would transform policymaking into a multiracial affair, white retrenchment has occurred throughout politics. White fear of black rule has affected administration of the act, leading Justice Department officials to provide token payoffs where substantial minority gains have been promised.[16] Moreover, this policy has been aggressively supported by the Republican party, an organization that clearly benefits from majority-minority districts and that some progressives see as "a white party, prepared to represent white Americans and defend their interests."[17] Finally, progressives suggest that some judges have themselves been infected with the desire to protect the "expectations of white voters at the expense of the aspirations of black voters."[18] Appealing to the sanctity of majority rule, the judiciary has frequently rebuffed efforts to reform the very electoral and legislative institutions that confine minorities to the political sidelines.

McCrary (1988), and Kousser (1992, pp. 164–76). See also, Guinier 1992a, pp. 1093–1101; Karlan 1991; Hacker 1992, pp. 199–219; and Jones 1985.

[15] This was particularly evident in the case of *Thornburg v. Gingles*, 478 U.S. 30 (1986), where the Court reduced the long list of vote dilution indicators given by the Senate Judiciary Committee in 1982 to a list of three quantitative measures.

[16] Jones (1985) is the strongest proponent of this claim.

[17] Hacker 1992, p. 201.

[18] Karlan 1991, p. 43.

Progressives conclude that the various sites of white resistance together foster an environment increasingly hostile to the goals of the Voting Rights Act. Indeed, as voting-rights litigator James Blacksher argues, the growing reliance on majoritarian rhetoric among political actors amounts to a "neo–white supremacist" movement, using a "tilt toward headcount democracy" to suppress the empowerment of historically subjugated minorities.[19] Only vigorous debate and active litigation can reverse the trend of retrenchment and restore the possibility of equitable power sharing.

THE REASONABLE MIDDLE GROUND OF THE CENTRISTS

On the whole, while conservatives and progressives are united in their rejection of the status quo, they diverge sharply in their reasons for seeking change. Both camps level indictments against a political process that has generated and sustained the Voting Rights Act. Yet, where conservatives see a politics that has been held hostage to the demands of civil-rights elites, progressives describe a politics increasingly dominated by white racism and retrenchment. Both camps also object to the development of the act itself, focusing their criticism on the proliferation of majority-minority single-member districts. Yet, again, where conservatives decry an affirmative-action program that balkanizes politics with racial quotas of power, progressives see the promise of equitable power sharing belied by the elevation of token minority representatives.

It is in this polarized context of claims and counterclaims that the centrists, led by Bernard Grofman, among others, attempt to fashion a reasonable middle position.[20] Dismissing both conservative and progressive claims as exaggerated rhetoric, centrists argue that the debate over the Voting Rights Act is actually quite narrow. While name calling and finger pointing have drawn the lion's share of attention, centrists claim that most of the disputants are actually concerned with achieving a color-blind society. Beneath the barbed polemics, controversies over minority representation amount to a disagreement over means rather than ends. To keep arguments focused on the actual question of appropriate means, the facts of the matter must be kept in full view. As Ber-

[19] Blacksher 1993, p. 34.

[20] Grofman and Davidson 1992, pp. 300–317; Grofman, Handley, and Niemi 1992; Grofman 1992; Grofman 1993; Davidson and Grofman 1994. See also Cain 1992; Issacharoff 1992; and Turner 1992.

nard Grofman and Chandler Davidson suggest, the "highly abstract" mode of the current debate only breeds misunderstanding and conflict; a better approach is to be found in "a consideration of the empirical evidence of the actual consequences of the [Voting Rights Act]."[21]

Centrists rely on such hard evidence to debunk the conservative critique.[22] Against the claim that the act is simply a vehicle for advancing special interests, centrists point out that patterns of racially polarized voting still persist, leaving minorities regularly opposed by white majorities in regions around the country. The reality of racially polarized voting means that the act speaks to the real barriers minorities encounter in electing representatives of their choice. The use of race-conscious, majority-minority districts to counteract racially polarized voting may, of course, be objectionable to some. For centrists, however, an understanding of the act's actual extent and impact does much to dispel objections. The comparatively low number of minority officeholders indicates that the creation of majority-minority districts is a limited brand of reform, far from a wholesale give-away of legislative seats. Without such majority-minority districts, minority candidates may rarely win elections; indeed, in the entire history of congressional elections, only six African Americans have won seats in districts with clear white majorities.[23] Moreover, the drawing of majority-minority districts seems to have done little to exacerbate racial divisions. In the absence of substantial evidence that the act's enforcement foments racial conflict, the exclusionary consequences of inaction must be weighed more heavily than the potential harms of action.

The facts not only demonstrate that the Voting Rights Act is not a vehicle for civil-rights elites but also show that the act is not a tool of the Republican party.[24] Centrists concede that Republicans have strongly supported minority voting rights in recent years. The Republican National Committee (RNC), for example, engaged in extensive voting

---

[21] Grofman and Davidson 1992, p. 301. Moreover, in their extensive analysis of the Voting Rights Act in the South, Davidson and Grofman explicitly avoid normative questions (1994, pp. 14–17, p. 447, n. 60). See also Cain 1992, p. 266.

[22] Grofman and Davidson 1992, pp. 303–4, 306–10, 312–13; Grofman, Handley, and Niemi, 1992, pp. 132, 136; Davidson and Grofman 1994, pp. 301–50; Cain 1992, p. 272; and Issacharoff 1992, pp. 1873–81.

[23] Lublin 1995, p. 112,

[24] Grofman 1993, pp. 1249–57. The claim that Republicans gain advantage under the current enforcement of the act is shared by progressives and conservatives; thus, centrist arguments apply against both camps.

rights litigation during the latest rounds of state and federal redistricting. Given the general Democratic dominance in state legislatures, the RNC found the prospect of litigation in federal courtrooms (brimming over with Republican-appointed judges) obviously appealing. Perhaps the main reason for the RNC strategy, though, was that many Republicans believed the creation of additional majority-minority districts would open opportunities to fashion more reliably Republican districts elsewhere.

Centrists react to the fact of RNC litigation by emphasizing that Republican hopes for success have not been the same as success itself. "The view that Republicans are *seeking to use* the Voting Rights Act for partisan gain," Grofman writes, "must not be confused with the much stronger claim that the Republicans have actually been *able to use* the Voting Rights Act in this way."[25] There is no systematic evidence to suggest that Republican-appointed judges favor Republican-submitted plans in minority voting-rights cases. Moreover, the evidence that does exist indicates that majority-minority districts do not necessarily play into Republican hands. Where Democrats can prevail (in the legislature or in court) or where the distribution of Republican voters is unfavorable, affirmative racial gerrymandering can just as easily be made to work against Republicans as for them.

According to centrists, progressive arguments fair no better than conservative ones once the appropriate facts have been marshaled.[26] Against progressive claims that the Voting Rights Act aims at equitable power sharing, centrists point out that Americans live under an essentially majoritarian system. Any guarantee of broad minority interest inclusion or, even worse, of fair legislative results, would destroy the stability and efficiency of the majoritarian system, solving problems of political inequality by generating more severe problems of political fragmentation. It is true that majority-minority districts do not themselves ensure proportionate minority influence. Once in office, minority representatives will doubtlessly find themselves on the losing end of many legislative struggles. Nonetheless, centrists contend that the relative ease of legislative compromise coupled with the likely election of minority representatives to ever higher offices will steadily enhance minority political strength. In the meantime, the real limits of politics must be recognized

---

[25] Ibid., p. 1256, emphasis original. This view is generally supported by Lublin 1995.
[26] Grofman, Handley, and Niemi 1992, pp. 135–36; Cain 1992, 262, 271–77.

and accepted. "To force the political system to be fairer," Bruce Cain observes, "people may try to define some things as voting rights that are not rights at all."[27] The franchise is hardly a panacea in our system and progressives must learn to expect less from it.

In the centrist view, then, the Voting Rights Act is neither a racially balkanizing nor a broadly empowering document. The debates, legislative amendments, and judicial decisions of the past thirty years actually amount to a far more pedestrian, "realistic politics of the second best."[28] In essence, the act takes limited steps to ameliorate specific and concrete inequities. Controversies over minority representation have failed to provoke widespread popular passion because the act itself is a model of moderation, "merely seek[ing] to provide an election system that permits all groups to be fairly represented."[29] Although the core provisions of the act have been repeatedly extended, they remain temporary and fact-contingent. Indeed, judicial interpretation of the act has kept voting-rights reform pragmatic and piecemeal, with federal intervention authorized only where it can be shown that minorities have actually been denied equal political opportunity.[30] In this sense, the act has been rendered "self-liquidating": once the facts that trigger voting-rights remedies can no longer be found, the act will cease to function.[31] More generally, the incrementalist, case-by-case nature of voting-rights policy means that remedial measures can be crafted without raising larger issues of democratic theory. As James Turner argues, "in the eyes of the law, the enforcement scheme [of the act] is to tailor remedies to fit discrete local problems. It does not perceive any requirement in sections 2 or 5 that adopts or promotes one theory of democratic representation over another."[32] Big questions such as "What is fair minority representation?" never need to be asked because judges and other federal officials are simply correcting what is obviously wrong given the specific facts at hand.

[27] Cain 1992, p. 275.

[28] Grofman, Handley, and Niemi 1992, p. 129.

[29] Grofman and Davidson 1992, p. 315. Compare the conservative claim that the lack of public knowledge about the act is a consequence of silent capitulation by politicians to the civil-rights agenda.

[30] Social science has played a key role in developing "clear and manageable" fact-based standards for intervention. See Grofman 1992, pp. 221–24, 227.

[31] Grofman, Handley, and Niemi 1992, p. 131.

[32] Turner 1992, p. 298.

A CRITIQUE OF CENTRISM

What can be made of the centrist attempt to steer a middle course between conservative and progressive claims? Centrists usefully eschew the conspiratorial overtones that characterize some conservative and progressive arguments. Instead of leveling indictments against civil-rights or racist cabals, centrists present the Voting Rights Act as the product of genuine legislative and judicial responses to the problem of minority exclusion. In this way, the centrist emphasis on measurable facts helps move the debate over minority representation past hyperbolic charges that our political system is on the verge of collapse.[33]

There is more to the centrist position, however, than the claim that the political process functions well. Centrists make the case for a responsive political process largely by insisting that the incrementalism of voting rights policy avoids theoretical questions. The very realism and reasonableness of the Voting Rights Act inheres in its atheoretical design. Thus, the centrist argument amounts to more than a simple corrective of exaggerated views. If the centrists are right, the entire polarized debate between conservatives and progressives should be set aside as a distraction. We will do just fine if the country and the courts continue to muddle through the issue of minority representation a case at a time.

On what grounds is the centrist evasion of theoretical issues warranted? The Voting Rights Act itself hinges on contestable issues such as "equal political opportunity," which Congress has defined only in the broadest manner. (Recall that the Senate Judiciary Committee suggested at least seven unranked criteria for assessing political opportunity.) Such imprecision would seem to encourage a wide range of judicial interpretations, suggesting an opportunity for judicial theorizing somewhat antithetical to the ideal centrist reform. Noting the breadth of statutory language is not, of course, the same as demonstrating the impossibility of atheoretical incrementalism. One could argue that so long as the interpretation and enforcement of the act remain tightly controlled by Congress, judicial interpretations might easily be steered away from conceptual questions. In this view, it does not matter if legislative language is capacious as long as Congress can keep close tabs on its judicial agents. The 1982 amendments to the Voting Rights Act dem-

---

[33] The model of such fact-centered analysis is Davidson and Grofman 1994. This volume carefully documents the impact of the Voting Rights Act on minority registration and officeholding in eight southern states.

onstrate that Congress is after all capable of redirecting an errant Court when it so desires. Delegation need not amount to abdication.

Unfortunately, the argument for strict congressional control is not very strong. Even in the area of statutory interpretation, where Congress may most readily reverse court rulings, the judiciary can have an important influence on how legislative terms are to be specifically understood. For example, while almost half of the Supreme Court's rulings involving statutory interpretation of federal laws receive some sort of congressional consideration, only 5 percent of these rulings are actually overridden.[34] The organizational demands of the political process help explain the relatively low number of reversals. Majorities in both houses of Congress as well as presidential support must be secured in order to reverse a Court ruling. The need to coordinate coalitions imposes significant barriers to Court reversals, barriers that may often be insurmountable. In fact, the more controversial the judicial interpretation of a statute is, the more difficult it may be to overturn, since groups on both sides are likely to lobby for congressional and presidential support.[35]

All of this suggests that the Court, circumscribed by the choices of other political actors, may nonetheless have an opportunity to play a key political role — an opportunity that may be especially great in civil-rights statutes where key terms remain open to a wide range of interpretations.[36] In the specific context of the Voting Rights Act, recall that the Court reduced the question of equal political opportunity from seven criteria to three in *Thornburg v. Gingles*. One of the Court-selected criteria (i.e., the requirement of geographic compactness) was not even listed in the legislative history of the 1982 amendments.[37] Although *Gingles* concerned only a single application of Section 2, its impact on voting-rights litigation and enforcement indicates the crucial difference the Court can make.

The centrist claim of atheoretical incrementalism may yet be defended. One could argue that so long as the Court is effectively constrained by its own canons of statutory construction, voting-rights reform need not plunge into any conceptual morass. The difficulty with such an argument is that the judiciary has historically employed a num-

[34] See, e.g., Eskridge 1991.

[35] Ibid., p. 366.

[36] Baum 1992a, pp. 191–92.

[37] Nor had geographic compactness been an element of the "totality of circumstances" rationale the 1982 amendments were meant to restore. See Karlan 1989.

61

ber of canons, many of which point interpretation in different directions. It is true that some legal commentators have spoken of the judge "worth his salt" or with the right "sense of the situation" who can negotiate among the various canons, consistently producing an accurate rendering of the statute's meaning or purpose.[38] Despite such claims, widespread consensus on what should count as the proper "sense of the situation" has not emerged. Easy agreement has proved elusive because the choice between interpretive strategies itself depends on what Cass Sunstein calls "background principles" — principles that express particular visions of how government ought to operate and, thus, provide the baseline against which statutes should be understood.[39]

The constellation of background principles employed by a judge makes all the difference in her approach to statutory interpretation. A background principle that seeks, for example, to maximize the harmony between government and private markets recommends interpretive canons very different from that of an alternative background principle that seeks to maximize public deliberation. The role played by background principles does not mean that the legal community will never reach some sort of consensus on the use of interpretive canons. The point is that any sort of consensus will rest on normative claims about how government ought to be conducted. In a word, then, statutory interpretation is hardly an area free of controversial conceptual choices. Rather than necessarily engendering atheoretical constructions, the selection of interpretive canons itself involves mediation between different principles offering alternative understandings of American government.[40]

---

[38] Frankfurter 1956, p. 47; Llewellyn 1950, p. 397.

[39] Sunstein 1989. For related arguments, see Sunstein 1987 and Melnick 1994, pp. 3–22.

[40] A number of scholars have recently appealed to public choice theory to provide a scientific account of government and, thereby, to set fixed guidelines for the judicial construction of statutes. Specifically, the argument has been made that statutes should be interpreted narrowly, according to the "plain meaning" of their language (see, e.g., Easterbrook 1983). One difficulty with such arguments is that scholars have yet to agree on the description of government public-choice-theory yields. (Shepsle [1992] argues that public-choice theory destroys the notion of legislative intent altogether; Farber and Frickey [1988] argue that public choice tells us more precisely what legislative intent actually is.) Even for those who attempt to unify the various lessons of public choice, the conclusion seems to be that public choice does not remove controversial conceptual choices from the interpretive enterprise. While public choice may provide a better notion of how government works, broader theories of democracy must be relied upon to tell us and the courts what to make of this information (See Eskridge 1988; 1992; Silverstein 1994; and I. Shapiro 1990).

Taken as a whole, the foregoing arguments give good reason to doubt the centrist portrait of voting-rights policy. The problem with centrism is not to be found either (i) in its claim that judicial interpretations of the Voting Rights Act have left the outlines of the majoritarian system largely untouched or (ii) in its insistence that the act itself has limitations that prevent it from addressing every political pathology. As simple matters of fact, both of these positions are valid.[41] The problem is that the debate over minority representation does not pivot on "simple matters of fact."

In general, one can say that the process of statutory interpretation is critically concerned with normative disputes over how the government ought to operate. The debate between progressives and conservatives — a debate over how a particular statute is to be interpreted — is similarly concerned with normative disputes.[42] By stressing measurable facts and hard evidence, the centrist argument as a whole sidesteps the debate's key issue. The progressive and conservative views are not simply "mistakes" that can be corrected by a more accurate set of facts. Each of these camps anchors its claims in different conceptions of fair representation, which serve as guides for how the Voting Rights Act's promise of equal political opportunity ought to be realized. Competing conceptions of representation lead conservatives and progressives to understand the facts of minority politics differently. Thus, conservatives and progressives do not simply disagree on what the "facts" of the debate are. More importantly, they disagree on what the same "facts" should mean in light of what fair minority representation is taken to be.[43]

The dispute between figures like Abigail Thernstrom and Lani Guinier is, at base, over how the political community ought to be constructed and how debate and decisions within that community ought to

---

[41] Following Browning, Marshall, and Tabb (1984, pp. 207–38), one could argue that no federal statute can provide the single lever needed to transform all of society because federal provisions will always interact differently with disparate local conditions.

[42] One would, however, expect these normative questions to be strongest and most important in the politics of representation, where the construction of the political community itself is at issue.

[43] On behalf of the centrists, the argument might be made that no larger theory of *fair* representation is necessary because the point is simply to strike down what is *unfair*. Yet, this claim simply places the need for an analysis of representation at one remove, for debate would still require some account of when representation is *not* unfair. For general treatments of this problem, see Dworkin 1985, pp. 293–334, and Beitz 1989, pp. 100ff.

be conducted. At this level, what matters are the different notions of political identity and judicial authority employed by each side.[44]

It is important to take some note of what this conceptual difference between conservatives and progressives means. Consider the conservative position. Conservative commentators repeatedly refer to an understanding of "politics as usual" that provides the standard against which the development of the Voting Rights Act has appeared illegitimate.[45] This notion of "politics as usual" is not an invention of the conservatives themselves; instead, it is drawn from older understandings of interest group pluralism.[46] Interest group pluralism envisions society as consisting of a multiplicity of groups, each with its own narrow interest. Democratic rule within such a social context is not rule by a monolithic majority but rather rule by a coalition of groups. As long as participation is open, elections frequent, and political entrepreneurs plentiful, any group shut out of the majority on one decision can hope to join it in the next.[47] Thus, the composition of the ruling coalition is dynamic, with coalition membership shifting from decision to decision.

This fluid process of political competition hinges on a particular un-

[44] A few other authors have looked at this matter differently. Rush (1994) claims that competing theories of representation separate the arguments of Guinier and the arguments made by the Court. Yet, not only does Rush fail to consider the arguments of either the centrists or the conservatives, he also distinguishes theories of representation largely on the basis of equal access and equal outputs. He offers no explicit analysis of political identity. King, Bruce, and Gelman (1993) rely on mathematical models as a means of examining representation directly. Yet, as the authors recognize, this kind of analysis does not obviate the need to address normative questions about political identity (pp. 2, 24–25). Cain (1990) looks explicitly at the different notions of political identity driving competing theories of minority representation. The primary aim of Cain's analysis, however, is to demonstrate the extent of controversy. He does not offer a systematic critique of conceptual claims nor does he recommend an alternative view of political identity, free of the problems that plague current debate. Maveety (1991, pp. 97–145) considers the Burger Court's approach to minority representation. Her analysis calls attention to the notions of political identity, interest, and competition in Court decisions. (Maveety and Cain both leave unexplored the interlocking issues of political identity and judicial authority.) The goal of Maveety's work is to demonstrate the consistency of the Burger Court's jurisprudence. To this end, she measures Court decisions against ideal types of representation drawn from the political science literature. Given my reading of representation as an essentially contested concept, I take Maveety's emphasis on consistency to work as a procrustean bed.

[45] Thernstrom 1987, pp. 4–9, 23, 234ff; Swain 1992; and Alexander 1989.

[46] Classic statements of this theory can be found in Truman 1971 and Dahl 1956 and 1961.

[47] Dahl 1956, pp. 124–51.

derstanding of political identity. Specifically, interest group pluralists hold that individual political identity is never solely defined by membership in a single group.[48] Individuals are taken to identify with a broad range of groups and interests. "As voters we are Democrats and Republicans, blacks and whites, males and females," Larry Alexander writes, "but we are also hawks and doves, redistributionists and laissez-faire advocates. . . . The list of our voting-relevant divisions is virtually endless."[49] The sheer number of competing political identities ensures that any given majority will be inherently unstable, forever threatened by potential majorities that could form along alternative group cleavages. The pluralist political market is flexible and dynamic, in other words, because the fungibility of political identity means that every player is potentially open to new deals.

The freewheeling bargaining process engendered by overlapping group membership must itself be somehow sustained. If individuals become unwilling or unable to step up to the bargaining table, the benefits of the political market can never be fully realized. Interest group pluralism locates the forces of market maintenance within a broad consensus on rules of the democratic game.[50] Social consensus keeps individuals wedded to the bargaining process as the means to make and enforce decisions, ensuring what Abigail Thernstrom calls "horizons of trust" among citizens.[51] The result is that groups in the minority need not fear that the majority coalition will use its strength to entrench itself, transforming the political victory of the moment into a position of lasting dominance.

Within the confines of the political market, judicial authority is properly minimized. The conservative account suggests that the Supreme Court can play a role in guaranteeing access to the political market. If the political market is clearly exclusionary, then the Court may well play an active role in restoring politics to its individualistic basis. Beyond that, however, conservatives remain essentially hostile to judicial intervention. Individual political identity is too protean to be captured in the judicial decision — as a result, there is little the Court can do to speak on behalf of the people. For conservatives, the Court that at-

---

[48] Ibid., pp. 104–5; Truman 1971, pp. 14–44, 501–35.

[49] Alexander 1989, p. 575.

[50] Truman 1971, pp. xxxvii, chap. 2; Dahl 1961, pp. 311–25. The classic statement of American consensus is Hartz 1955.

[51] Thernstrom 1987, p. 9.

tempts to assign political rights simply freezes a process that ought to remain fluid.[52] Again, as Abigail Thernstrom writes:

> If a community of citizens is an unattainable ideal, and if blacks and Hispanics are represented only by one of their own, then aggressive federal action to restructure methods of voting to promote minority officeholding is appropriate. But if the logic of politics works for inclusion (once basic enfranchisement has been assured), then a lighter touch, a more hesitant intervention, is possible.[53]

Judicial policies designed to ensure the election of minorities frustrates the political process and fosters racial balkanization where an integrated political community would otherwise be produced. Thus, the Court should limit itself to policing clearly egregious instances of racial discrimination, making it possible for the "logic of politics" to move smoothly from premise to conclusion. Through bargaining and coalition building, individuals will construct the political community on their own terms, giving different groups only the political representation that the pluralist market can bear.[54]

The conservative analogy between politics and markets finds no support in the progressive camp, which itself relies on very different notions of political identity and judicial authority to generate a distinct vision of representation.[55] Progressives repeatedly refer to the long history of racial discrimination in the United States—a history which they claim has created a cluster of minority group identities unshared by the white majority.[56] The progressive understanding of history directly contradicts the conservative model of "politics as usual," for progressives

---

[52] Recall that conservative Timothy O'Rourke took politics to be somehow at odds with the judiciary, rights, and equality.

[53] Thernstrom 1987, p. 242.

[54] Thus, Swain (1993) argues that African Americans can effectively be represented by white liberals. Left to its own devices, the political market facilitates representation along lines of party rather than of race. "Indirect influence" is the touchstone here (Dahl 1961, pp. 163–65; Thernstrom 1987, p. 48).

[55] Theories of pluralism need not rely so heavily on market metaphors. Walzer (1983) presents a notion of political pluralism rooted less in market-like bargaining than in separate social spheres connected by a shared sense of distributive criteria and processes. Yet, insofar as Walzer posits a set of already agreed-upon social meanings that govern exchanges between different social spheres, he describes a pluralism that is congenial to the conservative distrust of conducting politics on the basis of judicially assigned rights (Walzer 1983, pp. xv, 151–54; Thernstrom 1987, pp. 132n, 240).

[56] Guinier 1991a; Jones 1985; Parker 1990, pp. 6–7. For similar arguments, see Fiss 1976; Williams 1992; Young 1989 and 1990, pp. 27–38.

view minority identities as insufficiently fluid to serve as the currency of a smoothly functioning political market. Moreover, the gap between white and minority identities is emblematic of the disjuncture between political identities on the whole. At a certain level of specificity, political identities simply are not fungible. Citizens without direct ties to an elected official are in essence without political voice. In the words of Lani Guinier, "unless *all* the voters in the district vote for the winning candidate, some of their votes are wasted."[57]

The conservative language of overlapping membership and indirect influence is thus inappropriate. Groups in general and minority groups in particular must be able to articulate their interests through their own representatives, and other political actors must be persuaded to give these representatives a serious hearing. Genuine political deliberation cannot be achieved by forcing many groups to support a compromise candidate. Again, as Lani Guinier writes, the current "focus on developing consensus *prior to the election* means that issues are frequently not fully articulated or debated. Positions on controversial issues are often eschewed for palliatives designed to offend no one."[58] Each group deserves its own representative.

In this vein, the progressives effectively call for an alternative to the political market altogether. Ironically drawing on the political theories of John C. Calhoun, progressives such as Guinier argue that legislation in the interest of all can emerge only where decision making requires the consent of each nonfungible interest.[59] The disaggregation of majority power in legislative bodies yields a superior form of political deliberation. Once minorities are given veto power over the issues that specifically concern them, political interaction can no longer be conducted by

[57] Guinier 1993b, p. 1615, emphasis added. Guinier's view of political identity is quite hard-edged. She compares those who do not vote for a winning candidate as enjoying the same degree of representation as those who cannot vote at all — i.e., children, the mentally retarded, etc. (p. 1609). A citizen either has representation or she doesn't. Indeed, Guinier defines politically relevant groups in terms of the *unanimous* agreement among members about group interests (p. 1621). Thus, as Guinier has moved away from the specific issue of fair minority representation toward a more general advocacy of proportional representation, she has maintained the same notion of nonfungible political identity.

[58] Guinier 1993a, p. 1161, emphasis original.

[59] Calhoun 1953, pp. 21–28. Guinier 1991a, pp. 1112–28, 1140n, 1144–53; 1991b, pp. 1476–1514; Karlan 1989, pp. 237–48. The debt to Calhoun is ironic because Calhoun developed his view of concurrent majorities in the hope of protecting slaveholding states. It is worth noting that, contrary to Calhoun, progressives situate legislative restructuring primarily at local and state levels. See Guinier 1991b, p. 1487.

welding together narrowly self-interested groups into winning coalitions. The result is that a discourse of rights arises in place of the politics of bargaining. As Iris Marion Young argues, the need for virtual unanimity creates a political context in which actors "cannot simply assert that they want something; they must say that justice requires or allows that they have it."[60] Talk of rights and claims of equality are the medium of political debate. Questions of fairness, rather than issues of strategic calculation or affirmations of whatever the political market will bear, rule the day.

Within this revivified public space, progressives grant the judiciary a great deal of authority, giving the courts a power to restructure legislative procedure so that representatives of nonnegotiable interests might still hear one another out. Where the conservatives marginalize the Court, the progressives place the Court at the very center of politics. Indeed, for the progressives the governing metaphor for how a reconstituted legislature ought to work is the jury—a metaphor that is also found in the work of Calhoun.[61] Guinier writes:

> Jurors come collectively to their task under compulsion of law and are instructed to put aside their biases, deliberating only on the bias of the evidence. Their mission is to review the evidence and decide an outcome that is in the public interest rather than their self-interest. . . . Because of these rules and obligations, jurors may tend to respect each others' views to a greater extent than do other members of collective decision making bodies who fail to bond in the same way.[62]

The legislature qua jury will operate in the same manner, weighing each interest seriously and seeking a final consensus among all the representatives. In this way, progressives argue, politics will ultimately be reworked along more just lines, relying on the judicial system to furnish the means to as well as the model of fair representation.

The above review demonstrates, contrary to centrist claims, that much more than a question of means is at stake in the debate between conservatives and progressives.[63] In this sense, it is of little value for centrists to point out merely that the interpretation and enforcement of

[60] Young 1989, p. 263. See also Young 1990, pp. 183–91, 229–36, 251–56.

[61] Calhoun 1953, pp. 50–51; Guinier 1991b, pp. 1485–87.

[62] Guinier, 1991b, p. 1486.

[63] The centrists here repeat the mistake of those who argue that debates over affirmative action can be reduced to a question of means. In affirmative-action debates too, a sense of the relevant facts "turns" on one's values. See Edley 1986.

the Voting Rights Act has remained within the confines of the majoritarian system — for the crucial issue is what relationship minority rights and majoritarianism ought to continue to have.[64] Positing a multiplicity of political identities and a free political market, conservatives argue that judicially enforced fair representation ought to be eschewed altogether: the assertion of a right to representation will only sacrifice a unified community of citizens to a cacophony of group voices. On the other hand, stipulating a discrete set of group identities and a consensual model of political deliberation, progressives contend that a judicially enforced theory of fair representation ought to be embraced: it is only by identifying and protecting the representational rights of each group that a just political community can be constructed.

Centrists altogether fail to address such conceptual issues, neglecting to consider the relevance of political identity, much less to assess the kinds of judicial power claimed by the conservatives and progressives. Abjuring conceptual analysis, centrists fall well short of presenting a viable middle position. And if the centrist position does not hold, then conservative and progressive responses to the Voting Rights Act cannot be summarily pushed aside.

How might one finally adjudicate between conservative and progressive claims? Before that can be answered, the failure of the centrist arguments raises a more pressing question. Has the Supreme Court itself done any better in assessing the conceptual issues at stake in the politics of minority representation?

[64] In this vein, the argument has also been made that the act be reconfigured to respond more effectively to the particular problems of noncitizenship faced by Latinos (de la Garza and DeSipio 1993).

The Early Cases

How has the Supreme Court dealt with the conceptual issues at stake in the politics of minority representation? Because the public debate has pivoted on differing conceptions of political identity and judicial authority, the question of judicial action comes to the fore.

In this chapter, I begin my detailed study of Supreme Court opinions. Analysis of several key decisions handed down prior to the passage of the original Voting Rights Act reveals how justices initially envisioned the problem of minority representation, disclosing a fund of conceptual resources that informed later decisions. The Court's early interpretations of the Voting Rights Act added to the conceptual fund, introducing important new elements into the repertoire of judicial arguments. Finally, the Court's first direct efforts to ascertain the meaning of fair minority representation presented and developed fresh ideas about the "totality of circumstances."

The evolution of views across these judicial decisions was neither linear nor continuous. Members of the Court never fully converged on one uniform or universal theory of representation. Yet, the lack of consensus on the bench should hardly be surprising. Claims about judicial representativeness provide ways of justifying judicial authority, yielding various accounts of the political community in which different ranges of Court action are possible. The judicial decisions I examine in this chapter exhibit four primary understandings of political identity, organized around conceptions of popular vigilance, abstract individualism, legislative learning, and interest group competition. Each of these approaches furnishes a different rendering of the political contexts in which fair minority representation and legitimate judicial authority may be realized.

Of course, none of this is to suggest that all four approaches are unproblematic. The question remains: how well does the judicial reliance on a given notion of political identity ultimately preserve the capacity of the people to speak for themselves? Viewed from this perspective, each approach has its own difficulties.

THE VIGILANT PEOPLE AND MINORITY REPRESENTATION

The Supreme Court first confronted the general issue of representation during the reapportionment revolution of the early 1960s. Throughout this period, the Court employed a one-person–one-vote rule designed to equalize district populations. The conception of political identity that undergirded the one-person–one-vote rule was remarkable for its neglect of *all* groups, taking "the people" to be simply an assemblage of politically equal individuals. As a result, most reapportionment decisions were ill suited to explore the political status of any group. Nonetheless, the Court did address questions of minority representation in a handful of early reapportionment cases, and, in doing so, it laid important groundwork for the adjudication of representational conflicts under the Voting Rights Act.[1] The first request for Court intervention into reapportionment came in the case *Colegrove v. Green* (1946).[2] The case is the first skirmish in the reapportionment revolution and a critical precursor to the earliest judicial encounters with minority representation.

Colegrove concerned congressional districts in Illinois, which had not been reapportioned in more than forty years. Demographic shifts during this period had produced large population inequalities between districts. Three voters residing in the most populous districts filed suit against the state, seeking to prevent further congressional elections from being conducted in such a lopsided context.

Justice Felix Frankfurter, speaking for a plurality of the Court in *Colegrove*, rebuffed the novel request for judicial intervention.[3] His refusal rested on the claim that congressional reapportionment was exclusively a matter between Congress and "the people."[4] According to

[1] For my discussion of the one-person–one-vote rule, see chapter two. There is a thin line of minority voting-rights litigation beginning after the Civil War and continuing into the 1960s (see Elliot 1974, pp. 55–88, for an overview). These cases are clearly important — indeed, it was here that the Court struck down discriminatory devices like grandfather clauses and white primaries (see chapter one). Yet the main concern of these cases was basic political *access*. Cases explicitly raising issues of minority *representation* did not arise until the era of the reapportionment revolution.

[2] *Colegrove v. Green*, 328 U.S. 549 (1946). For an account of this case in the context of the reapportionment revolution, see M. Shapiro 1964, pp. 185–92.

[3] Frankfurter's opinion was joined by Justices Reed and Burton. Justice Rutledge filed a concurring opinion. These four members constituted a majority. The Court had only eight members (due to Justice Stone's death), and Justice Jackson took no part in the case.

[4] *Colegrove* at 552, 554.

Frankfurter, "the people" were a politically mature sovereign whose "vigilance" ensured that elected officials performed their duties.[5] Congress often altered the rules of reapportionment, for reapportionment was an area rife with "party contests and party interests."[6] Yet, for all its "embroilment in politics," apportionment remained firmly under the control of the vigilant people.[7] Even when Congress disregarded clear constitutional commands (failing, for example, to reapportion after a decennial census), Frankfurter asserted that "[i]t never occurred to *anyone*" to ask the Court to intervene and compel congressional action.[8] "If Congress fail[s] in exercising its powers, whereby standards of fairness are offended, the remedy ultimately lies with the people."[9] Congress answered to the vigilant people and every responsible citizen knew it.

In this sense, the petitioners in *Colegrove*, requesting judicial assistance when no legislative action had been forthcoming, could hardly be counted as part of "the people." Posing a sharp contrast to the vigilant people, Frankfurter presented the petitioners as impassioned individuals, urging "with great zeal" that population inequalities were "grave evils and offend[ed] public morality."[10] If the ardent petitioners were granted judicial relief, the Court would be working against "the people," forcing them to make a decision that they had refused make on their own. Indeed, Frankfurter predicted that judicial intervention would be "hostile to the democratic system," for it promised to leave Illinois with districtless elections, which Congress itself might refuse to honor.[11] "[D]ue regard for the effective working of our Government" simply required that the Court remain passive.[12]

In holding the Court back from the "political thicket" of reapportionment, Frankfurter's *Colegrove* opinion gave the vigilant people and their legislative representatives great latitude.[13] The problem was that Frankfurter failed to identify the contours of such latitude. Frankfurter took the will of the vigilant people to be manifest in whatever appor-

---

[5] Ibid. at 556.
[6] Ibid. at 554.
[7] Ibid.
[8] Ibid. at 555, emphasis added.
[9] Ibid. at 554.
[10] Ibid.
[11] Ibid. at 553–54.
[12] Ibid. at 552.
[13] Ibid. at 556.

tionment policy Congress adopted. Those who complained to the Court about district designs were summarily labeled as marginal figures, impassioned individuals unable to accept the rigors of responsible membership in the political community. At no point, however, did Frankfurter discuss the standards that allowed him to distinguish responsible citizenship from overzealous dissension. The notion of a "vigilant" people thus remained highly plastic, alternately amenable to sweeping legislative action and open to arbitrary judicial redefinition. As a predicate of judicial authority, then, Frankfurter's conception of political identity appeared to subvert the whole idea of limited government: in the name of the vigilant people, the Court could just as easily endorse either untrammeled legislative power or unconstrained judicial discretion.

In a dissenting opinion, Justice Hugo Black provided an alternative to Frankfurter's reasoning. He suggested that the central problem in *Colegrove* was not one of a few whining litigants but rather one of self-interested legislators refusing to recognize a substantial portion of the people.[14] Black argued that the legislature must be compelled to hear *all* the people, without any qualifications concerning responsibility or political maturity. "All groups, classes, and individuals shall to the extent that it is practically feasible be given equal representation in the House of Representatives, which, in conjunction with the Senate, writes the laws affecting the life, liberty and property of all the people."[15] In this vein, Black claimed that the districtless elections feared by Frankfurter would actually be beneficial, allowing at-large competition that would give "all the people an equally effective voice in electing their representatives."[16]

Calling for broadly inclusive representation, Black avoided the particular problem of standards that plagued Frankfurter. On Black's view, there was simply no need to identify the criteria of popular political vigilance because all interests were to be given legislative voice. Yet, even as Black eschewed the pitfalls of Frankfurter's position, his own argument ran into difficulties. Black asserted judicial authority on behalf of the people without considering the variety of ways in which "the people" could be characterized and the important choices that such variety engendered. For example, Black welcomed at-large congressional elections without acknowledging that at-large elections would not sim-

---

[14] Ibid. at 566–67. Black's dissent was joined by Justices Douglas and Murphy.

[15] Ibid. at 570–71.

[16] Ibid. at 574.

ply grant "all the people" an equally effective voice. At-large elections would certainly allow population majorities hobbled by existing districts to elect more representatives. But the gains in majority power would be purchased at the expense of local interests currently protected by districts.[17] Of course, the choice to protect majority interests over those of local subdivisions might well be reasonable; it would, however, be just that — *a choice* to preserve one political interest rather than another. Nowhere in his appeal for equal representation of all people did Black offer guidance about how such a choice ought to be made. Indeed, Black seemingly failed to recognize that his own opinion required such a choice in the first place.

As first cuts at the general issue of representation, the *Colegrove* opinions of Frankfurter and Black were clearly problematic. Both opinions nonetheless provided important claims that were to be invoked and reworked as the Court wrestled with questions of minority representation. The first such opportunity came for Frankfurter in *Gomillion v. Lightfoot* (1960).[18] *Gomillion* concerned Act 140 of the Alabama State Legislature altering the boundaries of the city of Tuskegee. Act 140 changed the shape of Tuskegee from a square to a twenty-eight sided figure, retaining every white resident while leaving all but a few of the city's African Americans outside the new boundaries. The excluded blacks, no longer residents of Tuskegee, lost their right to vote in municipal elections. They consequently filed suit on the grounds that Act 140 violated the Fifteenth Amendment, denying their right to vote on account of race.

Frankfurter began the opinion of the Court by noting that Act 140 "was not an ordinary geographic redistricting measure *even within* the familiar abuses of gerrymandering."[19] Act 140 was an almost "mathematical" exercise in discriminatory policymaking, "solely concerned with segregating white and colored voters by fencing Negro citizens out of town so as to deprive them of their pre-existing municipal vote."[20] Since this flagrant instance of discrimination involved race, it fell within

[17] This point was made by Frankfurter. Ibid. at 553.

[18] *Gomillion v. Lightfoot*, 364 U.S. 339 (1960).

[19] Ibid. at 341, emphasis added. Frankfurter was joined by Chief Justice Warren and Justices Harlan, Brennan, Stewart, Clark, and Black. Justices Whittaker and Douglas each filed separate concurrences. In his concurrence, Douglas simply noted his agreement with the majority and his continued adherence to Black's dissent in *Colegrove*.

[20] *Gomillion* at 341. Alabama failed to counter to this claim with an argument that Act 140 had any purpose other than racial discrimination (ibid. at 342).

the "conventional sphere" of Court business.[21] The Constitution contained special provisions against racial discrimination, evinced by the Fifteenth Amendment's protection of voting rights.[22] For Frankfurter, it took little effort to see that the systematic elimination of blacks from Tuskegee ran afoul of such constitutional provisions.[23]

Frankfurter recognized that his reasoning appeared to lead away from *Colegrove*. Contrary to his earlier opinion, he now ruled that the judiciary had the authority to evaluate reapportionment plans (in this instance, the plan reapportioning Tuskegee) and to strike down such plans if they violated Fifteenth Amendment guarantees.[24] In spite of this difference in result, however, Frankfurter maintained that his two rulings in no way conflicted.[25] Indeed, his emphasis on the extraordinary nature of Act 140 suggested that *Gomillion* was simply the exception that proved the *Colegrove* rule. The extreme degree of exclusion wrought by Act 140 actually changed the racial composition of the people: it silenced the political voice of a specific minority group, ejecting them from the political community.[26] Act 140 thus fell outside the broad political discretion granted to the "vigilant" people in *Colegrove*. Powerful as the vigilant people were, even they had to obey the Constitution. And, as a constitutional matter, the people simply could not organize themselves by expelling racial minorities.

In finding for the black litigants, then, Frankfurter's *Gomillion* ruling made sense of *Colegrove*, supplying an account of the limits beyond which a vigilant people and their obedient legislatures could not go. Yet, if Frankfurter's decision made the notion of political vigilance seem less arbitrary, it hardly freed the notion from difficulty. For all of Frankfurter's talk about the extreme political exclusion engineered by Act 140, it remained the case that the petitioners enjoyed the *same* vot-

[21] Ibid. at 347.

[22] Ibid. at 343, 345.

[23] Ibid. at 346.

[24] Frankfurter did not actually overturn Act 140 because the act's validity was not directly before the Court. Frankfurter focused instead on the prior question of whether such a lawsuit could be pursued at all. In this vein, the District Court had ruled against the black litigants on the grounds that only the state legislature not the court "act[ed] for the people" in the drawing of municipal boundaries (ibid. at 340–41). Frankfurter ruled in favor of the black litigants and reversed the judgment of the lower court. Thus, Frankfurter found the Court *could* at times act for "the people" in the area of reapportionment.

[25] Ibid. at 346–47.

[26] As Frankfurter noted, the issue in *Colegrove* was merely one of vote "dilution," while the issue in *Gomillion* was the actual deprivation of the vote (ibid. at 346).

ing privileges as all other Alabama voters residing outside of Tuskegee.[27] Regardless of their relationship to the Tuskegee city limits, black voters formed part of the "vigilant" people who (per *Colegrove*) presumably controlled the state legislature responsible for Act 140. To avoid deferring to the state legislature as the instrument of a vigilant people, Frankfurter needed either (i) to explain how the state electorate had failed to be properly vigilant; (ii) to indicate how the state legislature had failed to act on behalf of their constituency; or (iii) to demonstrate why something less than a minority group's total elimination from the political community required judicial intervention.

Frankfurter neglected to make any such arguments. Given that the aim of *Colegrove* was to keep the Court from grappling with complex representational issues, Frankfurter was clearly loath to investigate any broader political contexts. Still, without further development, his ambiguous notion of political vigilance, qualified only by prohibitions against the complete exclusion of minority groups, simply could not shoulder the burden that Frankfurter wished it to bear. Frankfurter wanted to avoid the thorny "political thicket" of representational politics by permitting the vigilant people to speak for themselves; but his reliance on a particular conception of "the people" had *already* drawn the Court into the position of making claims about the form and content of the political community.[28] The question was not whether the Court could remain aloof from representation but whether approaches to representation less problematic than Frankfurter's could be generated.

The Alternative of Abstract Individualism

The Court next considered the issue of minority representation in *Wright v. Rockefeller* (1964).[29] Like *Gomillion*, *Wright* concerned the validity of a reapportionment plan allegedly drawn on the basis of race.

---

[27] This point was made by Justice Whittaker in his brief concurrence (ibid. at 349).

[28] Of course, Frankfurter was not the only justice to involve the Supreme Court with the politics of representation. As I argued in chapter two, the Court has always trafficked in such politics. Frankfurter *did* recognize that the reapportionment revolution required the Court to deal with representational issues (see my chapter two discussion of his dissent in *Baker v. Carr*, 369 U.S. 186, 299–300 [1962]). His mistake was to insist that his own opinions were exempted from this requirement.

[29] *Wright v. Rockefeller*, 376 U.S. 52 (1964).

In 1961 the New York legislature had reapportioned congressional districts, creating four districts for Manhattan Island. Voters residing in the Manhattan districts challenged the reapportionment statute as a violation of the Fourteenth and Fifteenth Amendments, charging that the state had apportioned by concentrating minorities into three districts while leaving the fourth largely white.[30]

Even though *Wright* addressed an issue similar to that of *Gomillion*, members of the *Wright* Court did not frame the case directly in Frankfurter's terms. *Wright* focused attention on the distribution of minorities between electoral districts — a topic that Frankfurter avoided in his efforts to render *Colegrove* and *Gomillion* consistent. Worried about interdistrict comparisons, the petitioners in *Wright* complained that the state had reapportioned along racial lines and intentionally "ghettoiz[ed]" Manhattan by fashioning white and nonwhite districts.[31] The petitioners made no claim that minority groups had been deprived of the vote. Minorities clearly retained a political voice; it was the conditions under which this voice was exercised that remained the point of contention. Thus, the question was not one of political elimination but one of political segregation. Had minorities been intentionally crowded into a cluster of districts? If so, was it unconstitutional for minority groups to be represented in this way?

Justice Black, author of the majority opinion, responded to these questions on narrow grounds.[32] Limiting his attention to the issue of legislative intent, Black noted that some evidence appeared to suggest racial motivation, while other evidence did not. The Manhattan districts did not, for example, have equal shares of the minority population. But then again "the concentration of colored and Puerto Rican voters [living] in one area in the county made it difficult, even assuming it to be permissible, to fix districts so as to have anything like an equal division of these voters among the districts."[33] According to Black, such conflict-

---

[30] The "minorities" in question were people of Puerto Rican origin and African Americans. The districts had minority population percentages of 86.3, 28.5, 27.5, and 5.1. It is also worth noting that *Wright* was not a case simply pitting minority voters against the state. Adam Clayton Powell, the congressman representing the district with the greatest minority population, intervened as a defendant supporting the reapportionment statute.

[31] Ibid. at 54.

[32] Black was joined by Chief Justice Warren and Justices Clark, Brennan, Stewart, and White. Justice Harlan filed a brief concurring opinion, while Justices Douglas and Goldberg each filed dissents.

[33] *Wright* at 57.

ing pieces of evidence precluded a finding of intentional segregation. Since one could reasonably argue that Manhattan's districts were racially imbalanced because the city itself was racially segregated, Black ruled that the petitioners had failed to prove the legislature "was either motivated by racial considerations or in fact drew the districts on racial lines."[34]

Black's brief opinion clearly set a high threshold for proving discriminatory legislative intent. Yet the rationale for this threshold remained unclear. Black provided no real account of *how* legislative intent mattered in the context of reapportionment and minority representation. The New York legislature had admitted that race inevitably had some relevance in the process of reapportionment.[35] This meant that Manhattan's districts did not simply "happen" to reflect racially segregated residential patterns; at the very least, legislators knew that in drawing district boundaries as they did, large pockets of minority population would be placed in the same district. The legislature's racial cognizance introduced an important question about the *kind* of racial considerations at work in legislative deliberations. One could argue that the legislature either (i) intended *to create* racially homogeneous districts or (ii) intended *simply to recognize* racially homogeneous neighborhoods. In both cases, the results were identical (i.e., racially segregated districts), suggesting that Black found some crucial difference between the two kinds of legislative intentions. At no point, however, did Black spell out why one kind of legislative intention was harmful while the other was not.[36]

A more developed account of minority representation, replete with claims about political identity and judicial authority, materialized in Justice Douglas's dissent. Douglas dismissed Black's defense of the New York legislature. He argued instead that the legislature had carefully manipulated boundaries, producing irregularly shaped districts inexplicable on any terms other than racial ones.[37] But Douglas did not rest his opinion on the claim of overtly discriminatory motivation. According to Douglas, "[r]acial segregation that is state-sponsored should be nullified

[34] Ibid. at 56.

[35] Ibid. at 61.

[36] Compare Justice Goldberg. He thought that since the bulk of the evidence pointed toward the first sort of intent, the burden of proof ought to be shifted against the state (ibid. at 72–73).

[37] Ibid. at 60. Thus, where Black found indeterminacy, Douglas saw a prima facie case of willful segregation, which the state was required to rebut (ibid. at 61).

whatever may have been intended."[38] Whether the legislature willfully pushed minorities into specific districts or simply acknowledged existing patterns of racial segregation, racially sensitive reapportionment was invalid.[39]

Douglas rejected all forms of districting informed by race because they awarded representation directly to racial groups. He conceded that racial as well as religious group representation appeared to work in countries like India — where Sikhs, Muslims, Anglo-Indians, Europeans, and Indian Christians each enjoyed their own electoral districts.[40] But Douglas argued that such a system succeeded because the Indian people were so deeply torn by racial and religious differences that no other system could work.[41] The United States government was, by contrast, premised on the notion of a unified people. Douglas wrote:

> Racial electoral registers, like religious ones, have no place in a society that honors the Lincoln tradition — "of the people, by the people, for the people." Here the individual is important, not his race, his creed, or his color. . . . The racial electoral register system weights votes along one racial line more heavily than it does other votes. That system, by whatever name it is called, is a divisive force in a community, emphasizing differences between candidates and voters that are irrelevant in the constitutional sense. Of course, race, like religion, plays an important role in the choices which individual voters make from among various candidates. But government has no business designing electoral districts along racial or religious lines.[42]

Douglas's point was a complicated one. On the one hand, he acknowledged that in the United States, as in India, racial and religious differ-

---

[38] Ibid. at 61, emphasis added.

[39] Douglas recognized some limits to this broad rule. A racial bloc could be legitimately made into a district where the electoral unit *itself* was an "actual neighborhood" (ibid. at 67). When dealing with units any larger than the single neighborhood, the state could not draw districts along racial lines.

[40] Ibid. at 63. Douglas also briefly discussed the schemes of group representation used in Lebanon and Cyprus (ibid. at 65–66).

[41] To make this argument, Douglas relied on "The Joint Report of 1918," which he approvingly quoted as saying, "Some persons hold that for a people, such as they deem those of India to be, so divided by race, religion, and caste as to be unable to consider the interests of any but their own section, a system of communal electorates and class representation is not merely inevitable but it is actually best" (ibid. at 64, internal quotation marks omitted).

[42] Ibid. at 66, footnotes omitted.

ences overlapped closely with important political cleavages. On the other hand, he argued that the government could not explicitly recognize the reality of racial and religious politics in districting. To reapportion in racial or religious terms would be to exacerbate the worst sort of political divisions, dissolving "the people" into its constituent and contending groups.[43] To sustain a single people, Douglas insisted that the government treat all citizens as equal individuals abstracted from their racial or religious attachments. The American citizenry was not, of course, actually composed of such individuals. But, in Douglas's view, to treat the citizenry *as if* it were simply an assemblage of politically equal individuals was the only way to ensure that "the people" retained coherence.[44]

With this argument, Douglas reworked core elements of Black's dissent in *Colegrove*. While Black had demanded the representation of "all the people," he had failed to elaborate the terms on which the political community ought to be constructed. Douglas also called for the representation of "all the people," but he did so with a specific understanding of political identity in mind. Taking "the people" to be a collectivity of equal individuals, Douglas gave the judiciary a yardstick against which the representational claims of racial minorities could be measured. He thus empowered the Court to invalidate racially homogeneous districts, erasing the political traces of racial affiliations so that a single individualistic people could reign.

In developing Black's arguments, Douglas also offered a better alternative to Frankfurter's representational jurisprudence. Frankfurter's argument was only half-formed: he relied on an ambiguous notion of the vigilant people that alternately supported sweeping legislative power and arbitrary judicial action. Denying the judicial reliance on political identity, Frankfurter frustrated his own efforts to strengthen his position. Thus, even though his own opinions rested on problematic claims about who "the people" were and how they ought to be represented, he insisted that the Court had no business with the political affairs of the people. For his part, Douglas openly recognized the political entrepre-

---

[43] In Douglas's words, "When racial or religious lines are drawn by the State, the multi-racial, multireligious communities that our Constitution seeks to weld together as one become separatist; antagonisms that relate to race or religion rather than to political issues are generated; communities seek not the best representative but the best racial or religious partisan" (ibid. at 67).

[44] Defining "the people" as equal individuals (ibid. at 66), Douglas referred directly to the early reapportionment revolution case *Gray v. Sanders*, 372 U.S. 368 (1963).

neurship that Frankfurter disavowed. Douglas argued that legislatures, and the courts that reviewed them, jointly generated and enforced conceptions of "the people." His contention was that by enforcing nonracial apportionment schemes, legislatures and courts could actively fashion an integrated political community, free of the political fissures that would otherwise form around racial attachments.

Yet, even though Douglas's approach was an improvement over previous efforts, it was unclear whether his program of judicial action finally preserved the capacity of the people to speak for themselves. His argument hinged on the claim that racially homogeneous districts produced a highly polarized politics, marked by the election of representatives solely concerned with their own racial group. As a matter of political practice, however, it seemed that racially divisive politics could exist without being sustained by segregated districts. This possibility suggested that the judicial insistence on race-neutral apportionment plans might permit racially polarized politics to flourish, thereby disabling the individualistic people whom Douglas hoped to empower.

To see this, consider the at-large elections that Douglas (and Black) had shown enthusiasm for as early as *Colegrove*.[45] An at-large election placed voters of all races in a single district and, thus, seemed to satisfy Douglas's account of fair representation. Yet, even though at-large elections did not explicitly distinguish between groups of voters, they did not necessarily weld voters together into a single people. In fact, on the heels of *Wright*, the Court considered several cases in which complaints about the racially discriminatory impact of at-large elections were heard.[46] These complaints centered on a simple observation about racial-bloc voting: in an at-large district where a racial minority was submerged within a politically hostile white majority, minority voting strength could be easily canceled out, allowing whites to elect every representative. The racial neutrality of at-large elections had no talismanic value. Race-specific patterns of voting could balkanize politics and ensure racial exclusion, even within the context of ostensibly "integrated" at-large districts.

If Douglas was to rectify problems like minority submersion in at-large districts, then his conception of "the people" needed to be modified—for his pretense of a purely individualistic people ignored the ex-

---

[45] Douglas joined Black's dissent in *Colegrove*, which made an argument for at-large elections.

[46] See *Fortson v. Dorsey*, 379 U.S. 433 (1965), and *Burns v. Richardson*, 384 U.S. 73 (1966).

tent to which racial exclusion could be perpetuated by racially impartial means. Conversely, if Douglas was to accept the political consequences of at-large districts and other race-neutral devices, then he needed to develop a more sophisticated distinction between at-large districts and racially homogeneous single-member districts — for while only the latter would be invalid on Douglas's terms, both districting arrangements seemed capable of yielding the same exclusionary results.[47] In either case, Douglas needed to enlarge his understanding of how the judiciary should envision the political community and establish a role within it.

THE CONSTITUTIONALITY OF LEGISLATIVE LEARNING

The passage of the Voting Rights Act of 1965 ushered in a new era of heightened judicial concern for minority representation. The act featured a series of provisions designed to enforce the Fifteenth Amendment, protecting the right to vote from denial or abridgment on the basis of race or color. The heart of the act was in the temporary Sections 4 and 5.[48] Section 4 suspended literacy tests for five years in any political subdivision where such tests were in force and where voter registration or turnout was unusually low. The subdivisions "covered" by Section 4 were subject to "preclearance" under Section 5, requiring each subdivision to submit any changes in "voting qualification or prerequisite to voting, or any standard, practice or procedure with respect to voting" to the federal government for approval.[49]

The special enforcement mechanisms created by the act took the intent as well as the results of voting rules to be important. To bail out from Section 4 coverage, a subdivision had to prove in federal court that it had not used literacy tests during the past five years "for the purpose or with the effect of denying or abridging the right to vote on account of race or color."[50] Similarly, in order to comply with Section 5 preclearance, a subdivision had to show either the Attorney General or the D.C. District Court that its proposed rule change did "not have the

[47] This is a version of the problem faced by Black's majority opinion in *Wright*.

[48] I discussed the composition of the act at much greater length in chapter one. For the text of the act as originally passed, see *United States Statutes At Large*, 79 Stat. 437.

[49] Ibid. at 439.

[50] Ibid. at 438.

purpose and will not have the effect" of discriminating against racial minorities.[51]

By putting the federal government in the business of policing state and local legislatures, the act placed minority representation high on the political agenda. Of course, the assurance of political prominence was not the same as a guarantee that the act had addressed and resolved all the complexities of minority representation evident in *Gomillion* and *Wright*. As I illustrated at length in chapter one, the act itself contained no definition of what counted as a discriminatory intent or result, nor did it provide a broader understanding of "the people" or what it meant to represent them fairly. The result was that a good deal of room remained for continued debate and controversy.

Although the act was hardly a philosophers' stone, it nonetheless supplied a statutory context in which conflicts over minority representation could be readily examined and adjudicated. The question was how the Supreme Court was going to make sense of representational issues in this new context.

Shortly after the Voting Rights Act became law, South Carolina challenged the act's constitutionality in *South Carolina v. Katzenbach* (1966).[52] South Carolina's suit centered on Sections 4 and 5, attacking the suspension of literacy tests, the coverage of selected subdivisions, and the establishment of preclearance as unconstitutional exercises of congressional power.[53] Chief Justice Earl Warren, writing for an eight-member majority, defended the act against South Carolina's charges, holding the contested provisions to be "valid means for carrying out the commands of the Fifteenth Amendment."[54] Warren's ruling contrasted sharply with the Court's actions during the nineteenth century, a period when the judiciary systematically undermined congressional attempts to secure minority voting rights.[55] What was equally striking and, for my purposes here, more important, was that Warren's opinion also marked a departure from the Court's more recent treatment of minority representation.

---

[51] Ibid. at 439.

[52] *South Carolina v. Katzenbach*, 383 U.S. 301 (1966). The Court heard the case under original jurisdiction.

[53] For a full listing of South Carolina's contentions, see Ibid. at 315–23.

[54] Ibid. at 337. Warren was joined by Justices Brennan, White, Stewart, Harlan, Clark, Goldberg, and Douglas.

[55] For a brief discussion of the Court's nineteenth-century decisions, see chapter one.

Warren anchored his defense of the Voting Rights Act in a discussion of legislative deliberation. At the outset of his opinion, Warren noted that the act was introduced during eighteen days of committee hearings, featuring testimony from sixty-seven witnesses.[56] These hearings were followed by nearly thirty days of debate on the floors of both the House and Senate.[57] A "voluminous legislative history" was the result, exhaustively documenting the denial of minority voting rights.[58] Warren credited the massive infusions of information with persuading Congress that voting discrimination was deeply entrenched and resistant to simple remedies. The Voting Rights Act was the product of congressional learning. Indeed, Warren's entire opinion was heavily laced with the language of discovery and edification: looking over the sweep of American history, Congress "found" that case-by-case litigation was an inadequate response to voting-rights discrimination; Congress "learned" that voting-rights discrimination was especially pronounced in some areas; Congress further "learned" that such discrimination typically entailed the misuse of literacy tests; Congress not only "knew" that discriminatory literacy tests must be suspended, but also "knew" that many states had reacted to previous civil-rights measures by installing new discriminatory devices in the place of old ones; Congress thus "had reason to suppose" that subdivisions covered by the act would contrive new discriminatory schemes; in light of such knowledge, Congress subjected the covered subdivisions to on-going federal review.[59]

For Warren, congressional learning provided the ground on which the act's validity rested. Warren argued that Congress may generally "use any rational means to effectuate the constitutional prohibition of racial discrimination in voting."[60] The legislative record revealed to Warren that Congress had understood something new as it deliberated over the act. Viewed from the perspective of fresh congressional knowledge, the act's aggressive enforcement mechanisms made sense. That is,

[56] *South Carolina v. Katzenbach* at 308.

[57] Ibid. at 309.

[58] Ibid.

[59] Ibid. at 328, 331, 334, 335. Warren also presented the Court's own deliberations as analogous to the deliberations Congress went through to pass the act. At the direct invitation of the Court, twenty-six states (in addition to South Carolina) participated in the case (ibid. at 307–8). All of these states submitted or joined briefs and seven actually took part in oral arguments. According to Warren, the result of such broad participation was an inclusive, well-tempered proceeding in which "all viewpoints on the issues [were] fully developed" (ibid. at 308).

[60] Ibid. at 324.

given what Congress had come to know about the organization and operation of the political community, the Voting Rights Act was reasonable and, hence, constitutional.

One could argue that Warren's account of congressional deliberation served as more than a means of justifying the Voting Rights Act. Consider Warren's discussion of the preclearance provisions in Section 5. Warren recognized that the preclearance was perhaps the most formidable of the act's enforcement mechanisms.[61] Preclearance would prohibit covered subdivisions from unilaterally determining the fundamental rules of political organization. Instead of fashioning the political community as they wished, covered subdivisions would be forced to justify changes in political rules to the federal government. Preclearance would thus compel covered subdivisions to perform a political task that they had historically neglected — to deliberate on behalf of the entire people without discriminating on the basis of race or color.[62] Warren ruled preclearance to be constitutional and, in doing so, acknowledged the need to oversee state and local deliberation.

But Warren gave more than his endorsement to preclearance. He implicitly provided a model of the nondiscriminatory deliberation that preclearance was meant to ensure. The model was Congress. According to Warren, Congress had conducted broadly inclusive hearings, gathered enormous amounts of new information, staged lengthy debates, and recommended reasonable measures to repair a racially fractured political community. The passage of the Voting Rights Act was virtually an archetype of fair deliberation undertaken in the name of ensuring fair political opportunities. By orchestrating his opinion around the admirable example of Congress, Warren seemed to suggest that for covered subdivisions to survive preclearance, proof of having conducted Congress-like deliberations ought to be required. The suggestion was, in other words, that preclearance required covered subdivisions to justify new political procedures much as Congress had — by demonstrating an understanding of what was in the interest of the people as a whole.

Warren did not develop the connection between congressional deliberation and subdivisional deliberation in any detail.[63] Yet the general

---

[61] Ibid. at 334–35.

[62] As I noted above, the same standard would have to be met for a covered subdivision to bail out of Section 5 and thus forego preclearance.

[63] The incompleteness of Warren's argument made a certain amount of sense. After all, the primary question in *South Carolina v. Katzenbach* concerned the validity of the act;

implication of his opinion, indicating that deliberation in covered subdivisions was to be reconfigured, did not pass unnoticed. In the lone *South Carolina v. Katzenbach* dissent, Justice Black rejected Section 5 (and Warren's defense of it) *precisely* because preclearance promised to compel covered subdivisions to deliberate on terms dictated by the federal government. Whatever terms federal officials might name, Black argued that merely to give them "the power to veto state laws they do not like [was] in direct conflict with the clear command of our Constitution that 'The United States shall guarantee to every State in this Union a Republican Form of Government.'"[64] Selected states and localities could not be forced to deliberate without robbing them of self-rule and treating them as "little more than conquered provinces."[65] For Black, the Voting Rights Act was "reminiscent" of the political abuses that led to the American Revolution, an oppressive move taken by a tyrannical sovereign against a few self-governing communities.[66]

Black maintained his objections against Warren's opinion and the Voting Rights Act until he left the Court in 1971.[67] Although Black persistently pressed his case, his position remained weak, without an effective response to the extensive evidence of voting-rights discrimination that informed the act. If certain states and localities consistently excluded racial minorities from the political community, why should their claim to unsupervised self-rule go unchallenged? On what grounds could such political subdivisions be allowed to continue to abridge voting rights on the basis of race? Black had no answers. At one juncture, he did attempt to sidestep these questions by arguing that the persecution of southern states, not the protection of racial minorities, was the

---

having resolved this question, Warren had little cause to produce a comprehensive treatise on the probable operation of the act.

[64] Ibid. at 359.

[65] Ibid. at 360.

[66] Ibid. at 359n.

[67] See his dissents in *Allen v. State Board of Elections*, 393 U.S. 544 (1969); *Gaston County v. United States*, 395 U.S. 285 (1969); and *Perkins v. Matthews*, 400 U.S. 379 (1971). Black did deliver the Court's opinion in *Oregon v. Mitchell*, 400 U.S. 112, (1970), the decision in which the Court upheld most of the 1970 amendments to the Voting Rights Act. But questions of minority representation were marginal in *Oregon v. Mitchell*. The primary bone of contention was whether Congress had the authority to lower the voting-age requirement in state elections to the age of eighteen. A majority of the Court ruled that Congress could not—a decision that was not only overturned by the Twenty-sixth Amendment to the Constitution, but also a decision that had no effect on the act's provisions dealing with minority voting rights.

central motivation of the act.[68] But Black's attempt fell flat: by the time he began to stress the act's southern focus, the act had been amended so that it covered parts of the country ranging from Maine to Wyoming.[69]

The failure of Black's argument did not mean that Warren's opinion was unassailable. Warren had suggested that the aim of the Voting Rights Act was to enforce nondiscriminatory deliberation — a kind of deliberation that was evident in Congress's own efforts to produce the act. But how was such broad legislative learning to be realized under the act? What was the relationship between legislative learning, fair minority representation, and judicial authority? In the end, did Warren's nondiscriminatory deliberation preserve the capacity of the people to speak for themselves?

Three years after *South Carolina v. Katzenbach*, Warren had an opportunity to confront these questions in *Allen v. State Board of Elections* (1969).[70] *Allen* combined four separate cases in which different covered subdivisions had failed to submit new political rules for federal preclearance.[71] The contested rules included a switch from single-member to at-large districts, the transformation of elective offices into appointive ones, and the alteration of procedures governing write-in and independent candidates. Considering whether such changes were subject to preclearance, the Court was presented with an opportunity to flesh out its understanding of the act, a chance to ascertain the range of matters over which covered subdivisions could be forced to deliberate.

Warren began the opinion of the Court by recalling the extensive legislative history discussed in *South Carolina v. Katzenbach*, emphasizing that Congress had documented a virtually endless variety of discriminatory schemes.[72] In recognition of this variety, Warren argued that the act had been designed to root out "subtle" as well as "obvious" forms

---

[68] *Perkins v. Matthews* at 406–7.

[69] See chapter one for a discussion of the act's 1970 amendments.

[70] *Allen v. State Board of Elections.*

[71] Ibid. at 550–54.

[72] Ibid. at 548. Warren was joined by Justices Brennan, Fortas, Stewart, and White. Justice Marshall, joined by Justice Douglas, filed an opinion that concurred in part and dissented in part. Justice Harlan did the same. Justice Black filed his usual dissent. Warren also defended the validity of the cases that made up *Allen*. Noting that these cases were initiated by individuals (rather than by the attorney general), Warren interpreted the act to allow private suits (ibid. at 554–57). Private suits were permissible, he argued, because they were consistent with the act's general efforts to keep the burdens of litigation on covered subdivisions. He used similar reasoning to allow individuals to bring voting rights suits in local district courts (ibid. at 557–60).

of discrimination.[73] This meant that the terms of Section 5 were all-inclusive, requiring covered subdivisions to preclear *every* change in political procedures no matter how minor. In this vein, Warren ruled that each of the changes at issue in *Allen* should be subject to federal review.[74] Without drawing any firm conclusions about actual discrimination, Warren observed that both the creation of appointive offices and the alteration of candidate qualifications could affect political opportunities and, as a consequence, might be used to circumscribe minority voting power. The same could be said for the switch from district to at-large elections. As Warren reasoned, "the right to vote can be affected by a dilution of voting power as well as by an absolute prohibition on casting a ballot. . . . Voters who are members of a racial minority might well be in the majority in one district, but in a decided minority in the county as a whole. This type of change could therefore nullify their ability to elect the candidate of their choice just as would prohibiting some of them from voting."[75]

Warren's comprehensive reading of preclearance fit easily with his understanding of legislative learning. In *South Carolina v. Katzenbach*, Warren had gestured toward a model of nondiscriminatory deliberation, which the Voting Rights Act was meant to enforce, compelling covered subdivisions to justify rule changes with some knowledge of common interests. In *Allen*, Warren suggested further that covered subdivisions were required to justify themselves across a wide range of matters.[76] Much as Douglas had in *Wright v. Rockefeller*, Warren realized that legislatures, and the courts that reviewed them, jointly forged the political community. He thus held subdivisions broadly responsible for securing minority voting rights. Unlike Douglas, however, Warren focused on the *actual* political status of minority groups. He explicitly noted that minority voting strength could be canceled out by race-neutral rules and thus denied that a covered subdivision could defend itself by citing simple formulas. According to Warren, covered subdivisions had to demonstrate that their decisions not only reflected an under-

---

[73] Ibid. at 566. Indeed, the act defined "voting" to include "*all* action necessary to make a vote effective" in any election (sec. 14, emphasis added).

[74] *Allen* at 569–71.

[75] Ibid. at 569.

[76] Indeed, in one of the cases at issue in *Allen*, the Mississippi legislature had passed new electoral laws without *any* public debate at all (Davidson and Grofman 1994, p. 32). In Warren's view, such silent legislation was clearly illegitimate.

standing of the people as a whole, but also avoided the actual diminution of minority voting power.

Yet, for all his emphasis on the concrete conditions of minority power, Warren appeared to possess only a vague notion of the political community he hoped the act would achieve. Warren wished to subject covered subdivisions to close supervision, obliging them to deliberate on behalf of the entire people as each rule change was debated. This much could be inferred from *South Carolina v. Katzenbach* and *Allen*. But Warren failed to furnish any substantive sense of "the people" that the covered subdivisions were meant to take into account. Warren maintained that Congress had deliberated in the interests of all, yet this Congress was virtually all white. If Congress as it stood in 1965 could be speak on behalf of the whole, how much could the Court gainsay the efforts of covered subdivisions? Indeed, how was the Court to know deliberation when it saw it? The analogy linking congressional learning to covered subdivisions—an analogy that promised to provide a model of nondiscriminatory deliberation under the act—was incomplete and abstract. Covered subdivisions might be compelled to prove that they had learned about the entire people, but without a more definitive understanding of who "the people" were and what counted as legislative learning, the consequences of Warren's approach were indeterminate.

It was into this lacuna that Justice John Harlan stepped with a specific conception of "the people" and a reading of preclearance to match. Dissenting in *Allen*, Harlan began by claiming that Section 5 "march[ed] in lockstep" with Section 4, which prohibited the use of literacy tests and similar barriers to equal political access.[77] In tightly linking the two sections, Harlan suggested that Section 5 was intended merely to preserve what Section 4 had accomplished. For Harlan, this meant that preclearance could be used to review only "those techniques that prevented Negroes from voting *at all*."[78] Such an interpretation of the act was required because Congress had enacted Section 4 (as well as Section 5) "on the premise that once Negroes had gained free access to the ballot box, state governments would then be suitably responsive to their voice, and federal intervention would not be justified."[79] Congress

---

[77] *Allen* at 584.

[78] Ibid. at 585, emphasis added.

[79] Ibid.

had assumed that the people could take care of themselves so long as no racial group was clearly eliminated from the political community.

This was, of course, the argument that Justice Frankfurter had made in *Gomillion v. Lightfoot*. Harlan recognized the connection. He argued that the act was based on the Fifteenth Amendment and that the Fifteenth Amendment itself was to be understood (by both Congress and the Court) in terms of *Gomillion*'s emphasis on complete minority exclusion.[80] In light of *Gomillion* — or, more precisely, in light of who *Gomillion* took "the people" to be — Harlan concluded that preclearance could only be used to oversee decisions affecting the conditions of basic political access. Once such decisions had been made, the vigilant people and their obedient legislatures were to be left alone. The logic of *Gomillion* thus kept the Court away from the judicially intractable questions of minority representation with which Warren wished to grapple.[81]

In adopting this position, Harlan failed to mention, much less resolve, the problems plaguing Frankfurter's original opinion. He ignored the ways in which the issue of minority exclusion remained muddled in *Gomillion*, reflecting the poorly developed conceptions of "the people" and judicial authority on which Frankfurter had relied. All of this suggested that the strength of Harlan's dissent was not that it featured a faultless conception of "the people" but that it featured such a conception at all. Even as Warren had called for the close examination of political conditions in covered subdivisions, he had failed to describe who "the people" were or how their interests were to be represented. This failure left Warren's opinion vulnerable to alternative readings of the Voting Rights Act that were explicitly grounded in conceptions of "the people." Offering such an alternative reading of the act, Harlan did not close off the debate over minority representation so much as indicate the terrain on which the debate would occur. Harlan reminded

[80] Ibid. at 589.

[81] For example, Warren would have the judiciary scrutinize the choice to hold at-large rather than district elections. Harlan thought that such a choice defied intelligent judicial assessment. He wrote, "Under one system [i.e., at-large], Negroes have *some* influence in the election of *all* officers; under the other, minority groups have *more* influence in the selection of *fewer* officers" (ibid. at 586, emphasis original). In this vein, Harlan called attention to the lack of real relief in *Allen*. (Warren simply remanded the cases for further consideration, rather than issuing a injunction against future elections.) Harlan implicitly suggested that Warren did not take stronger action because there were in fact no standards to guide his judgment (ibid. at 593–94).

the Court of the question that had always been at the center of its decisions: what notion of "the people" ought to inform the judiciary's participation in the politics of minority representation?

INTEREST GROUP COMPETITION AND THE TOTALITY OF CIRCUMSTANCES

Warren's rulings in *South Carolina v. Katzenbach* and *Allen v. State Board of Elections* seemingly placed Section 5 of the Voting Rights Act at the forefront of the minority representation debate. Yet, the most controversial and complex questions of representation did not immediately surface in the context of preclearance cases. Throughout the 1970s, Section 5 adjudication was constrained for several reasons. First, the enforcement of preclearance proved to be somewhat less than perfect, with covered subdivisions neglecting to report electoral changes or to comply with the attorney general's decisions. Gaps in preclearance enforcement simply meant fewer representational conflicts for the federal government and the courts to consider.[82] Second, and more importantly, preclearance itself was limited to the review of *changes* in political rules. This fact allowed the Court to evade the most comprehensive representational issues — for if rule changes were the sole focus of preclearance, then Section 5 could not be used to address the discriminatory impact of any voting procedures *already in place*.[83] The result was that preclearance inquiries were reduced to the issue of political backsliding, leaving broader issues of fair minority representation unexplored.

---

[82] This is not to say that Section 5 was a dead letter. A significant number of rule changes were submitted to the Justice Department during the 1970s. Moreover, the Court took steps to plug the holes in preclearance. Recall that in *Allen*, the Court permitted private individuals to sue covered subdivisions for failing to submit rule changes. Also in *Georgia v. United States*, 411 U.S. 526 (1973), the Court broadly supported Justice Department regulations governing the enforcement of preclearance.

[83] See my discussion of *Beer v. United States*, 425 U.S. 130 (1976) in chapter one. See also *City of Lockhart v. United States*, 460 U.S. 125 (1983). Prior to *Beer* the Court handed down several decisions holding that Section 5 could not be used outright to maximize minority power. Where a covered subdivision took an action that unintentionally lessened minority voting power, the subdivision need only ensure that its new districting plan fairly reflected the voting strength of the minority community. See *City of Petersburg v. United States*, 354 F. Supp. 1021 (1972), affr'd 410 U.S. 962 (1973); and *City of Richmond [Va.] v. United States*, 422 U.S. 358 (1975).

In spite of the limitations of preclearance, the sweeping judicial review promised in *South Carolina v. Katzenbach* and *Allen v. State Board of Elections* was not lost. Representational questions that were not raised in the context of Section 5 were directly confronted in a series of constitutional cases. It was in these that the Court established the "totality of circumstances" test as a tool for directly assessing minority presence in the political community. It was in these cases, in other words, that the Court continued the battle over competing conceptions of "the people."[84]

The Court first articulated its "totality of circumstances" test in *Whitcomb v. Chavis* (1971).[85] *Whitcomb* was primarily concerned with the complaints of minority voters residing in Marion County, Indiana.[86] Under Indiana's apportionment scheme, Marion County formed one at-large district electing eight state senators and fifteen state representatives. Minority voters filed suit against Indiana, alleging that the multimember district "invidiously diluted the force and effect" of their vote.[87] More specifically, minority voters argued (i) that residents of a "ghetto area" within Marion County shared "particular demographic characteristics rendering them cognizable as a minority group interest group with distinct interests in specific areas of the substantive law;" (ii) that the at-large district, coupled with strict party control of nominating procedures, led to the election of few candidates from the ghetto; and (iii) that ghetto residents had " 'almost no political force or control over legislators because the effect of their vote [was] canceled out by other contrary interest groups' " in Marion County.[88] Reviewing these com-

---

[84] To examine the Court's constitutional decisions is not, of course, to forsake the study of the act. The Court's constitutional decisions of the 1970s shaped the Court's Voting Rights Act decisions during the 1980s and 1990s. This was so because the division between constitutional and statutory approaches to minority representation substantially dissolved (see chapter one). In 1982, Congress used the "totality of circumstances" test as its standard for amending Section 2 of the act. By 1987, the Justice Department had officially incorporated the amended Section 2 into Section 5 preclearance requirements. Some important differences between the constitutional and statutory approaches to minority representation did remain, largely due to the case *Mobile v. Bolden*, 446 U.S. 55 (1980). I discuss *Bolden* in chapter five.

[85] *Whitcomb v. Chavis*, 403 U.S. 124 (1971).

[86] *Whitcomb* also featured a challenge from an Indiana voter residing in a multimember district smaller than Marion County, alleging that Marion County voters had greater voting power because they voted for more representatives. The Court rejected this claim on the grounds that it lacked empirical validation (ibid. at 145–47).

[87] Ibid. at 128.

[88] Ibid. at 129.

plaints, the lower court investigated the interests of the ghetto area, the manner of legislative election, and the actual performance of representatives. The lower court ruled in favor of the minority voters, recommending the creation of single-member districts intentionally designed to represent minority interests.[89]

Justice Byron White, writing for the Supreme Court, overturned the lower court ruling.[90] White acknowledged that the issues posed in *Whitcomb* forced the judiciary to squarely consider the "quality of representation afforded by the multi-member district as compared with single-member districts."[91] To assess representational quality, the Court needed to determine whether ghetto residents "had less opportunity than did other Marion County residents to participate in the political processes and to elect legislators of their choice."[92] To this end, the lower court had rightly gathered extensive information about local political conditions. The difficulty was that these political findings had been misconstrued. According to White, the lower court had focused on the low proportion of representatives elected from the ghetto, even though ghetto residents as a whole appeared to have strong ties with the Democratic party.[93] Indeed, White found it "reasonable to infer that had the Democrats won all of the elections or even most of them, the ghetto would have had no justifiable complaints about representation."[94] Few representatives had come from the ghetto because few elections had been won by Democrats.

White suggested that the lower court had erred because it misunderstood what equal political opportunity for *any* group was in the first place. The lower court had worried that ghetto residents had been unable to elect candidates of their choice. But as "our system has it," White observed, "*one* candidate wins, the others lose."[95] Political defeat

---

[89] Ibid. at 134–40. The lower court's order ultimately resulted in the reapportionment of the entire state by the Indiana legislature. This reapportionment featured single-member districts throughout the state, including in Marion County.

[90] White's opinion was joined in its entirety by Justices Black, Blackmun, and Burger. Justice Stewart concurred in all but one part of White's opinion. Justice Douglas, joined by Justices Brennan and Marshall, concurred in part and dissented in part. Justice Harlan filed a dissent.

[91] *Whitcomb* at 142.

[92] Ibid. at 149. This language would serve as the template for the 1982 amendments to Section 2 of the Voting Rights Act.

[93] Ibid. at 148–51.

[94] Ibid. at 152.

[95] Ibid. at 153, emphasis added.

was commonplace in a nation filled with many different interest groups that found themselves unable to dominate either multimember or single-member elections.[96] White pointed out that even the apportionment plan ordered by the lower court would leave Republicans and Democrats with predictably "safe" seats, permitting "political, racial, or economic minorities in those districts [to be] 'unrepresented' year after year."[97] Such patterns of political loss made certain that some group interests would be disregarded by the legislature. Indeed, since majority-rule elections ensured that legislatures would be "predetermin[ed]" against losing groups, White labeled the lack of inclusive representation an "inherent" tendency of our political system.[98]

In White's view, then, the lower court had missed the degree to which ordinary politics was defined by interest group competition, defeat, and exclusion. In this context, ghetto residents were to be viewed simply as members of an interest group unless the totality of circumstances suggested otherwise. White reasoned that the ties between ghetto residents and the Democratic party were sufficiently strong to refute any claim that minority voters had suffered special discrimination. He consequently took ghetto dwellers to be an interest group like any other. This meant that the claim of minority vote dilution was invalid, "even assuming bloc voting by the [Marion County] delegation [was] contrary to the wishes of the ghetto majority."[99] A record of interest group defeat was no cause for judicial intervention. According to White, the "mere fact that one interest group or another concerned with the outcome of Marion County elections has found itself outvoted and without legislative seats of its own provides no basis for invoking constitutional remedies. . . ."[100]

When the totality of circumstances showed a racial minority to be different from any other interest group, White was willing to intervene. Writing for the Court in *White v. Regester* (1973), White applied his *Whitcomb* reasoning to at-large elections in Dallas and Bexar Counties, Texas.[101] White noted that Dallas County had a long history of racial

---

[96] Ibid. at 156, 159–60. White cited "union oriented workers" and "the university community" as examples of such interest groups.

[97] Ibid. at 153.

[98] Ibid. at 155.

[99] Ibid.

[100] Ibid. at 154–55.

[101] *White v. Regester*, 412 U.S. 755 (1973). *Regester* also concerned district population variances across the whole of Texas. The parts of White's opinion that addressed at-large

discrimination as well as a series of electoral rules that solidified the electoral clout of the white majority.[102] Moreover, a white-dominated organization ran the Democratic party in Dallas County and maintained tight control over the candidate slating process. Given this context, White concluded that the election of only two Dallas County blacks to the state legislature since Reconstruction was not an instance of ordinary interest group defeat.[103] He reached the same conclusion after considering the political position of Latinos in Bexar County. Like Dallas County blacks, Bexar County Latinos had endured a long history of discrimination, punctuated by "the most restrictive voter registration procedures in the nation."[104] The language barrier acted as an additional hurdle to Latino participation, helping to explain why only five Bexar County Latinos had been elected to the state legislature since 1880. On the strength of these findings, White agreed with the lower court ruling that Latinos had been "'effectively removed from the political processes of Bexar County.'"[105] White further held that the lower court had rightly ordered the Texas legislature to reapportion Dallas and Bexar Counties into single-member districts. Such a move was necessary to bring minorities "into the full stream of political life."[106]

What was to be made of White's totality-of-circumstances argument? As Douglas had done in *Wright* and as Warren had done in *South Carolina v. Katzenbach* and *Allen*, White clearly rejected Frankfurter's claim that the Court had no role to play in the construction of the political community.[107] Indeed, White believed that conflicts over minority representation could not be successfully adjudicated if the Court failed to evaluate the actual conditions of representation. For White, there simply were no "vigilant people" to whom the judiciary owed deference.

---

elections were joined by all justices (Burger, Stewart, Blackmun, Powell, Rehnquist, Brennan, Douglas, and Marshall).

[102] In addition to holding elections for the Texas House of Representatives on an at-large basis, Dallas County required a majority vote to win primaries and relied on a "place" balloting rule to ensure head-to-head contests for each office (thus allowing whites to coordinate their opposition to minority candidates). See Ibid. at 766.

[103] Ibid. at 767.

[104] Ibid. at 768.

[105] Ibid. at 769.

[106] Ibid.

[107] Harlan made this point in his separate (and dissenting) opinion in *Whitcomb*. Harlan claimed that White had in fact become "trapped" in the "political thicket" of representational politics, which Frankfurter had wisely refused to enter in *Colegrove* and *Gomillion* (see *Whitcomb* at 170).

White did defer, however, to the panoply of competing interest groups that he thought comprised the political community. His conception of interest group competition distinguished White's arguments from those of both Douglas and Warren. Unlike Warren, White paid little attention to the quality of legislative debate or learning. White argued that American government was fundamentally disposed against broadly inclusive deliberations. Legislatures routinely gave some interests short shrift, debating and acting against groups that had failed to elect representatives of their choice. White found evidence showing a lack of legislative responsiveness to be significant only when coupled with additional findings about the patterns of political defeat. On their own, arguments that claimed that the legislature had ignored minority group interests and, as a result, had failed to learn about everyone's interests, were of negligible value.[108]

White differed even more strongly with Douglas. White appeared to deny that there was anything unusual or dangerous about recognizing the reality of racial divisions in reapportionment. He observed that government at every level featured districts controlled by a single political party or interest. This was so because reapportionment was a political process intimately connected with the larger political environment in which it occurred. Thus, the entrenchment of some interests was simply a consequence of a system in which groups often found themselves without legislative seats of their own. According to White, the Court could not hope to purge districting of these political dynamics; the reapportionment process would inevitably recognize and reward some groups rather than others.[109] Instead, the judicial task was to ensure that no racial group had its voting strength invidiously minimized. Where the totality of circumstances suggested that such minimization had occurred, the Court responded merely by redirecting the flow of normal politics, instructing legislatures to protect a slightly different constellation of interests than they ordinarily would.

In sum, one could say that White assimilated the dilemmas of minority representation to a more general politics of interest group competi-

[108] More generally, White insisted on the importance of surrounding circumstances when examining claims of racial discrimination in contexts other than voting. See his dissent in *Palmer v. Thompson*, 403 U.S. 217 (1971) and his majority opinion in *Washington v. Davis*, 426 U.S. 229 (1976).

[109] White made this point most clearly in *Gaffney v. Cummings*, 412 U.S. 735, 753–54 (1973), decided at the same time as *Regester*, where he openly accepted legislative efforts to reward political parties with "safe" districts.

tion, making sense of the former in terms of the latter. With this approach, White could easily account for the racial divisions bedeviling those (like Douglas) who strove toward an individualistic and race-neutral politics. What was missing from White's argument, however, was some explanation for why interest group competition yielded a status quo worth preserving. If ordinary politics was characterized by the exclusion of some groups and the entrenchment of others, in what sense was such a politics fair?

White did argue that judicial solicitude for excluded groups would generate tremendous legal activity, as political losers besieged the courts in pursuit of greater representation.[110] Yet White failed to indicate why increased litigation was not an appropriate response to political exclusion and entrenchment. White never argued that certain groups *deserved* to lose.[111] The political system did not select inimical interests for defeat; on the contrary, the political system handed out defeat indifferently, producing a series of districts dominated by one interest group or another. White used the notion of widespread defeat as a baseline for measuring the extent of minority representation, arguing that minority groups should be allowed to suffer the same political losses as everyone else. But White had no general account of how political losers were connected to or could expect to be represented by the political winners; his opinions simply painted a portrait of distinct political classes. His totality-of-circumstances reasoning thus presented minority groups with the stark choice of either dominating their own districts or being dominated by some other interest group. In other words, where "the people" were understood to be nothing more than a competitive pool of interest groups, judicial action taken on behalf of the people routinely left the entire citizenry unable to speak for itself.

Of course, White was not the only Justice to offer a flawed approach to minority representation. As I have argued, Frankfurter, Warren and Douglas also presented schemes for adjudicating representational controversies that relied on questionable notions of political identity and judicial authority. Problematic as they were, however, all of these approaches would be revisited and reconfigured in the crucible of continuing judicial debate.

[110] *Whitcomb* at 157.

[111] Compare White's view with that of James Madison (see chapter two). Madison thought the system of representation would work to frustrate an entire range of passionate (and dangerous) political interests.

The Later Cases: The Polarization
of Judicial Debate

THE EARLY JUDICIAL ENCOUNTERS with minority representation generated a variety of approaches, each of which yielded claims of judicial
authority that impaired democratic sovereignty. In time, the Court
gradually moved away from their problematic early efforts. More specifically, reactions against White's interest group approach led different
justices to divergent conceptions of political identity and judicial authority, producing distinctly "individualist" and "group" renderings of
fair minority representation. The clash between individualist and group
conceptions drove judicial debate throughout several decisions, even as
members of the Court offered new accounts of minority representation
cast in terms of discriminatory intent and adverse effects.

The conceptual polarization of judicial arguments has only grown
more apparent in recent years. In response to the congressional rejection
of discriminatory intent in 1982, the Court developed a functionalist
view of the political process that helped streamline the diagnosis of minority vote dilution. The very simplicity of the Court's functionalism
helped expose the conceptual conflict at the root of judicial debate,
clearing a space in which individualist and group understandings of
"the people" could clash more openly. In this context of evident disagreement, justices have at times adopted alternative strategies of full-
scale retreat and measured advance. Yet both these strategies fail to
address underlying conceptual divisions and, thus, leave open the question of how the Court should proceed.

SKETCHING THE LINES OF OPPOSITION

With his opinions in *Whitcomb v. Chavis* and *White v. Regester*, Justice
White established the totality-of-circumstances approach. Anchored in
an interpretation of the Constitution, White's approach provided an independent means of litigating minority representation that was often

used in lieu of or in addition to the Voting Rights Act.[1] Yet, even as White's arguments were more frequently relied upon during the late 1970s and early 1980s, they also became targets of attack, serving as points of departure for justices who rejected the appeal to interest group competition.

The paths away from White's position began to be cleared in the case *UJO v. Carey* (1977).[2] *UJO* concerned the design of state senate and assembly districts in New York City. Kings, Bronx, and Manhattan Counties had become subject to Section 5 following the 1970 amendments to the Voting Rights Act. As a consequence, New York sought preclearance from the attorney general for its 1972 redistricting of the covered counties. The attorney general rejected the 1972 plan, finding that certain districts in Kings County appeared "to have an abnormally high minority concentration while adjoining minority neighborhoods [were] significantly diffused into surrounding districts."[3] Such a concentration of the nonwhite population clearly diluted minority voting strength. New York moved to meet the attorney general's objections by producing a revised redistricting plan in 1974. While the 1972 plan had contained three state senate districts with minority populations of roughly 91, 61, and 53 percent, the 1974 plan featured three districts with more efficient minority majorities ranging from 70 to 75 percent. The 1974 plan similarly evened out the distribution of minorities in the county's seven majority-minority assembly districts.[4]

As part of the 1974 revisions, a community of about thirty thousand Hasidic Jews, which had been located entirely in one senate and one assembly district, was split between two senate and two assembly districts. Once New York submitted the 1974 plan to the attorney general for preclearance, members of the Hasidic community filed suit, claiming that the plan not only assigned them to electoral districts solely on the basis of race (thus violating the Fifteenth Amendment), but also diluted their voting strength (thus violating the Fourteenth Amendment).[5] The

---

[1] For example, as many as forty lower court cases were litigated within the totality-of-circumstances framework from 1973 to 1980 (see chapter one).

[2] UJO is the acronym for United Jewish Organizations of Williamsburgh, Inc. Thus, the full name of the case is *United Jewish Organizations of Williamsburgh, Inc., v. Carey*, 430 U.S. 144 (1977).

[3] Ibid. at 150, n. 6. The attorney general as well as the lower court took Puerto Ricans and African Americans to be a single minority group (ibid. at 150, n. 5).

[4] Ibid. at 151–52.

[5] Ibid. at 152–53.

District Court dismissed the Hasidic complaint, rejecting their claim of vote dilution and upholding race-conscious districting pursuant to the Voting Rights Act. The Court of Appeals affirmed.[6]

Writing for a divided Supreme Court, Justice White affirmed the lower court rulings.[7] He reduced the Hasidic argument to four basic propositions: (i) the use of racial criteria in districting was impermissible; (ii) even if racial criteria were permissible, they should be employed only to remedy past discrimination — and there was no evidence of past discrimination in this case; (iii) whatever else, the use of a "racial quota" in redistricting was never acceptable; and (iv) the attorney general and New York relied on a 65 percent minority threshold and thus used an unconstitutional racial quota.[8] White argued that these propositions were clearly contradicted by a straightforward reading of the act and the Court's earlier cases. White pointed out that the act's preclearance provisions were fashioned to prevent *new* forms of voting discrimination from arising; as a result, preclearance was not dependent on proving past discrimination.[9] Moreover, White noted that since the protection against new voting discrimination might require remedial action, the Court had long recognized that compliance with preclearance might entail some race-conscious districting.[10] Such race-conscious districting necessarily demanded covered subdivisions to determine the level of minority population needed to guarantee effective political opportunities.[11] Far from being unconstitutional, White found "it was reasonable for the attorney general to conclude in this case that a *substantial* nonwhite population majority — in the vicinity of 65 percent — would be required to a achieve a nonwhite majority of eligible voters."[12]

On the whole, White reasoned that the 1974 redistricting plan could be upheld because New York had done no more than comply with the

[6] Ibid. at 153–55.

[7] White was joined by Justice Stevens. Justices Brennan and Blackmun joined all of White's opinion except his constitutional argument. Justice Rehnquist joined only White's constitutional argument. Justice Stewart, joined by Justice Powell, concurred in judgment and Chief Justice Burger dissented. Justice Marshall took no part in the case.

[8] Ibid. at 156.

[9] Ibid. at 157.

[10] Ibid. at 160–61. Here White cited *South Carolina v. Katzenbach, Allen v. State Board of Elections, Beer v. United States, City of Richmond (Va.) v. United States,* and *City of Petersburg v. United States.* See chapter four for my discussion of these cases.

[11] *UJO* at 162.

[12] Ibid. at 164, emphasis original.

Voting Rights Act.[13] Even so, White could not rest his argument here. White's enumeration and refutation of the basic Hasidic claims simply did not reach the nub of the case. With his reading of the act, White illustrated how the political voices of minorities like African Americans and Puerto Ricans might be legitimately protected by race-conscious districting. Yet his interpretation of the act ignored the central issue of whether the Hasidic community could be justifiably fragmented as part of the remedial process. Even if the act sanctioned the creation of majority-minority single-member districts, could these districts be drawn in a way that harmed groups like the Hasidim?[14]

In response to this question, White recurred to his totality-of-circumstances analysis. White noted that while New York had deliberately enhanced the opportunity to elect minority candidates, there simply was "no fencing out of the white population [as a whole] from participation in the political process."[15] Indeed, the 1974 plan still left white majorities in nearly 70 percent of the senate and assembly districts, even though whites comprised only 65 percent of the countywide population.[16] White acknowledged that some white voters, including the Hasidim, found themselves in new districts with nonwhite majorities. But, as he had done in his original totality-of-circumstances opinions, White argued that defeat was an essential element of American politics, where "[s]ome candidate, along with his supporters, always loses."[17] Governmental efforts to inflict extreme degrees of political loss warranted judicial scrutiny and intervention. In this case, however, the state sought "to alleviate the consequences of racial voting at the polls and to achieve a fair allocation of political power between white and nonwhite voters in Kings County."[18] In White's view, the 1974 plan was a measure that merely altered the mix of political winners without forcing any

---

[13] Ibid. at 165.

[14] The Hasidic petitioners did not press any special claim to a group voice *as Hasidim* nor did they claim that the 1974 plan was specifically motivated by anti-Semitism (ibid. at 178, 178, n. 7). Instead, the Hasidic petitioners spoke as those who had been harmed by a plan explicitly designed to benefit racial minorities. In his brief concurrence, Justice Stewart suggested that this failure to identify the Hasidim as a cognizable minority interest was a key weakness (ibid. at 179).

[15] Ibid. at 165.

[16] Ibid. at 166.

[17] Ibid.

[18] Ibid. at 167.

group to suffer extraordinary levels of defeat.[19] It made little difference that the Hasidic fragmentation arose as a consequence of race-conscious districting. Race was, after all, part and parcel of ordinary political practice.[20] New York's redistricting plan had simply conformed with the alternating patterns of exclusion and entrenchment that comprised the politics of interest group competition.

As a standard application of totality-of-circumstances reasoning, White's opinion exhibited the same difficulties that plagued his earlier opinions. White measured the Hasidic complaint against a baseline of political defeat and racial division without explaining why such a baseline was worth defending in the first place. To the question of how his conception of interest group competition might be justified, White appeared to have no answer.

Or, more accurately, he appeared to have no substantially developed answer. White did make a small move toward offering a justification, suggesting that the defeats which punctuated interest group competition were not as complete as they might seem. White stipulated that "the white voter who as a result of the 1974 plan is in a district more likely to return a nonwhite representative *will be represented*, to the extent that voting continues to follow racial lines, by legislators elected from majority white districts."[21] Without their own electoral districts, the Hasidim would nonetheless possess an effective political voice, as their "white" political interests were championed by whatever whites happened to hold power.

Justice White made no real effort to expand this view of indirect representation; yet, even in its incipient form, his defense of interest group competition appeared only to heighten the need for further justification. White minimized the extent of Hasidic exclusion only by emphasizing the depth of racial divisions. By assigning racial attachments such high political valence, he could argue not only that racial divisions were an essential part of interest group competition but also that racial divisions explained why interest group competition was fair. Thus, contrary to Justice Douglas (whose *Wright v. Rockefeller* opinion argued that the

[19] In this vein, White compared the Hasidim directly to the Democrat and Republican minorities submerged in districts controlled by majorities of the opposing party. Since apportionment by party was allowable, so too apportionment by race (ibid.). Compare *Whitcomb v. Chavis*, 403 U.S. 124, 153 (1971).

[20] As White wrote, "voting for or against a candidate because of his race is an unfortunate practice . . . [b]ut it is not rare." (*UJO* at 166).

[21] Ibid. at 166, n. 24, emphasis added.

divisive politics of race ought to be overcome), White relied on racial representation as an essential justification for judicial and legislative decision making. To be sure, Justice Douglas's own prescriptions for achieving a nonracial politics were problematic. But White's easy embrace of racial representation was hardly an improvement. Working with a vision of fixed racial blocs, White at minimum raised a serious question of judicial legitimacy: If judicial authority was predicated on a capacity to speak for the people as a whole, what judicial action could there be when the very notion of a "whole people" was denied?

It was precisely because White's efforts to justify his interest group baseline remained problematic that Justice Brennan refused to concur with White's totality-of-circumstances analysis. Brennan was struck by the "starkly clear fact" that "an overt racial number was employed to effect [Hasidic] assignment to voting districts."[22] While White was willing to accept race-conscious districting as part of ordinary interest group competition, Brennan insisted that race should *not* be viewed as "the keystone of the political trade."[23] For Brennan, racial and political divisions remained importantly different from one another. It was not enough for the Court to proclaim the benign purpose of a race-conscious policy or to console adversely affected groups with the claim that politics entailed defeat. Unlike other factors that played explicit roles in the districting process, race required special forms of justification because its use introduced a host of special problems. Brennan noted generally that where states used racial classifications to benefit minorities, a strong risk remained that such "preferential" racial discrimination might disguise a plan that in fact harmed the supposed beneficiaries.[24] Even if preferential discrimination actually served a remedial purpose, it might nonetheless stimulate race consciousness or stigmatize the recipient groups.[25] Finally, apart from the possible harms to the intended beneficiaries, preferential discrimination raised a serious question of whether other races could justly be made to bear the costs of advancing minority interests, especially given the Fourteenth Amendment's guarantee of equal protection.[26]

Brennan's argument, then, was not that race-conscious policies had no place in politics, but that such policies could only be used if properly

[22] Ibid. at 169.
[23] Ibid. at 171, n. 1.
[24] Ibid. at 172.
[25] Ibid. at 173.
[26] Ibid. at 174.

justified.[27] Brennan saw little in White's totality-of-circumstances reasoning that spoke to the special justificatory needs created by preferential discrimination. Instead of attempting to extend White's limited defense of interest group competition, Brennan claimed it was the Voting Rights Act itself that "substantially minimize[d] the objections to preferential treatment, and legitimate[d] the use of even overt, numerical racial devices in electoral districting."[28] Brennan emphasized that the act had been "the product of substantial and careful deliberations" that signified nothing less than "an unequivocal and well-defined congressional consensus on the national need for 'sterner and more elaborate measures' to secure the promise of the Fourteenth and Fifteenth Amendments. . . ."[29] Such comprehensive congressional proceedings attenuated any claim that the act's measures directly stigmatized or insulted racial groups. Indeed, the length and breadth of congressional consideration strongly suggested that "[w]hatever may be the indirect and undesirable counter-educational costs of employing such far-reaching racial devices, Congress . . . confront[ed] these considerations before opting for an activist race-conscious remedial role supervised by federal officials."[30]

Brennan's appeal to the deliberative basis of the Voting Rights Act marked a return to Warren's earlier understanding of legislative learning. As Warren had before him, Brennan took the act to be a product of broad-based deliberation, expressing a distinct understanding of what was in the interest of the people as a whole. The link between the act and common interests permitted Brennan to account for race-conscious remedies in terms unavailable to White. Brennan argued that racial districting was justified, not because it reflected the most salient cleavage among competing interest groups, but because Congress had learned that racial districting was necessary to help move the entire polity toward the goal of equal political opportunity. In this vein, Brennan could claim that the act ultimately *worked through*, rather than simply *reinforced and relied upon*, the racial divisions in any given jurisdiction, aiming at an egalitarian political community in which citizen voices were not racially constrained.

Of course, this kind of justification left open the question of how the politics engendered by the act actually worked to ensure equal opportunities. Warren's opinions provided Brennan with little guidance on

[27] Ibid. at 171.
[28] Ibid. at 175.
[29] Ibid. at 176, citations omitted.
[30] Ibid.

this question. Warren largely restricted his attention to the passage of the act and neglected to elaborate his implicit view of how deliberative politics ought be conducted in covered subdivisions (see chapter four). Brennan made an effort to move beyond Warren, suggesting how politics under the act could be said to deploy racial distinctions in the name of common interests. Brennan asserted that the fact of New York's coverage gave the politics of districting a public-interest orientation, for it indicated that the state's prior political practices had diluted the minority vote.[31] In this sense, the fact of coverage implied that nonminorities in New York had *already* benefited from discriminatory procedures and, thus, were not mere innocents now forced to pay the price of reform. The involvement of the attorney general in formulating the 1974 plan similarly shaped reapportionment politics. Brennan argued that the preclearance process itself transformed the attorney general into the "champion" of minority interests—a role that enabled him to detect and invalidate malign reapportionment plans that covered subdivisions might try to pass off under benign pretenses.[32] This meant that the attorney general's intervention in New York diminished the possibility that race-conscious districting might actually harm minorities.

Unfortunately, Brennan did not develop these few remarks concerning the public-interest possibilities of Voting Rights Act politics. Instead, he concluded his opinion by invoking the very same notion of indirect racial representation that he criticized in Justice White's majority opinion. Brennan argued that even though the Hasidim had been "relegat[ed]" to nonwhite districts, they remained "indirectly 'protected' by the remaining white assembly and senate districts within the county, carefully preserved in accordance with the white proportion of the total county population."[33] Brennan tried to qualify his ultimate reliance on racial representation, claiming that "[w]hile these considerations obviously do not satisfy [the Hasidim], I am persuaded that they reinforce the legitimacy of this remedy."[34] But the attempt to situate racial representation within his larger justificatory framework stirred up

[31] Ibid. at 177–78. In making this claim, Brennan was careful not to contradict White's point that preclearance was designed expressly to prevent *new* forms of voting discrimination. While Brennan agreed that the process of preclearance did not hinge on proof of past discrimination, he merely added that preclearance would not apply in the first place if some indica of racial discrimination were not present (ibid. at 177, n. 6).

[32] Ibid. at 175.

[33] Ibid. at 178.

[34] Ibid.

difficulties that a single qualification could not hope to resolve. Brennan had demonstrated the general legitimacy of racial districting by describing the common interests that the act served; now he claimed to "reinforce" this argument by appealing to the capacity of each race to protect its own particularistic interests. The problem was that Brennan did not explain how the pursuit of such narrow and divisive interests would secure, rather than sideline or subvert, the shared interests that informed his broader analysis. The account of the whole people that Brennan had supplied with one hand, he swiftly removed with the other. It is true that, unlike White, Brennan sketched an approach to fair minority representation that did not depend on interest group competition—an approach that took racial cleavages to be quite different from political ones and that required special justifications to support preferential discrimination. Yet, much as White had, Brennan simply failed to indicate how racial districting pointed beyond the patterns of racial division and exclusion that stimulated the act in the first place.

A second alternative to White, with its own distinctive promise and pitfalls, was articulated by Chief Justice Warren Burger. Writing in dissent, Burger quickly cast doubt on the legitimacy of racial districting. Burger read *Gomillion v. Lightfoot* to mean that the "drawing of political boundary lines with the sole, explicit objective of reaching a predetermined racial result cannot *ordinarily* be squared with the Constitution."[35] In the case at hand, Burger argued that the New York legislature had ignored the *Gomillion* standard, formulating the 1974 plan in "an atmosphere of hasty dickering" without any substantial evidence of past discrimination (which the plan might remedy) or of racial bloc voting (which was necessary if the plan was to ensure the election of any nonwhite representatives at all).[36] For Burger, in short, the New York legislature had not demonstrated that any race-conscious measure outside the ordinary run of policymaking was required.

Burger's contention that extraordinary evidence was necessary to sustain racial districting seemed to echo Brennan's call for special forms of justification. Beyond this point of correspondence, however, the two justices differed profoundly. Where Brennan grounded his opinion on the premise that racial and political divisions were distinct, Burger dis-

[35] Ibid. at 181, emphasis added. In spite of this initial reference to *Gomillion*, Burger did not rely on Frankfurter's notion of popular vigilance. As will become clear below, Burger's efforts had far more in common with Douglas's appeal to abstract individualism in *Wright v. Rockefeller*.

[36] *UJO* at 184–85, internal quotation marks omitted.

carded the very idea of racial cleavages and the group identities they purportedly engendered. Burger rejected the notion of competing racial groups in part because he felt its affirmance represented "a retreat from the ideal of the American 'melting pot'" — a retreat that would itself "sustain the existence of ghettos by promoting the notion that political clout is to be gained or maintained by marshaling particular racial, ethnic, or religious groups in enclaves."[37] More importantly, Burger denied claims about racial identities because he believed that such identities did not actually exist in a politically meaningful way. According to Burger, the "assumption that 'whites' and 'nonwhites' in the county form homogeneous entities for voting purposes is entirely without foundation. The 'whites' category consists of a veritable galaxy of national origins, ethnic backgrounds, and religious denominations."[38] To construct racial categories was to conceal the "galaxy" of diversity that comprised the electorate; more precisely, to construct racial categories was to endorse a mistaken view of race-based politics forcefully "repudiated in the election of minority members as mayors and legislators in numerous American cities and districts overwhelmingly white."[39]

Burger's insistence on the absence of cognizable racial identities had one clear advantage: it freed his argument of the counterfactual claims that had weakened Douglas's appeal to abstract individualism in *Wright v. Rockefeller*. There was no need to argue that "the people" should be treated *as if* they were simply an assemblage of equal individuals, for Burger claimed that "the people" *already* were such an assemblage.

Yet Burger's thorough-going individualism also had clear disadvantages. Although Burger sharply criticized the entire notion of racial identity and group rights, he did so in defense of a districting scheme that itself had already conferred political recognition on the group identity of the Hasidim. If the legislature could legitimately choose to recognize the Hasidic community, why was it improper for it to offer such recognition to a different group? Burger attempted to respond to this question, admitting that he had no "quarrel with the proposition that the New York Legislature may choose to take ethnic or community union into consideration in drawing district lines."[40] But Burger was quick to claim that legislative choice had its limits: "While petitioners

---

[37] Ibid. at 186–87. I have slightly reordered the quotes.
[38] Ibid. at 185.
[39] Ibid. at 187.
[40] Ibid. at 186.

certainly have no constitutional right to remain unified within a single political district, they do have, in my view, the constitutional right *not* to be carved up so as to create a voting bloc composed of some other ethnic or racial group."[41] The difficulty with this position was that Burger's promotion of a group-respecting status quo appeared to contravene the ideal of the "American melting pot" as well as the claim that racial and ethnic identities had no significant political valence. Without a more detailed account of why New York's previous districting plans did not violate his individualistic understanding of "the people," Burger's argument reduced to the bare assertion that while Hasidic Jews could be favorably placed in electoral districts, African Americans and Puerto Ricans could not.

LINKING INTENT TO INDIVIDUALS AND EFFECTS TO GROUPS

With their arguments in *UJO*, Brennan and Burger jointly rejected White's efforts to locate racial divisions within a context of interest group competition. Both Brennan and Burger claimed that issues of racial representation required a special degree of judicial attention lacking in the totality-of-circumstances approach. In their view, it was not enough for the Court simply to note patterns of minority defeat and to alter the mix of political winners accordingly.

Beyond this shared rejection of White, of course, Brennan and Burger differed sharply in their understanding of how the judiciary ought to proceed. Brennan argued that judicial attention should be tightly focused on the special dimensions of racial division and identity, enforcing processes of justification with the aim of reintegrating excluded minority groups into the political community. For his part, Burger insisted that judicial analysis should remain focused on real individuals rather than hypothesized groups; to reward minority groups with representation was to generate racial cleavages where none had previously existed.

Neither Brennan nor Burger offered arguments that were free of problems — indeed, each justice reached conclusions that subverted his own premises. In spite of such flaws in form, however, the opinions of Brennan and Burger expressed a basic conflict between "group"

[41] Ibid., emphasis added.

and "individualist" approaches that was increasingly to dominate the Court's decisions.[42]

The seeds planted in *UJO* began to bear fruit in *Mobile v. Bolden* (1980).[43] *Bolden* concerned at-large municipal elections in Mobile, Alabama. Since 1911 Mobile had been governed by a City Commission consisting of three members elected at-large and exercising all legislative, executive, and administrative powers. Although African Americans comprised more than one-third of Mobile's population, no black had ever been elected to the City Commission.[44] Several black residents filed suit against Mobile, alleging that the at-large election of city commissioners unfairly diluted their vote in violation of Section 2 of the Voting Rights Act, the Fourteenth Amendment, and the Fifteenth Amendment. The District Court upheld the charge of minority vote dilution and ordered Mobile to replace the City Commission with a City Council whose members were to be elected from single-member districts.[45] The Court of Appeals affirmed.[46]

Writing for a plurality, Justice Potter Stewart reversed the lower court rulings.[47] Stewart premised his reversal on the claim that the black appellees had simply failed to prove a denial of their voting rights. He argued first that Section 2 of the Voting Rights Act was no more that a restatement of the Fifteenth Amendment, leaving appellees with only a constitutional complaint.[48] Considering this constitutional complaint, Stewart argued further that both the Fourteenth and Fifteenth Amend-

---

[42] In this sense, the opinions of Brennan and Burger played the same role that Frankfurter's and Black's opinions in *Colegrove v. Green* had played earlier. As first cuts at the issue of minority representation, Frankfurter's and Black's arguments were clearly problematic. Yet, notwithstanding such difficulties, the claims of Frankfurter and Black were invoked and reworked by the Court in its subsequent encounters with minority representation (see chapter four).

[43] *Mobile v. Bolden*, 446 U.S. 55 (1980).

[44] Ibid. at 58, n. 1. In addition to being at-large, Mobile elections also featured numbered posts (i.e., designated seats for which candidates had to run rather than simply running for the City Commission as a whole), which prevented blacks from pooling their votes for one City Commissioner (ibid. at 60).

[45] The District Court's plan also provided for a mayor (ibid. at 58).

[46] Ibid. at 59.

[47] Stewart was joined by Justices Powell and Rehnquist as well as by Chief Justice Burger. Justice Blackmun concurred in the result and Justice Stevens concurred in judgment. Justices White, Brennan, and Marshall each dissented.

[48] Ibid. at 60–61.

ments required proof of discriminatory intent before any state action could be overturned.[49]

In this vein, Stewart claimed that providing proof of discriminatory intent was not the same as showing that legislators could foresee how at-large elections might foreclose the selection of minority commissioners. Instead, Stewart ruled that the notion of discriminatory intent "implies more than intent as volition or intent as awareness of consequences. . . . It implies that the decision maker . . . selected or reaffirmed a particular course of action at least in part 'because of,' not merely 'in spite of,' its adverse effects upon an identifiable group."[50] Stewart accepted the District Court's finding that the City Commission itself had engaged in discriminatory practices.[51] But such a finding hardly proved that the legislators who framed Mobile's electoral laws in 1911 acted with a clear discriminatory intent. Given that minorities could vote "without hindrance" and that Mobile's electoral laws were "readily explainable on grounds apart from race," Stewart concluded that the Court lacked a constitutional warrant for intervention.[52]

Stewart's reliance on intent was not unprecedented in the Court's minority-representation cases. Recall that Justice Black upheld a reapportionment plan in *Wright v. Rockefeller* on the grounds that the legislature had not acted with an openly discriminatory intent. Black's argument proved to be problematic, largely because he failed to provide any rationale for the kind of discriminatory intent he used. Contrary to Black, Stewart not only recognized that discriminatory intent might be conceptualized in different ways but also insisted that the Court seek out intent in its most stringent form. Even so, one could argue that Stewart followed in Black's footsteps by neglecting to offer an explicit justification for his claims. Stewart devoted the main body of his opinion merely to reiterating the assertion that "the law" required clear proof of strong discriminatory intent. Without giving reasons for *why* the law should require the most rigorous type of intent, his position appeared inexplicable.[53]

---

[49] Ibid. at 62–70. In Stewart's view the Fifteenth Amendment required a showing of discriminatory intent only where, as in this case, the statute in question was racially neutral on its face.

[50] Ibid. at 71, n. 17, ellipses original. Stewart was quoting from *Personnel Administrator of Mass. v. Feeney*, 442 U.S. 256, 279 (1979).

[51] *Bolden* at 71, 73–74.

[52] Ibid. at 73, 70, internal quotation marks omitted.

[53] Three separate justices made a similar observation (see Stevens, concurring in judg-

Yet, if a direct justification for Stewart's claims was missing, traces of an indirect justification could still be discerned. Consider the final section of Stewart's opinion, where he presented a critique of Justice Marshall's lengthy dissent. Marshall argued that fair minority representation ought to be appraised in terms of the *adverse effects* that electoral laws had on minority political opportunity.[54] Stewart dismissed Marshall's argument in part because it eschewed language of discriminatory intent. While Stewart agreed that the Fourteenth Amendment conferred "a substantive right to participate in elections on an equal basis," he thought it was a "basic fallacy" for Marshall to read this guarantee as anything more than a protection against intentional political exclusion.[55]

Stewart also criticized Marshall's argument for reasons that had little to do with the avoidance of discriminatory intent — and it was here that Stewart indirectly defended his own position, suggesting how alternatives to his approach were unworkable.[56] According to Stewart, Marshall's argument boiled down to the proposition that "every 'political group,' or at least every such group that is in the minority, has a federal constitutional right to elect candidates in proportions to its numbers."[57] Stewart found this proposition to be shot through with uncertainties, all stemming from the essential ambiguity of the term *political group*. Making his point with a series of questions, Stewart asked:

> Can any "group" call itself a "political group"? If not, who is to say which "groups" are "political groups"? Can a qualified voter belong to more than one "political group"? Can there be more than one "political group" among white voters (e.g., Irish-American, Italian-American, Po-

---

ment [ibid. at 84, 84, n. 3]; White, dissenting [ibid. at 94, 101]; and Marshall, dissenting [ibid. at 133–34]).

[54] Ibid. at 104.

[55] Ibid. at 77, 77, n. 24.

[56] At the beginning of his opinion, Stewart adumbrated a different indirect justification. He pointed out that "literally thousands of municipalities" used the at-large electoral system found in Mobile (ibid. at 60). The implication of this observation seemed to be that if the Mobile system were struck down, thousands of cities would find themselves without a government. While the specter of systemic disorder could be read as an indirect justification for Stewart's position, he never developed this argument at any length. Moreover, the potential for broad change in itself does not completely justify judicial restraint. One could argue that it is precisely in the context of a widespread denial of rights that strong judicial action is required (compare Justice White in *Whitcomb v. Chavis*, 403 U.S. 124, 157 [1971]).

[57] *Bolden* at 75.

lish-American, Jews, Catholics, Protestants)? Can there be more than one "political group" among nonwhite voters?[58]

Stewart viewed this litany of questions as "largely unanswerable."[59] The range of groups in the electorate was so vast and complex that the Court simply could not construct a coherent definition of *the* "political group." On the contrary, it was only when the government intentionally acted to isolate and exclude a particular cluster of individuals that the notion of a distinct "political group" took on meaning. Thus, for Stewart, as for Burger in *UJO*, judicial action was to be directed toward the concrete rights of diverse individuals rather than the so-called claims of hypothesized groups. The key difference between Stewart and Burger was that Stewart's emphasis on discriminatory intent kept judicial attention tightly focused on the manifold reality of individual political attachments. While Burger's approach reduced to a unargued preference for one group-conscious districting plan over another, Stewart could cast himself as a consistent advocate of individualism, acknowledging something beyond individual claims only where government action had purposely called a group into being.

Stewart's dependence on an individualistic conception of "the people" raised questions about the role of political identity in Marshall's dissent. Did Marshall rely on a different conception of "the people"? If so, did this different conception account for the conclusions that he reached?

At first glance, Marshall's opinion appeared to be free of claims about political identity. Marshall argued that the Court's vote dilution cases protected "a fundamental right to equal electoral participation."[60] While Stewart wished to link violations of this fundamental right to discriminatory intent, Marshall believed that "'[t]o have a right to something is to have a claim on it irrespective of why it is denied.'"[61] Laws establishing at-large elections, for instance, might be justified in "good government" terms, but the mere possibility of such a justification did nothing to diminish the "harsh effects" that at-large elections could produce.[62] Only by focusing on these "harsh effects" could the Court effectively protect the fundamental rights of electoral minorities,

[58] Ibid. at 78, n. 26.
[59] Ibid.
[60] Ibid. at 114.
[61] Ibid. at 121, n. 21.
[62] Ibid. at 106, n. 4.

sheltering them from the "political impotence" engendered by certain electoral systems.[63]

Yet, for all of Marshall's efforts to defend a fundamental political right against the threat of adverse circumstances, his argument ultimately relied on a specific understanding of "the people." Throughout his opinion Marshall maintained a distinction between his concern for adverse effects and a general call for proportional representation. He spoke of protecting electoral minorities from "political impotence," but he did so with the qualification that such impotence was not a problem that threatened all groups alike. Marshall wrote:

> Unconstitutional vote dilution occurs *only* when a discrete political minority whose voting strength is diminished by a districting scheme proves that historical and social factors render it largely incapable of effectively utilizing alternative avenues of influencing public policy.[64]

Marshall claimed that most political groups would have a difficult time proving they were "sufficiently discrete to suffer vote dilution."[65] If a given group was not truly insulated and insular, then dominant political factions could not readily ignore it. Marshall thought racial groups would easily be able to muster proof of their "discreteness." Racial considerations had historically been "far more powerful and pernicious than . . . considerations of other divisive aspects of the electorate."[66] This meant the experience of racial groups like African Americans had differed "in kind, not just in degree," leaving such groups especially prone to political exclusion when they failed to elect representatives of their choice.[67]

For Marshall, then, it was precisely because "historical and social factors" had so marked the identity of specific racial groups that the judiciary needed to shield them from adverse political effects, regardless of intent. The point was to help *particular* groups. Much as Brennan had in *UJO*, Marshall tailored his argument around the unique status of racial groups, defining the scope of judicial authority with an eye toward reintegrating excluded people of color. The difference between Marshall and Brennan was that Marshall made no attempt to embed his "group" notion of racial identity within the deliberative framework of

---

[63] Ibid. at 112.
[64] Ibid. at 111, n. 7, emphasis added. See also ibid. at 122.
[65] Ibid. at 120, n. 19.
[66] Ibid. at 138, n. 37.
[67] Ibid., internal quotation marks omitted.

the Voting Rights Act.[68] Instead of trying to work racial divisions through an elaborate deliberative process, Marshall attached his claim of distinct racial identities to a fundamental right, positing a single yardstick of equal electoral participation against which the political success of racial groups could be measured.

Marshall's approach had the advantage of simplicity: it avoided the identification and analysis of special justifications, which Brennan had emphasized. According to Marshall, the issue was not to address the distinctive difficulties raised by race-conscious remedies, but simply to protect a right that had been infringed. The problem was that Marshall purchased this simplicity at an unreasonable price. Marshall drew the fundamental right of equal electoral participation from the reapportionment decisions of the 1960s.[69] These reapportionment decisions clearly concerned issues of representation, but they did so with a notion of political identity antithetical to Marshall's "group" approach. The conception of "the people" that undergirded the Court's "one person, one vote" rule was remarkable for its neglect of *all* groups and their interests, taking "the people" to be merely an assemblage of politically equal individuals. Marshall's dependence on the individualistically conceived right of equal participation built an instability into the foundation of his argument. On the one hand, he wished to preserve the political voice of discrete racial groups; on the other, he invoked a standard that assumed that no such groups existed. Thus, Marshall affirmed contradictory assertions of individual and group identity, failing either to recognize the tension between these assertions or to identify a means of reconciliation.[70]

SEARCHING FOR MIDDLE GROUND

Taken as a whole, the preceding analysis suggests that while *Bolden* involved a superficial dispute over intent and effects, the central dis-

[68] Marshall avoided the Voting Rights Act altogether, accepting Stewart's claim that the Section 2 complaint presented in *Bolden* was indistinguishable from the Fifteenth Amendment complaint also presented (ibid. at 105, n. 2). Still, in his very brief *Bolden* dissent, Brennan supported Marshall's reasoning (ibid. at 94).

[69] Ibid. at 115–17.

[70] See chapter two for my account of the reapportionment revolution. Stewart questioned Marshall's use of the reapportionment decisions, but on the grounds that *Bolden* had nothing to do with the unequal district populations that drove the reapportionment revolution (ibid. at 77–78). Stewart simply missed the contradiction between notions of political identity, although some students of the Court have not (e.g., see M. Shapiro 1985).

agreement actually hinged on a deeper discord between conceptions of who "the people" were.[71] Stewart clearly emphasized discriminatory intent, but he justified his emphasis with an individualistic notion of political identity, arguing that in the absence of readily recognizable groups no other standard of judicial analysis was workable. For his part, Marshall used an understanding of distinct racial identities to create a context within which the appeal to adverse effects made sense. Marshall thus translated a right to equal electoral participation into special protection for racial groups, claiming that such groups had unique histories that left them predisposed to political exclusion.

To be sure, both Stewart's and Marshall's opinions had their difficulties. Yet, to the degree that they were organized around "individualist" and "group" notions of political identity, these opinions fleshed out a conceptual continuum first outlined by Brennan and Burger in *UJO*. This conceptual continuum provided a discrete space across which the meaning of fair minority representation could be debated, either by developing better versions of the individualist or group approach or by articulating a third approach between the two.

In *Bolden* itself, Justices White and Stevens each attempted the latter strategy, seeking an alternative position between Stewart and Marshall. The problem was that both White and Stevens cast their attempts in terms of intent and effect, without grasping the underlying questions of political identity.

White's evasion of conceptual issues was in keeping with his usual totality-of-circumstances approach. White argued that discriminatory intent and adverse effects fit together within a single analytical framework, for "an invidious discriminatory purpose could be inferred from the totality of facts."[72] White claimed that Stewart had separated intent from effect, rejecting "the inference of purposeful discrimination apparently because *each* of the factors relied upon by the courts below [was] alone insufficient to support the inference."[73] To compartmentalize the evidence was, in White's view, to frustrate the search for *patterned* political loss that undergirded the totality-of-circumstances analysis. Stewart sought the smoking gun of discriminatory intent and simply missed

[71] In calling the intent/effects dispute "superficial," I do not mean to suggest that *Bolden* was unimportant. My discussion in chapter one indicates that Stewart's intent standard had a strong impact on minority representation cases.

[72] *Bolden* at 95. In his brief concurrence, Blackmun endorsed White's reasoning (ibid. at 80–82).

[73] Ibid. at 103, emphasis added.

the significance of "the fact that racial bloc voting at the polls [made] it impossible to elect a black commissioner."[74]

Throughout his dissent, White struggled to explain the source of Stewart's mistaken views, calling Stewart's argument alternately "inexplicabl[e]," "cryptic," and "remarkable."[75] Stewart's opinion remained elusive for White because he overlooked the conceptual differences that distanced him from Stewart in the first place. Working from his notion of interest group competition, White sought to protect groups from extraordinary patterns of loss. Stewart, on the contrary, wished to protect politically protean individuals from the imposition of fixed group identities. Without identifying or exploring this contrast in conceptual baselines, White not only left his criticism of Stewart incomplete, but also left his own position inadequately justified. To the question of why judicial analysis should begin with *either* an "individualist" or a "group" notion of "the people," White (once again) had no answer.

Like White, Stevens exhibited a brand of conceptual neglect as he attempted to steer a middle course between Stewart and Marshall. Stevens argued that the judiciary should "focus on the objective effects of the political decision rather than the subjective motivation of the decisionmaker."[76] Stevens believed that since some kind of discriminatory intent played a role in most districting processes, intent could not distinguish one districting plan from another.[77] Setting aside Stewart's quest for intent, Stevens also denied Marshall's claim that the mere showing of an adverse impact on "historically and socially disadvantaged racial group[s]" could carry a case.[78] Stevens claimed that past vote dilution cases had sidestepped discussion of specific group histories or experiences; what mattered instead was how the legislature had manipulated the voting strength of *any* group to achieve a specific electoral result.[79]

---

[74] Ibid.

[75] Ibid. at 94, 95, 101.

[76] Ibid. at 90.

[77] Ibid. at 91–92. As Stevens wrote, "I do not believe otherwise legitimate political choices can be invalidated simply because an irrational or invidious purpose played some part in the decisionmaking process" (ibid. at 92).

[78] Ibid. at 85–86.

[79] Ibid. at 86–88. Stevens based his view on the fact that the *Gomillion v. Lightfoot* holding was explained in terms of the Fifteenth Amendment (by Frankfurter) as well as in terms of the Fourteenth Amendment (by Whittaker, writing in concurrence). For Stewart, the use of both amendments "indicat[ed]" that vote dilution was not about any particular group (ibid. at 86).

Between the indeterminacy of discriminatory intent and the color-blindness of adverse effects, Stevens identified a constitutional standard of vote dilution that he thought would allow "the political process to function effectively."[80] When weighing the claim of vote dilution, Stevens claimed the Court should consider (i) whether the electoral system arose as part of "a routine or a traditional political decision," (ii) whether the system "was unsupported by any neutral justification," and (iii) whether the system had "a significant adverse impact on a minority group."[81] Applying these criteria to the case at hand, Stevens concluded that there was "substantial neutral justification" for Mobile's electoral system and, thus, the system could be retained even though it diminished minority voting strength.[82]

With this three-pronged standard, Stevens hoped to replace the competing appeals to intent and effects. Yet Stevens struck his balance on undefended, substantially biased grounds. Privileging "traditional" or "routine" political decisions, Stevens skewed his standard toward the status quo, a move that automatically worked against minority groups already disadvantaged by existing political rules.[83] Perhaps more importantly, Stevens implicitly attached his understanding of "neutral justification" to an individualistic (or at least a nongroup) notion of "the people." He remained highly critical of any quick claims about distinct group identity: to warrant protection against gerrymandering, groups first had to demonstrate their commonality through concerted political action.[84] This group-skepticism created a specific context in which justifications were to be sought, allowing Stevens to treat as "neutral" an electoral system that was not only adopted when blacks had no political voice but also was maintained as blacks consistently failed to elect a candidate of their choice.[85]

Stevens was, of course, free to anchor his opinion in whatever conception of "the people" he wished. Yet the fundamental disagreements in *Bolden*, defined by competing individualistic and group conceptions

---

[80] Ibid. at 85.

[81] Ibid. at 90. I have slightly reordered Stevens' criteria.

[82] Ibid. at 92, n. 14. Stevens did not elaborate on the "substantial neutral justification," but he did note, as Stewart had, that thousands of other cities used Mobile's commission system (ibid. at 92).

[83] Marshall also made this point (ibid. at 138, n. 37).

[84] Ibid. at 89.

[85] As Marshall noted, blacks had been "totally disenfranchised" by the Alabama Constitution of 1901 (ibid. at 136, n. 34).

of "the people," demanded that Stevens do more than simply choose an understanding of political identity. The choice itself required justification. Unfortunately, Stevens, like White, neglected the deeper issues of political identity on which the debate over fair minority representation depended.

In the years immediately following *Bolden*, opinions cast in the spirit of White and Stevens decided several cases.[86] These opinions boldly experimented with different blends of discriminatory intent and adverse effects, all the while ignoring the underlying conflicts over political identity. The result was a crop of ambiguous arguments and bitter dissents that left the Court largely incapable of charting a coherent jurisprudential course. Indeed, even as a majority of justices proclaimed their fidelity to Stewart's *Bolden* opinion, the Court struck down a commission system virtually identical to the one upheld in *Bolden*.[87] The judicial debate over fair minority representation had come to a critical pass.

IMPACT OF THE 1982 AMENDMENTS

Bolden set the stage for the 1982 amendments to the Voting Rights Act (see chapter one). With debate centering on whether Stewart's opinion ought to be overturned, Congress explicitly rejected the intent standard and amended Section 2 to prohibit any test or procedure that "result[ed] in a denial or abridgment" of minority voting rights.

Congress elaborated its new prohibition against adverse results at some length. According to the amended Section 2, a violation of the right to vote existed wherever racial or language minorities had "less

---

[86] *City of Rome v. United States*, 446 U.S. 156 (1980), arguing that adverse effects alone can be dispositive because one could conclude that where effects are present, so too is the risk of discriminatory intent; *City of Port Arthur v. United States*, 459 U.S. 159 (1982), arguing that proof of intent in a previous case (involving the same locality) can be carried over to a subsequent case where only effects have been shown, all as part of a "reasonable hedge" against the persistence of intent; *Rogers v. Lodge*, 458 U.S. 613 (1982), arguing that intent can be inferred from the totality of facts.

[87] *Rogers*, 616–28. The tangled state of the debate here was further illustrated by Stevens's lengthy dissent in this case. Stevens criticized the majority for focusing exclusively on intent and thus failing to take into account a host of "additional factors" (e.g., presence of numbered posts) when investigating the charge of vote dilution (ibid. at 638–40). The problem was that the majority did in fact take into account such additional factors; indeed, the presence of intent was inferred directly from the presence of such factors (ibid. at 624–27). If Stevens's criticisms applied to anything, it was to the majority opinion in *Bolden*—the decision that the *Rogers* majority substantially overturned.

opportunity than other members of the electorate to participate in the political process and to elect representatives of their choice." While "the extent to which members of a protected class have been elected to office" was to be considered in determining political opportunity, Section 2 disavowed any "right to have members of a protected class elected in numbers equal to their proportion in the population."[88] The report of the Senate Judiciary Committee supplemented Section 2 with nine additional factors to be used in measuring minority voting strength.[89] The Senate report left the additional factors unranked. Indeed, at no point in either Section 2 or the Senate Report did Congress articulate the necessary and sufficient conditions for satisfying the new results standard. Congress simply urged judges to use their "overall judgment" in their assessment of minority representation.[90]

In a sense, then, one could argue that the 1982 amendments resolved the post-*Bolden* quandary in a single stroke. The Supreme Court would no longer debate the relationship between discriminatory intent and adverse effects because the act itself had been rewritten in favor of effects. What the Court had proposed, Congress now disposed.[91]

Nonetheless, there remained much that the 1982 amendments left unfinished. As the reference to the Court's "overall judgment" indicated, Congress had delegated large issues of application and interpretation to the judiciary. Moreover, Congress had said little to connect the 1982 amendments to some broader notion of who "the people" were. While the decision for some kind of effects-oriented test was clear, the linkage between this test and any fundamental conception of political identity or fair representation had yet to be drawn.

All of this suggested that the amended act, much like the original act, would not terminate conflicts over minority representation so much as supply a new context in which such conflicts could be explored and adjudicated. As it had been in 1965, the question after 1982 was how the Court was going to make sense of representational issues in a new statutory context.

---

[88] I draw this quotation and the one in the previous sentence from the reprint of the Voting Rights Act in Grofman and Davidson 1992, p. 319.

[89] See chapter one for an enumeration of these additional factors.

[90] U.S. Senate 1982a, p. 29.

[91] It is worth noting here that the 1982 amendments affected only the *statutory* definition of vote dilution (i.e., what counted as vote dilution under the terms of the Voting Rights Act). At the constitutional level (i.e., what counted as *unconstitutional* vote dilution) *Bolden*, as "upheld" in *Rogers v. Lodge*, remained authoritative.

The Court offered its first interpretation of the new Section 2 in *Thornburg v. Gingles* (1986).[92] *Gingles* concerned the 1982 redistricting plan for the North Carolina State Senate and House of Representatives. African American voters challenged one single-member district and six multimember districts in the North Carolina plan, claiming that the districts violated the amended Section 2 by effectively impairing their ability to elect candidates of their choice.[93] Relying on the nine factors outlined in the Senate Judiciary Report, the District Court found that all seven districts resulted in the dilution of minority voting strength.[94]

Writing for the Supreme Court, Justice Brennan upheld the lower court findings of vote dilution in four of the five contested multimember districts.[95] Brennan began by noting that the amended Section 2 aimed to replace *Bolden*'s search for discriminatory intent with an analysis of concrete results.[96] Although Congress identified a wide range of flexible factors for consideration under Section 2, Brennan argued that the "results test" had clear limits. Brennan emphasized that Congress had not presupposed the existence of any given factor or claim. The Senate report had assumed neither that particular electoral rules always generated dilutive effects nor that members of a minority group always voted as a bloc.[97] Given this legislative background, Brennan took the results test to be essentially fact-contingent, requiring all relevant factors be proved in each case.

Brennan argued that if one concentrated on the specific question of how minority vote dilution should be measured in multimember districts, the core requirements of the results test became even more distinct.[98] This was so, Brennan asserted, because the results test was not

---

[92] *Thornburg v. Gingles*, 478 U.S. 30 (1986). It is worth pointing out that Justice Marshall called attention to the importance of the amended Section 2 as early as 1983 (See *City of Lockhart v. United States*, 460 U.S. 125, 145–46 [1983]).

[93] *Gingles* at 34.

[94] Ibid. at 37–38.

[95] North Carolina appealed the District Court's ruling only with respect to five of the seven originally contested districts. The majority of Justice Brennan's opinion was joined by Justices Marshall, Blackmun, Stevens, and White. Justices Marshall, Stevens, and Blackmun rejected Brennan's ruling that one district did not dilute minority voting strength. White accepted Brennan's ruling on this point, but dismissed Brennan's view that the race of candidates was unimportant under Section 2. Justice O'Connor, joined by Chief Justice Burger and by Justices Powell and Rehnquist, concurred in judgment.

[96] *Gingles* at 43–44.

[97] Ibid. at 46.

[98] Focusing on the multimember context, Brennan avoided questions of whether minor-

only fact-contingent but also "functional" in its orientation, seeking solely to determine whether a particular electoral mechanism impaired minority voting strength.[99] The commitment to functionalism meant that *only* the interaction between voter behavior and electoral structure mattered; broader explanations of *why* a minority group had problems electing representatives merely deflected attention away from the central question of whether such problems could be said to exist at all.[100] Thus, the point was not to prove that whites outvoted minorities because of racial hostility (or any other reason) but to demonstrate that the electoral structure allowed whites to outvote minorities in the first place. Translating the functionalist imperative into the multimember context, Brennan identified three "necessary preconditions" for substantiating a minority vote dilution claim: (i) the minority group must be sufficiently large and geographically compact to constitute a majority in a single-member district; (ii) the minority group must be politically cohesive; and (iii) whites must vote as a bloc often enough that the minority's preferred candidate usually loses. Where these conditions did not obtain, a minority group simply could not attribute their political weakness to the structure of the multimember district itself.[101]

Brennan's functionalism clearly simplified voting rights litigation, reducing the process of proving multimember vote dilution to a matter of verifying a few factual circumstances.[102] Functionalism focused judicial analysis on the concrete operation of electoral politics, calling attention to the results of using a particular electoral rule or procedure in a given

---

ity groups could be unfairly fragmented across single-member districts or whether especially small or dispersed minority groups could make a vote dilution claim (ibid. at 46, n. 12). The Court has subsequently ruled (i) that Brennan's criteria should serve as a starting point for these additional questions and (ii) that Brennan's criteria will have to be modified in unspecified ways to make sense in such cases (see *Voinovich v. Quilter*, 507 U.S. 146 [1993] and *Growe v. Emison*, 113 S.Ct. 1075 [1993]).

[99] *Gingles* at 49, n. 15.

[100] Ibid. at 63, 66, 68, 73.

[101] Brennan reasoned that if the size and compactness criteria were not met, "as would be the case in a substantially integrated district," then "the multi-member form of the district [in and of itself] cannot be responsible for minority voters' inability to elect candidates." He also reasoned that "[i]f the minority group is not politically cohesive, it cannot be said that the selection of a multimember electoral structure thwarts distinctive minority group interests." Finally, Brennan claimed that where the pattern of minority loss did not prevail, the minority group could not distinguish its fate from merely bad political fortune (ibid. at 49–51).

[102] As I pointed out in chapter one, Brennan's streamlining of Section 2 litigation led to a near doubling of voting dilution cases in the wake of *Gingles*.

context. Thus, the functionalist approach placed a premium on the measurement of results, prompting Brennan to spend much of his opinion discussing the proper way of gauging political cohesion and racially polarized voting. In fact, the importance of measurement gave Brennan's arguments a technical tone and suggested that the thorniest questions of fair minority representation would be answered once an objective standard of polarized voting was properly identified.

But Brennan's opinion did not completely turn on technical questions. Apart from the issue of empirical measurement, functionalism relied on the framework within which results were given meaning — for the debate over how measurements ought to be devised itself hinged on the selection of baseline factors that were to be measured. Brennan treated the choice of baseline factors as a relatively unproblematic one and devoted little time to the whole issue. Indeed, he merely took the single-member district to be the touchstone of his functionalist analysis, asserting that the "single-member district is generally the appropriate standard against which to measure minority group potential to elect because it is the *smallest* political unit from which representatives are elected."[103]

This argument from "district size" had little to recommend it. Brennan gave no reason why district size provided the relevant criterion for sorting between competing standards of minority group potential. And even if one were to accept this criterion, it would be unclear why the Court was restricted to the smallest *existing* political unit rather than the smallest *possible* unit. Brennan did not entertain any such objections, but his argument did suggest that this line of criticism might be moot — for where Brennan felt that well-represented minorities might still suffer unequal political opportunities, he was quick to jettison the single-member district standard.

Brennan's readiness to shift baselines surfaced at the end of his opinion. In one of the contested multimember districts, black voters had enjoyed sustained electoral success, consistently achieving proportional representation in the past six elections.[104] Although Brennan rejected the District Court's finding of vote dilution in this district, he did not do so on the functionalist grounds that blacks had repeatedly elected their preferred candidates and, therefore, could not blame the multimember

---

[103] Ibid. at 50, n. 17, emphasis added. Brennan's reliance on such a standard was most obvious in the way he restricted judicial analysis to only those minority groups sufficiently large and compact to control their own single-member district.

[104] *Gingles* at 77.

district per se for any political disadvantages. Instead, Brennan based his reversal of the lower court on the lack of any broader explanation for why the record of political success did not accurately reflect the minority's electoral ability.[105] For all his arguments against forsaking functionalism by furnishing some larger account of minority political opportunity, Brennan remained willing to call for a searching examination of the reasons behind electoral victory.

What was the significance of Brennan's failure to follow his own functionalist line? Brennan clearly cut through the tangled web of discriminatory intent and adverse effects that had characterized *Bolden* and its progeny. But in doing so, Brennan never reached the conflict between "individualist" and "group" conceptions of political identity that undergirded these cases. Instead, he mapped out a new "results test" merely by stipulating the smallest electoral district as the appropriate standard of fair minority representation. Brennan's own ambivalence toward this standard indicated that the emphasis on district size had missed the real target of debate.[106] Without some broader notion who "the people" were to guide his analysis, Brennan dealt with the limits of his poorly justified representational standard simply by abandoning it.

Yet, if Brennan's austere functionalism did not crack the nut of political identity, it did explicitly call judicial attention to the importance of representational baselines for the first time.[107] This important point was grasped by Justice O'Connor. Concurring in judgment, Justice O'Connor identified the selection of an appropriate baseline as the central task of representational adjudication. She wrote:

> In order to evaluate a claim that a particular multimember district or single-member district has diluted the minority group's voting strength to

---

[105] Ibid. at 77, 77, n. 38.

[106] In this sense, Brennan's failure was analogous to the failure of the centrist arguments explored in chapter three. The centrists failed to achieve the consensus they sought because they missed the conceptual depth of the politics of minority representation, claiming that "simple facts" would resolve a debate that actually turned on competing notions of political identity.

[107] Of course, I have argued throughout this book that various judicial claims *should* call one's attention to deeper, conceptual issues. But this was the first time a justice had directly suggested such a position. (More accurately, Brennan emphasized representational baselines for the first time in the *minority* voting cases I have considered. As I pointed out in chapter two, Justice Frankfurter *generally* recognized the importance of such baselines in *Baker v. Carr*, 369 U.S. 186 [1962].)

a degree that violates Section 2 . . . [it is] necessary to construct a measure of "undiluted" voting strength. . . . Put simply, in order to decide whether an electoral system has made it harder for minority voters to elect the candidates they prefer, a court must have an idea in mind of how hard it "should" be for minority voters to elect their preferred candidates under an acceptable system.[108]

O'Connor argued that Brennan's single-member district standard of representation effectively maximized minority strength, a move that O'Connor thought ran afoul of the Section 2 proviso against proportional representation.[109] More generally, O'Connor claimed that Brennan had attempted to articulate a single representational baseline when it was neither "necessary [n]or appropriate to decide in this case whether Section 2 require[d] a uniform measure of undiluted minority voting strength in every case."[110] Brennan had understood the importance of having a representational baseline; the problem was he had failed to choose the right one.

O'Connor herself did not indicate what the proper representational baseline should be in *Gingles* or in future decisions.[111] Nor did she raise any questions of political identity. She ventured only that *whatever* representational baseline might be determined, the Court ought to gauge departures from that baseline by broadly examining minority political opportunities, basing its judgments of vote dilution on more than just levels of minority electoral success.[112] The imperative for broad-based analyses simply followed, O'Connor believed, from the tradition of totality-of-circumstances reasoning begun by Justice White and reaffirmed by the 1982 amendments.[113]

Without defending a representational baseline of its own, O'Connor's opinion was valuable primarily for its critical insight.[114] O'Connor saw

---

[108] *Gingles* at 88.

[109] Ibid. at 97. In Brennan's defense, it should be noted that single-member districts generally fail to yield substantial proportional representation.

[110] Ibid. at 94. O'Connor overstated her distance from Brennan with this point, for Brennan's functionalism paid attention *only* to cases involving multimember districts. The possibility of broadly examining minority political opportunities in different contexts remained real (see chapter one and below).

[111] *Gingles* at 105.

[112] Ibid.

[113] Ibid. at 93ff.

[114] One might argue that O'Connor's argument implicitly made a more positive contribution. In invoking the totality-of-circumstances approach, O'Connor seemed to suggest

that Brennan's functionalism was made possible by selecting a measure of what counted as fair minority representation. By highlighting this fact, O'Connor fastened judicial attention on the question of how representational baselines ought to be identified and defended. To be sure, O'Connor did not provide any kind of detailed answer to the important question she had identified. But her efforts did help ensure that the decisions following *Gingles* would not be simple elaborations of functionalism so much as investigations of the contestable grounds on which functionalism was anchored.

THE BATTLE OVER BASELINES

With *Gingles*, the stakes of voting rights adjudication became more clear and, in *Gingles*'s wake, open disputes over representational baselines became an increasingly prominent feature of the Court's decisions.

In 1991, the Court ruled that the amended Section 2 applied to judicial elections (*Chisom v. Roemer*).[115] Much of the Court's opinion was devoted to the narrowly interpretive question of how the Voting Rights Act could be applied to judges when Section 2 spoke only of opportunities to elect "representatives."[116] Also important, however, was the broader issue of what representational baseline the courts should use when examining judicial elections. The *Chisom* dissenters claimed that "one person, one vote" was the Court's *only* working standard of representation; if judicial elections were exempt from such a rule (as the Court had long held), they were necessarily exempt from *any* meaningful claim of vote dilution.[117] The *Chisom* majority countered the dissenters by arguing that the 1982 amendments as a whole aimed at pro-

---

that the appropriate representational baseline would ultimately be drawn from Justice White's understanding of interest group competition. But there were no substantial indications that O'Connor was in fact making such an implicit claim.

[115] *Chisom v. Roemer*, 111 S.Ct. 2354 (1991). Justice Stevens delivered the Court opinion.

[116] Ibid. at 2360–61. The Court resolved this question by reading "representatives" to mean "winners of popular elections" (Ibid. at 2366).

[117] Justice Scalia wrote, "it is the principle of 'one person, one vote' that gives meaning to the concept of 'dilution.' . . . I frankly find it very difficult to conceive how it is to be determined whether 'dilution' has occurred, once one has eliminated both the requirement of actual intent to disfavor minorities [as the 1982 amendments did], *and* the principle [of 'one person, one vote']" (ibid. at 2374–75, emphasis original).

viding *greater* voting-rights protection than had previously existed.[118] While the majority refused to set forth a new representational standard, it avowed that the generation of such standards was the difficult task that Congress had left to the courts.[119]

The fight over representational baselines flared up again in *Presley v. Etowah County Commission* (1992).[120] Writing for the majority, Justice Kennedy held that Section 5 covered only those rule changes that bore a "direct relation to voting or the election process."[121] More specifically, Kennedy ruled that alterations in the power of elected officials — alterations that Etowah County Commission had used to strip responsibilities from a newly elected minority member[122] — fell outside the purview of federal preclearance. Kennedy limited Section 5 coverage on the theory that there was no representational standard against which shifts in political authority could be measured. Local and state governments carried out "limitless minor changes in the allocation of power," but they did so for the sake of "efficient governance."[123] To insist on representational fairness where the criteria of efficiency held sway was to expand Section 5 beyond reasonable bounds, forcing preclearance of all the adjustments necessary for routine government function.

Writing in dissent, Justice Stevens rejected Kennedy's appeal to efficiency.[124] Stevens pointed out that the Justice Department had already subjected a significant number of authority transfers to preclearance.[125] Even if one were to argue that *Presley* called for a novel extension of preclearance, the fact remained that the history of Section 5 was a "continuous process of development in response to changing conditions in

[118] Ibid. at 2368.

[119] Ibid. The majority also rejected the assertion that vote dilution was necessarily based on the one-person–one-vote rule (ibid. at 2368, n. 32).

[120] *Presley v. Etowah County Commission*, 502 U.S. 491 (1992).

[121] Ibid. at 503. Kennedy was joined by Chief Justice Rehnquist as well as by Justices O'Connor, Scalia, Souter, and Thomas.

[122] Each member of the commission originally exercised control over road repairs for his district. Although the commission voted collectively on the division of funds, each member set spending priorities for his own district. In 1986, commission elections were restructured as a consequence of a successful minority vote dilution suit. Two new commissioners were subsequently elected, one white and one black. In the wake of these elections, the holdover members of the commission reconfigured commissioner responsibilities, removing all budgeting authority from individual members and placing it in the hands of the commission as a whole (ibid. at 492–500).

[123] Ibid. at 506.

[124] Stevens was joined by Justices White and Blackmun.

[125] *Presley* at 512.

the covered jurisdictions."[126] In either case, whether authority transfers fell under Section 5 routinely or for the first time, Stevens argued that such changes should be precleared because they could easily dilute minority voting strength by transforming elected officials into "mere figurehead[s]."[127] The appropriate baseline here was not one of efficiency, but rather one of equal political opportunity. While the precise definition of such opportunity might be elusive, Stevens reasoned that "at the very least" reallocations of decision-making authority that occurred (i) after the victory of a minority candidate, and (ii) after the successful conclusion of a lawsuit designed to improve minority representation deserved to be precleared.[128]

An emphasis on the importance of representational baselines, coupled with a hesitancy to suggest what the baseline might be and a reluctance to explore questions of political identity, marked both *Chisom* and *Presley* as the heirs of *Gingles*.[129] All of these decisions debated the selection of representational standards without quite referencing the competing notions of "the people" which were ultimately at stake. Still, whatever the limits and lacunae of *Gingles*, *Chisom*, and *Presley*, the long-standing debate over "individualist" and "group" conceptions of political identity had not simply passed away. The continued vitality of this debate was demonstrated in *Shaw v. Reno* (1993), where the struggle over representational baselines and its links to conflicting notions of "the people" were placed on clear display.[130]

Shaw concerned the design of congressional districts in North Carolina. Following the 1990 census, North Carolina had received an additional congressional seat. The North Carolina General Assembly drew

---

[126] Ibid. at 514. In this vein, Stevens argued that it made little sense to limit Section 5 to its past applications, because the whole point of preclearance was to root out *new* forms of discrimination (ibid. at 518).

[127] Ibid. at 520.

[128] Ibid. at 523. It is worth noting here that the decision to subject a rule change to preclearance turns on the question of whether such a change has the *potential* for discrimination; whether the change in fact receives preclearance turns on the separate question of whether the change actually has a discriminatory purpose or effect (Ibid. at 521, n. 22).

[129] Of course, Scalia's dissent in *Chisom* did rely on the one-person–one-vote rule — a rule that I have argued rests on an individualistic understanding of "the people" (See chapter two). But Scalia made no positive attempt to apply this rule or to unpack its meaning. His use of one person, one vote was largely negative: the important fact for him was that judicial elections had *not* been subject to this rule (whatever the rule might mean itself).

[130] *Shaw v. Reno*, 509 U.S. 630 (1993).

up a new districting plan to accommodate the additional seat and submitted this plan to the attorney general for preclearance.[131] The attorney general objected to the North Carolina plan, arguing that even though the plan featured one majority-minority district, a second such district could be created "to give effect to black and Native American voting strength" in the southeastern region of the state.[132] The general assembly responded with a new plan that featured a second majority-minority district — but it was a district located in the north-central part of the state, apart from the more concentrated minority population of the southeastern region.[133]

The north-central district, District 12, followed the Interstate 85 for nearly 160 miles linking together disparate minority neighborhoods (the district population was 54.7 percent African American).[134] For much of its length, the district was no wider than the I-85 corridor. At points, District 12 was even narrower than the highway itself, making northbound and southbound drivers constituents of different Congress members. District 12 was also distinguished by Melvin Watt, the man elected by district voters in 1992 and the first black member of Congress from North Carolina since Reconstruction. Five white voters ultimately filed suit against District 12, alleging that it was a racial gerrymander, which violated the Equal Protection Clause of the Fourteenth Amendment.

The facts of *Shaw* bore an obvious resemblance to those found in *UJO v. Carey* nearly twenty years earlier. In both cases, white voters complained that legislative districts drawn to enhance minority representation were unconstitutional racial gerrymanders. In spite of this similarity, however, Justice O'Connor insisted in her majority opinion that *UJO*'s framework simply did not apply to the "analytically distinct claim" that *Shaw* presented.[135] Justice White's opinion in *UJO* consid-

---

[131] Forty of North Carolina's one hundred counties were covered by Section 5. Since the new districting plan affected the covered counties, the state sought preclearance (ibid. at 634).

[132] Ibid. at 635.

[133] Ibid. The placement of District 12 had much to do with the fact that Democrats controlled the General Assembly. Indeed, the first suit against District 12 was filed by the Republican party, claiming that the district was an unconstitutional *political* gerrymander designed to profit Democrats. This claim was dismissed (Ibid. at 636). For a general discussion of the role played by partisanship in voting rights enforcement, see chapter three and Grofman 1993. For a discussion of bipartisanship, see chapter six.

[134] Ibid. at 671, n. 7.

[135] Ibid. at 652. O'Connor was joined by Chief Justice Rehnquist as well as by Justices Scalia, Thomas, and Kennedy.

ered whether white voters (as a group) suffered an egregious degree of political defeat due to the creation of majority-minority districts. On the other hand, according to O'Connor, *Shaw* considered whether a reapportionment plan could be so irregular and irrational that it could not "be understood as anything other than an effort to separate voters into different districts on the basis of race, and that the separation lacks sufficient justification."[136]

O'Connor did not rule that District 12 actually violated the novel claim made in *Shaw*; but she did rule that such a claim could be legitimately made. She wrote:

> [W]e believe that reapportionment is one area in which appearances do matter. A reapportionment plan that includes in one district individuals who belong to the same race, but who are otherwise widely separated by geographical and political boundaries, and who may have little in common with one another but the color of their skin bears an uncomfortable resemblance to political apartheid.[137]

O'Connor was careful to argue that this claim did not hold the design of legislative districts to some strict criteria of shape. The constraints traditionally applied to district shape (e.g., compactness, contiguity, and respect for political subdivisions) *were not* constitutionally required.[138] The goal was to avoid "political apartheid"—a goal that might well be advanced (although not necessarily secured) by paying attention to compactness, contiguity, and other traditional districting criteria.

If the "political apartheid" standard did not simply require districts of a specific shape, what did it require? Put differently, what kind of representation was to be achieved when a reapportionment plan successfully eschewed political apartheid? O'Connor answered this question by listing two related "harms" engendered by political apartheid— harms that could not be part of any fair representational scheme. First, she claimed that political apartheid reinforced impermissible stereotypes, strengthening the perception that all members of the segregated racial group "think alike, share the same political interests, and will prefer the same candidates at the polls."[139] Second, O'Connor contended that racially segregated districts sent a "pernicious" message to elected officials, encouraging them "to believe that their primary obliga-

[136] Ibid. at 649.
[137] Ibid. at 647.
[138] Ibid.
[139] Ibid.

tion is to represent only the members of [the segregated minority] rather than their constituency as a whole."[140]

Thus, O'Connor's notion of political apartheid supplied a distinct representational standard, adumbrating a view of how citizens ought to be given political voice by identifying a set of harms to which they could not be subjected.[141] Even with the articulation of a representational standard, however, O'Connor's opinion still remained incomplete. This was so because O'Connor had not justified the harms of political apartheid so much as stipulated them. She insisted that the government could inflict damage on the citizenry by designing the political community in a particular way. Yet O'Connor's mere insistence begged an important question: who were "the people" such that they could be harmed as O'Connor claimed?

The harms O'Connor enumerated made sense if one adopted an individualistic understanding of political identity, similar to the understandings outlined by Burger in *UJO* and Stewart in *Bolden*. O'Connor's assertion that District 12 could reinforce impermissible stereotypes (stereotypes that in turn distorted the responsiveness of elected officials) was essentially a version of the more general claim that the government could impose restrictive "group" identities upon the fluid assemblage of equal individuals comprising the electorate. Indeed, O'Connor's commitment to individualism was clear from the beginning of her opinion, where she refused to acknowledge the race of the five voters contesting District 12. According to O'Connor, the appellants did not claim that North Carolina had diluted "white" voting strength, for the appellants "did not even claim to be white."[142] The appellants objected to District 12 precisely because they believed it gave racial identities political meaning, erasing the "constitutional right to participate in a 'colorblind' electoral process."[143] In this vein, O'Connor maintained that any racially sensitive districting merited strict scrutiny, regardless of which racial group was supposedly helped by such districting.[144] There were no

---

[140] Ibid. at 648.

[141] Indeed, O'Connor claimed that such harms "threaten[ed] to undermine our system of representative democracy" (ibid. at 650).

[142] Ibid. at 641.

[143] Ibid. at 642. It is worth noting that the debate over a "colorblind" Constitution is not restricted to the Court's minority-voting-rights decisions. At least since *Regents of the University of California v. Bakke*, 438 U.S. 265 (1978), the issue of colorblindness has been central to the Court's affirmative-action decisions.

[144] *Shaw* at 651–52. Here O'Connor cited Brennan's remarks in *UJO* that preferential

special racial identities to which the political system should respond; instead, the aim was to avoid the generation of such identities in the first place, invalidating districting plans that would "balkanize us into competing racial factions."[145]

O'Connor's reliance on an individualistic conception of "the people" meant that her ruling was, in an important sense, hardly new. What *was* new was that O'Connor elaborated an individualistically grounded standard of representation in a context where the entire debate over representational standards had now become explicit. This difference was reflected in the three separate opinions filed by the dissenting justices — opinions that openly rejected O'Connor's political apartheid standard and the notion of political identity on which it rested.[146]

Justice White penned the longest dissent, providing a restatement of his totality-of-circumstances approach. For White, the issue in *Shaw* was not one of irregular or irrational districts but one of the political exclusion suffered by *specific groups*.[147] Where the charge of unconstitutional vote dilution was leveled, the Court "insisted that members of the political or racial group demonstrate that the challenged action have the intent and the effect of unduly diminishing their influence on the political process."[148] White pointed out that North Carolina had "made no mystery of its intent," which was to respond to the attorney general's objections made pursuant to the Voting Rights Act.[149] Even if this constituted a discriminatory intent (a claim that White very much doubted), the fact remained that the white appellants had not furnished proof of discriminatory effects. As a group, whites still comprised a majority in a

---

discrimination might perpetuate disadvantageous treatment of the supposed beneficiaries (ibid. at 643). Tellingly, O'Connor failed to cite Brennan's extensive arguments about how both the deliberative background of the Voting Rights Act and the special historical experience of racial minorities effectively countered the risks of preferential discrimination.

[145] *Shaw* at 657. Thus, O'Connor, like Burger and Stewart before her, rejected the counterfactual argument (i.e., racial identities do exist but districting should be conducted *as if* they did not) made by Douglas in *Wright v. Rockefeller*. O'Connor did cite Douglas approvingly, but her citation omitted his recognition that racial cleavages were a fact of American political life (*Shaw* at 648–49).

[146] Justices White, Blackmun, Stevens, and Souter all dissented. Blackmun filed only a brief opinion stating his agreement with White.

[147] Thus, White maintained that *UJO* could not be sidestepped as O'Connor wished (ibid. at 664–68).

[148] Ibid. at 660.

[149] Ibid. at 666.

disproportionate number of North Carolina's congressional districts.[150] To deem this situation a violation of white voters' constitutional rights was to embrace a "fiction."[151] White concluded that while white voters "might be dissatisfied at the prospect of casting a vote for a losing candidate—a lot shared by many, including a disproportionate number of minority voters—surely they cannot complain of discriminatory treatment."[152]

In his own dissent, Justice Stevens explicitly seconded White's appeal to a "group" conception of political identity. Stevens noted that both the irregular shape of District 12 and North Carolina's intent to enhance minority representation were "unarguable facts."[153] Given these facts, the question was not whether North Carolina's districting plan imposed a specific identity upon the mass of equal individuals, for the politics of representation was not really about such individuals. According to Stevens, "[p]oliticians have always relied on assumptions that people in *particular groups* are likely to vote in a particular way."[154] What O'Connor took to be the "impermissible racial stereotypes" reinforced by District 12 were nothing more than the facts of political life.[155] Any realistic representational standard accounted for the centrality of groups in the political process. For Stevens, this meant that the Court properly worked to prevent "a group with power over the electoral process [from defining] electoral boundaries solely to enhance its own political strength at the expense of any weaker group."[156] The contrary capacity to facilitate the political strength of minorities was one that the Court ought to foster.

Finally, in his dissent, Justice Souter joined White and Stevens in clearly endorsing a group rendering of "the people." Souter argued that our very "ability to talk about concepts like 'minority voting strength' and 'dilution of minority votes'" implicitly suggested that members of

---

[150] Whites constituted roughly 76 percent of the voting age population in North Carolina yet held a majority in 83 percent (ten of twelve) of the congressional districts (ibid. at 666).

[151] Ibid. at 659. Indeed, White argued that the aim of North Carolina's plan was not to minimize the strength of a particular group but to enhance it (ibid. at 674).

[152] Ibid. at 666–67.

[153] Ibid. at 676.

[154] Ibid. at 678, emphasis added.

[155] Stevens claimed that the *Gingles* requirement of political cohesion meant that the Court actually demanded that O'Connor's stereotypes must be proven to be true (ibid. at 678–79, n. 3).

[156] Ibid. at 678.

racial groups have a "commonality of interest."[157] Souter argued further that the reality of coherent racial group identities (and the importance of protecting these identities) must be understood in the special context of districting. Unlike other areas in which preferential discrimination was used, "the mere placement of an individual in one district instead of another denie[d] *no one* of a right or a benefit provided to others."[158] This was so because the efficacy of an individual's vote never depended on an "individual's political power viewed in isolation, but on the political power of a group."[159] As a result, the recognition of a racial group in districting was unconstitutional only where it "devalue[d] the effectiveness of a voter compared to what, as a group member, he would otherwise be able to enjoy."[160] Without proof of such a "cognizable harm," districting plans should be allowed to stand.[161]

Taken together, the opinions of White, Stevens, and Souter were free neither of internal difficulties (e.g., White had not addressed any of the problems with the totality-of-circumstances approach) nor of external differences (e.g., White and Stevens stressed the similarities between racial and other group affiliations, while Souter emphasized the special nature of districting). Nonetheless, these dissents did exhibit a common feature that was absent from previous voting-rights cases. Each justice openly discussed the question of representational baselines and explicitly anchored his position in a specific notion of how "the people" should be understood. In making such arguments, the dissenting justices helped lay bare the polarization between conceptions of political identity that had come to underlie the judicial debate over fair minority representation.

Shaw provided slim hope that any sort of mediated solution to this conceptual conflict was possible. The opposing opinions appeared to talk past one another, trading charges of impermissible stereotyping with assertions of protected group voice. The disjuncture between positions

---

[157] Ibid. at 680. I have reordered the quotes.

[158] Ibid. at 681–82, emphasis added. Thus, Souter thought that electoral districting required a different kind of equal protection analysis than other governmental decisions (ibid. at 684–85).

[159] Ibid. at 682.

[160] Ibid. at 684.

[161] Ibid. In this vein, Souter rejected O'Connor's claim that District 12 somehow stigmatized voters (ibid. at 686, n. 9). Interestingly, Souter read O'Connor to claim that *whites* had been stigmatized, even though she plainly argued that minority voters within District 12 were the ones threatened by the stain of stigma.

surfaced clearly in O'Connor's treatment of the dissenting arguments. Responding to Souter's discussion of vote dilution, O'Connor merely reiterated the harms of stigma and skewed representation allegedly engendered by racially segregative districting. The difficulty was that Souter had failed to "explain why *these harms* are not cognizable under the Fourteenth Amendment."[162] According to O'Connor, then, Souter had simply missed the conceptual drift of the majority opinion. Given the terms in which *Shaw* had been framed, it seemed little more could be said.

Of course, the fact that clear lines of conceptual division had been drawn did not mean that every question of application had been answered. Unlike Justice Brennan in his *Thornburg v. Gingles* opinion, O'Connor spent very little time explaining how the analytically distinct claim in *Shaw* might play itself out in subsequent litigation. Anchored in an individualistic understanding of "the people," would *Shaw* ultimately invalidate all racial redistricting or only certain extreme instances? If *Shaw* eliminated only extreme racial gerrymanders, how could such gerrymanders be identified in a principled manner?[163]

The Court considered the reach of *Shaw* in *Miller v. Johnson* (1995).[164] *Miller* concerned a 1992 congressional district created under the preclearance provisions of the Voting Rights Act. Striving to meet the requirements of the Justice Department, the Georgia legislature had drawn its third majority-minority district 260 miles in length, grouping together black neighborhoods of metropolitan Atlanta with the poor black populace of the Georgia coast. Five white voters living in this district filed suit, claiming that the district was a racial gerrymander, which violated the Equal Protection Clause of the Fourteenth Amendment. Writing for the five-member majority, Justice Kennedy restated the potential harms of race-based districting enumerated in *Shaw*. He noted that racial redistricting not only reinforced "the demeaning and offensive assumption" that all members of a same race "think alike" but also threatened to "balkanize us into competing racial factions" by encouraging elected officials to represent only the interests of racially segregated minorities.[165] With such harms in mind, Kennedy ruled for

[162] Ibid. at 650, emphasis added.

[163] A number of scholars have concentrated on the question of exactly how *Shaw* might be applied to future cases. See for example, Pildes and Niemi 1993 and Karlan 1994.

[164] *Miller v. Johnson*, 115 S.Ct. 2475 (1995). On the same day, the Court also decided the minority-voting-rights case *United States v. Hays*, 115 S.Ct. 2431 (1995).

[165] *Miller* at 2486. Justice Kennedy was joined by Chief Justice Rehnquist and Justices O'Connor, Scalia, and Thomas.

the white voters, arguing that the Equal Protection Clause was compromised wherever "race for its own sake, and not other districting principles, was the legislature's dominant and controlling rationale in drawing its district lines."[166]

As means of clarifying *Shaw*'s reach, the *Miller* decision enjoyed limited success.[167] Where *Shaw* took district shape to be the prime indicator of "political apartheid," *Miller* took the legislative reliance on race as a "predominant factor" to be the touchstone of political apartheid and its associated harms. District shape was thus simply one of many possible indicators of the role played by race in the districting process.[168] If the relevant indicators showed that race was indeed used as a predominant factor, the districting plan would be presumed unconstitutional — meaning that the plan could be upheld only if it could be demonstrated that it was narrowly tailored to satisfy a compelling interest.[169] While it was clear that most plans would fail to meet such a high standard once the predominance of race was proved, it was far less clear how such predominance should be proved in the first place. Given that legislators were typically *aware* of race during the process of redistricting, how could courts consistently discern the instances when race had *motivated* redistricting decisions?

In his opinion, Kennedy claimed that the distinction between "awareness" and "motivation" would be difficult to make in the context of redistricting, but his claim provided insufficient guidance for some members of the majority.[170] Writing a brief concurrence, Justice O'Connor insisted that the *Miller* standard was a "demanding" one that would subject only "extreme" instances of racial gerrymandering to judicial review.[171] O'Connor's insistence on the sharp limits of *Miller* effectively reasserted the same question of application that had emerged in the wake of *Shaw*: Just how far would the judicial crusade against "political apartheid" be pushed?

Yet, if the question of application was left open in *Miller*, the question of political identity was not. The debate among members of the Court in *Miller* was built around the same polarized notions of "individualistic" and "group" political identity that had informed judicial

[166] Ibid.
[167] For an extended discussion of this point, see Issacharoff 1996.
[168] *Miller* at 2487.
[169] Ibid. at 2490–94.
[170] Ibid. at 2488.
[171] Ibid. at 2497.

135

reasoning since *UJO v. Carey*. Just as O'Connor had in *Shaw*, Kennedy used his *Miller* opinion to render the harms of political apartheid against the backdrop of an individualistic people. Kennedy argued that race-based districting allowed the government to impose a restrictive "group" identity on the electorate. The imposition of this group identity was not impermissible because voters always lacked shared interests; indeed, Kennedy readily acknowledged that the recognition of shared "communities of interest" was a legitimate redistricting principle.[172] The point was that Kennedy conceived of shared interests and race in ways that *precluded* racial membership from forming the basis of a meaningful political identity.

Detailing the evidentiary requirements for contesting race-based districting, Kennedy drew an opposition between "communities defined by actual shared interests" and "racial considerations": plaintiffs must show that the former had been "subordinated" to the latter.[173] Such an opposition was possible because Kennedy viewed legislative reliance on "racial considerations" as a matter of insisting on a rigidly fixed identity (an invidious assertion that voters of the same race literally "think alike"), while he saw legislative reliance on "community interests" largely as a matter of recognizing loose ties among neighbors.[174] While the stipulation of racial interest entailed a stereotyped assertion of homogeneity, the recognition of community interests did not entail the claim that neighbors were of a single mind on every issue. Among residents of the same town, there was clearly some diversity of interests; nonetheless, one could reasonably believe that these interests would overlap when it came to broader issues of community good. Where the legislature acknowledged such a loose confluence of interests, no insult was leveled against the fluid assemblage of individuals residing in the district. By the same reasoning, where members of a single racial group lived together—where they could be assumed to have diverse, yet overlapping interests—they too could be said to enjoy a "community of interest." As Kennedy wrote, a "state is free to recognize communities that have a particular racial makeup, *provided* its action is directed toward some common thread of relevant interests. [W]hen members of a racial group live together in one community, a reapportionment plan that concentrates members of the group in one district and excludes

[172] Ibid. at 2488.
[173] Ibid.
[174] Ibid. at 2490.

them from others may reflect wholly legitimate purposes."[175] When members of a racial group did not reside in the same community, the legislature lacked a legitimate reason for placing them in the same district. Indeed, Kennedy seemed to suggest that when members of the same race lived apart, the *only* interests they could have in common would be the result of a monolithic, state-imposed group identity.

The dissenters in *Miller* organized their arguments around a sharply different conception of the relationship between race and political identity.[176] Where Kennedy denied the political valence of racial membership, Justice Ginsburg argued that "ethnicity *itself* can tie people together . . . even people with divergent economic interests."[177] Racial identities were not imposed by the state; instead, such identities were already at work in the electorate, serving as the locus of distinct political attitudes and concerns. As a consequence, Ginsburg argued that race-based districting did not enforce invidious assumptions, so much as "accommodate the reality of ethnic bonds."[178] Individuals included in "ethnic districts reflecting felt identity" did not ordinarily take offense or feel demeaned.[179] Indeed, the entire fear of individual insult was misplaced because districting was not about individuals in the first place. On the contrary, the design of district lines turned on the identification and recognition of coherent groups. As Ginsburg wrote, the reapportionment process simply did "not treat people as individuals. . . .

---

[175] Ibid., emphasis added, internal cites and quotation marks omitted. Kennedy's emphasis on actually living together remained crucial even though he cited Plaintiff's Exhibit No. 85 (report of Timothy G. O'Rourke, Ph.D.) to make the claim that residents of the contested district were politically, economically, socially, and culturally fractured (*Miller* at 2484, 2490). This claim was overdrawn. O'Rourke based his conclusions on a host of measures (e.g., urban/rural environment, socioeconomic characteristics, shared metropolitan areas), which acted as proxies for geographic compactness (see O'Rourke report, pp. 10–27). At no point did O'Rourke investigate the presence or absence of shared political attitudes (what Carol Swain has called the "subjective" component of shared interests — Swain 1993) among district residents. Far from demonstrating the complete fragmentation of the district population, O'Rourke simply reproduced Kennedy's dichotomy between communities of interest and racial considerations.

[176] Two dissenting opinions were filed, one by Justice Stevens and another by Justice Ginsburg (joined in full by Justices Stevens and Breyer, and in part by Justice Souter).

[177] *Miller* at 2504, emphasis added. This is not to say that Ginsburg took traditional principles of districting (e.g., compactness, protection of incumbents) to be unimportant. She simply argued that the Georgia district, in spite of its irregularities, was "not an outlier district shaped without reference to familiar districting techniques" (ibid.).

[178] Ibid. at 2505.

[179] Ibid.

Rather, legislators classify voters in groups — by economic, geographical, political, or social characteristics — and then reconcile the competing claims of [these] groups. "[180] Some racial and ethnic groups had suffered from a history of discrimination, but that hardly disqualified them from the group struggles of reapportionment politics.[181] The history of discrimination instead demanded "vigilant judicial inspection to protect minority voters."[182] According to Ginsburg, the real danger of redistricting was that one group would use its power to shut out another group — there simply was no other kind of harm in this context.[183] To substantiate their claim against the Georgia district, appellees had to show that white voters *as a group* had been locked out of the political process.

FULL-SCALE RETREAT VERSUS CAUTIOUS ADVANCE

By the end of the 1995 term, the judicial debate had become dominated by two visions of minority representation rooted in conflicting notions of political identity. Drawing on an individualistic understanding of "the people," Justices Kennedy and O'Connor, backed by Scalia, Thomas, and Rehnquist, curbed the race-conscious districting under the Voting Rights Act, arguing that majority-minority districts could inflict special harms by imposing monolithic group identities upon the politically protean mass of individual voters. For their part, Justices Souter, Stevens, and Ginsburg, at different times joined by Justices White and Breyer, defended the practice of race-conscious districting, claiming that majority-minority districts did not manufacture group identities so much as recognize the identities already in the electorate. The clash between these two blocs of justices left important questions of degree unresolved, with the five-member bloc of individualistic justices unable to agree on the precise scope of their opposition to racial redistricting. Yet, whatever uncertainties attended questions of degree, the post-*Gingles* decisions repeatedly presented determinant answers to the question of political identity: the choice has been a categorically stark one between individualistic and group conceptions of "the people."

[180] Ibid. at 2506, internal cites and quotation marks omitted.

[181] See ibid. at 2500–2501, where Ginsburg reviewed the history of vote discrimination against African Americans.

[182] Ibid. at 2506.

[183] Justice Stevens also made this point in his dissent. See ibid. at 2497–99.

The Court's most recent decisions have hewed to the same lines. Striking down three majority-minority districts in 1996, the plurality rejected the use of race as a proxy for political interests, arguing that the reliance on race would only disrupt the ordinary bases of political identity.[184] In turn, the dissenters criticized the plurality's single-minded search for racial factors, insisting that the intersection between political identity and racial membership was an obvious fact of American politics.[185] Revisiting long-standing disputes in North Carolina and Georgia, the Court once again divided along individualist and group cleavages, with the majority refusing to grant race any political valence and the dissenters situating racial membership within the American mosaic of group political identities.[186]

Interestingly enough, there has been one major post-*Gingles* case in which the justices adopted a different tack.[187] In *Holder v. Hall* (1994), most members of the Court avoided discussion of the deep conceptual divisions that *Shaw* revealed, which *Miller* and later decisions would subsequently reiterate.[188] *Holder* concerned the government of Bleckley County, Georgia, where a single commissioner has always held all legislative and executive authority. In 1985, the Georgia legislature authorized Bleckley County voters to reorganize their government by referendum, replacing the single commissioner with five officials elected from single-member districts and a chair elected at-large. The voters defeated

[184] *Bush v. Vera*, 116 S.Ct. 1941, 1956, 1962 (1996). Writing for the Court, Justice O'Connor explicitly linked the *Gingles* standard of vote dilution to *Shaw* and *Miller* (ibid. at 1961). Brennan's functionalism was thus made to serve an individualistic understanding of identity.

[185] See Justice Stevens's dissent (*Bush v. Vera* at 1979, 1988) and Justice Souter's dissent (ibid. at 1999–2000, 2004–6, 2010–12).

[186] *Shaw v. Hunt*, 116 S.Ct. 1894 (1996); and *Abrams v. Johnson*, 65 U.S.L.W. 4478 (1997).

[187] As I noted earlier, neither of the post-*Gingles* decisions *Chisom v. Roemer* nor *Presley v. Etowah County* featured a clear clash between individualistic and group positions. I nonetheless distinguish *Holder v. Hall*, 114 S.Ct. 2581 (1994) from both *Chisom* and *Presley* because the former decision suggests strategies explicitly designed to avoid the complexities of the debate over political identity (see my discussion of Thomas's *Holder* dissent below). While *Chisom* and *Presley* fail to explore the linkage between representational baselines and political identity, neither decision suggests a means by which the exploration of that linkage can ultimately be foregone. For this reason, I treat *Holder* separately.

[188] *Holder v. Hall*, 114 S.Ct. 2581 (1994). *De Grandy v. Johnson*, 114 S.Ct. 2647 (1994) was decided on the same day as *Holder*. I only consider *Holder* here, although *De Grandy* exhibited the same alternatives of full-scale retreat and cautious advance.

this proposal, although they had previously approved a five-member district plan for the county school board. Six African American voters living in Bleckley County subsequently filed suit, claiming that the single-commissioner system denied them equal political opportunity in violation of the Fourteenth Amendment, the Fifteenth Amendment, and Section 2 of the Voting Rights Act. The District Court rejected these claims, but the Court of Appeals held that Section 2 had been violated and suggested the single-commissioner government be modeled after the new five-member school board.[189]

Writing for a plurality, Justice Kennedy reversed the Court of Appeals.[190] Kennedy focused his opinion on the question of whether the size of a governing authority could be challenged under Section 2. Citing O'Connor's *Gingles* opinion, Kennedy argued that the question of governmental size, like all questions of vote dilution, required the Court to "find a reasonable alternative practice as a benchmark against which to measure the existing practice."[191] Kennedy did not attempt to provide any general sense of how the "reasonableness" of a benchmark ought to be understood. Unlike the sharp arguments that had divided the Court in *Shaw* and *Miller*, Kennedy's remarks steered well clear of any broad claims about who "the people" were and how their interests ought to be represented. Instead, Kennedy simply pointed out that "in certain cases, the benchmark for comparison in a Section 2 dilution suit is obvious."[192] In the specific case of governmental size, however, reasonable baselines remained elusive because there was "no principled reason why one size should be picked over another as the benchmark for comparison."[193] Kennedy acknowledged that governmental size could be reviewed under Section 5. But this was so because Section 5 preclearance worked on the principle of nonretrogression: the benchmark was given "by definition" because the aim was only to determine if a proposed change in political rules left minorities worse off than before.[194]

Like all justices writing in the wake of *Gingles*, Kennedy showed a

---

[189] *Holder* at 2585.

[190] Kennedy was joined by Chief Justice Rehnquist and, with the exception of his argument distinguishing Sections 2 and 5, by Justice O'Connor. O'Connor filed a separate opinion, concurring in part and concurring in judgment. Justice Thomas, joined by Justice Scalia, also filed a concurrence in judgment.

[191] *Holder* at 2585.

[192] Ibid. at 2586.

[193] Ibid.

[194] Ibid. at 2587.

certain awareness of the representational issues at stake in vote dilution litigation; indeed, he organized his entire argument around the question of how the appropriate representational baseline ought to be identified and defended. Yet Kennedy was also careful to keep his discussion limited to the case at hand. Moreover, even as the dissenters in *Holder* rejected Kennedy's claim that the there was no meaningful benchmark to be found, they also shared Kennedy's commitment to seeking out the appropriate representational standards on a case-by-case basis.[195] The dispute between Kennedy and the dissenters thus turned on the question of whether the specific customs and practices of the jurisdiction under examination indicated a reasonable representational standard. The broader linkages between representational baselines and deeper understandings of political identity were simply pushed aside, displaced by a belief that the knot of minority representation could only be unraveled one case at a time.

As a recognition of judicial limitations, the decision to defer sweeping statements of judicial policy was reasonable enough. The Court could hardly hope to resolve all the complexities of minority representation on an a priori basis. Still, there remained an important difference between a commitment to the process of case-by-case adjudication and a refusal to investigate the conceptual issues raised by representational litigation. In one form or another, understandings of "the people" had informed judicial debate over the meaning of fair representation for nearly fifty years. And efforts to deflect judicial attention from questions of political identity did not reduce their importance so much as ensure that such questions would be answered in an indirect and inadequate fashion.

In his lengthy *Holder* concurrence, Justice Thomas showed some awareness of this point by emphasizing the enduring centrality of political theory in representational jurisprudence.[196] Citing Frankfurter's dissents from the reapportionment revolution of thirty years before, Thomas argued that judicial efforts to correct problems of minority vote dilution had long compelled the Court to consider theories of meaningful participation.[197] While Kennedy's pragmatic analysis sug-

---

[195] See Blackmun's dissent, ibid. at 2622. Blackmun was joined by Justices Stevens, Souter, and Ginsburg.

[196] Thomas was joined by Justice Scalia.

[197] Ibid. at 2593–94. Thomas saw political theory first entering the judicial analysis of minority representation in *Allen v. State Board of Elections* (1969). For my discussion of *Allen*, see chapters one and four.

gested that there was no reasonable representative baseline in *this* case, his opinion did little to sort through the "infinite number of theories of effective suffrage, representation, and the proper apportionment of political power" that could be used as guides in subsequent cases.[198]

Thomas thus dismissed the incrementalist strategy that Kennedy and the other justices embraced. He argued that the weighing of political theories was an altogether "hopeless project" that courts were "inherently ill-equipped" to undertake.[199] Concepts of political equality came in "a dizzying array," which the Voting Rights Act did not even attempt to sort through.[200] Blindly groping its way through the thorniest of political thickets, the Court had "given credence to the view that race defines political interest" and had engineered "the enterprise of segregating the races into political homelands."[201] The Court often claimed to base its rulings on a variety of factors, but for Thomas such "dissembling" and "puffery" could not hide the "political choice" for proportional racial representation at the heart of the Court's decisions.[202] Thomas saw no reason why judicial policy would not continue to move from bad to worse, for "it is only the limits on our 'political imagination' that place restraints on the standards we may select."[203] The only possible response to this judicial debacle was to restrict Section 2 of the Voting Rights Act to "state enactments that limit citizens' *access* to the ballot."[204] According to Thomas, the most "natural" and "plain" readings of the act demonstrated that "access" formed the boundary of Section 2. Indeed, to read Section 2 to allow anything more would be to claim that Congress had transformed the Court into either "mighty Platonic Guardians" or a "centralized politburo," entitled to "dictate to the provinces the 'correct' theories of democratic representation."[205]

Thomas's opinion was extremely problematic.[206] His claim that the Court had consistently misread the Voting Rights Act since the late

[198] *Holder* at 2596.

[199] Ibid. at 2592.

[200] Ibid. at 2608, 2594.

[201] Ibid. at 2597–98. According to Thomas, the path to proportional representation was the "most logical" once the Court began delving into political theory (ibid. at 2614).

[202] Ibid. at 2614, 2616.

[203] Ibid. at 2601.

[204] Ibid. at 2592, emphasis added.

[205] Ibid. at 2602.

[206] I describe only a few of the problems with Thomas's argument. For additional criticisms, see the separate opinion filed by Justice Stevens (joined by Justices Blackmun, Souter, and Ginsburg), ibid. at 2625–30; and Guinier 1994.

1960s ignored the fact that Congress had reenacted and expanded the act on four occasions without identifying the "mistakes" that Thomas found so glaring and intolerable. Thomas did insist that the Court had sampled legislative history selectively, arriving at an interpretation that did not give full credit to the "compromise" that made the 1982 amendments possible.[207] Nonetheless, Thomas's own reading of the act flouted the idea of legislative compromise by enshrining the views of a single senator.[208]

In any case, for all of Thomas's appeals to the "plain" terms of the act, he admitted that such terms did not, in and of themselves, foreclose the application of Section 2 to vote dilution.[209] His restriction of Section 2 to the conditions of access thus made sense only because (i) there was simply no way for the Court to adjudicate between competing representational standards and (ii) in trying to do the impossible, the Court had been inexorably drawn to a destructive doctrine of proportional racial representation. Whatever the force of the first argument might be, Thomas characterized the second as more serious (or "worse").[210] But Thomas undercut his claims about the Court's "destructiveness" with a rhetorical sleight of hand. The facts that Thomas drew from *Shaw* to illustrate judicial devastation were not the "facts" of *Shaw* at all; they were merely assertions that Justice O'Connor had made about the kind of harm that *might* result from certain districts.[211]

Perhaps the most problematic aspect of Thomas's opinion was its attempt to resurrect the untenable approach of Justice Frankfurter in *Colegrove v. Green*. Where Justice Kennedy and the *Holder* dissenters failed to mention the importance of conceptual issues in the politics of minority representation, Thomas wished to keep such issues entirely insulated from debate. Like Frankfurter before him, Thomas denied that the judiciary should make claims about the form and content of the political community. Yet also like Frankfurter, Thomas insisted on a particular rendering of the political community to which the judiciary ought to adhere. In the end, then, it was not the judicial endorsement of political theories to which Thomas objected, so much as the endorsement of *particular* political theories that called into question his preferred understanding of fair minority representation.

---

[207] *Holder* at 2612–13.
[208] Ibid. at 2613. The senator in question was Robert Dole.
[209] Ibid. at 2608.
[210] Ibid. at 2592.
[211] Ibid. at 2592, 2598. Compare *Shaw* at 647–48.

If both of the strategies adopted in *Holder* were indeed ill-advised, how was the Court to proceed? In the context of conceptual polarization that characterized *Shaw* and *Miller*, how was the debate over minority representation to be advanced? Did either approach permit the Court to speak on behalf of the people without preventing the people from finally speaking for themselves? These questions are the subject of the concluding chapter.

The Possibilities of Legislative Learning

MY ARGUMENT has traveled full circle. First, I showed that the conservative and progressive views of minority representation hinged on different conceptions of political identity (chapter three). The conservatives saw "the people" as a mass of protean individuals with fungible interests, capable of striking whatever bargains the open political market would bear. By contrast, the progressives took "the people" to be a patchwork of distinct groups, capable of relating to one another only where each group interest could be fully articulated and seriously heard. The development of judicial debate (chapters four and five) resembles the larger ideological debate.[1] Abandoning an original variety of approaches, members of the Court have embraced individualist and group conceptions of "the people" that parallel conservative and progressive claims. Just as conservatives wish to roll back the Voting Rights Act, keeping the fluid political process free of rigid judicial strictures, judicial advocates of individualism have attempted to shield the electoral process from race-conscious Court interventions—interventions that supposedly threaten to displace the American melting pot with a network of racial enclaves.[2] And, just as progressives insist on a group-directed process of political decision making actively enforced by the Court, ju-

[1] The resemblance is not exact. At points, the views of conservatives and progressives outstrip judicial discussion; no member of the Court has, for example, endorsed the scheme of proportional representation and minority vetoes championed by Lani Guinier. But the judicial debate also has unmatched extremes. In *Holder v. Hall* (114 S.Ct. 2581 [1994]), Justice Thomas claimed the Voting Rights Act should be rolled back *even further* than leading conservatives have suggested (see Thernstrom 1987, p. 30, granting some value to the notion of minority vote dilution). Still, these differences in policy recommendations on and off the bench should not obscure a more important similarity in fundamental frameworks.

[2] Individualists on the bench have not shied away from judicial activism altogether. They have called for some aggressive judicial action—all with the aim of *restoring* fluidity to the political process. This is consistent with the conservative claim that the courts will be restricted to the margins in a well-ordered political market. See, e.g., Burger's opinion in *UJO v. Carey*, 430 U.S. 144 (1977); Stewart's opinion in *Mobile v. Bolden*, 446 U.S. 55 (1980); O'Connor's opinion in *Shaw v. Reno*, 509 U.S. 630 (1993); and Kennedy's opinion in *Miller v. Johnson*, 115 S.Ct. 2475 (1995).

dicial advocates of group identity have tried to stamp race-conscious measures with the Court's imprimatur, attempting to reconfigure the political process with the aim of integrating excluded people of color.[3]

Both the debates on and off the bench have also been marked by unsuccessful efforts to downplay political identity. Relying on a broad base of empirical data, centrists have attempted to defuse the conflict between conservatives and progressives, arguing that voting-rights policy is actually an incremental, atheoretical enterprise. For their part, various members of the Court have adopted a strategy of measured advance that looks much like a judicial brand of centrism. While both these approaches have some value, neither manages to identify a viable alternative position. The centrists fail *not* because reliable empirical information is unimportant but because the key question is what such information should mean given what fair representation is taken to be. Likewise, the appeal to cautious advance fails *not* because case-by-case adjudication is a worthless ideal but because the strict insistence on judicial incrementalism neglects the conceptual issues that have animated the jurisprudence of minority representation. The judicial and public debates thus teach the same lesson: without the recognition and assessment of political identity, no approach to minority representation is tenable.[4]

The question, then, is how one should evaluate the polarized positions that have dominated the discussion of minority representation. While acknowledging the conceptual issues at stake in this area, should the Court simply embrace one pole of the existing debate? Or is there a better alternative, a third approach to representational politics that does not depend on *either* individualist or group understandings of "the people"?

---

[3] See, e.g., Marshall's opinion in *Bolden*; the separate opinions of White, Stevens, and Souter in *Shaw*; and Ginsburg's opinion in *Miller*.

[4] One might agree that debates over "the people" are central to representational politics yet argue that such debates are so entangled that they defy resolution. In this view, it would be reasonable to support centrism because a denial of conceptual issues is the only practical way to make progress (see Peterson 1995). The problem with this view, of course, is that few justices share it. From the strong conservative claims of Justice Thomas to the more progressive approaches of Justices Souter and Ginsburg, members of the Court have repeatedly anchored their opinions in assertions about political identity. As conducted in judicial decisions, the debate over "the people" is certainly contentious, but it cannot be side-stepped.

These questions can be answered by assessing the Court's political entrepreneurship, by considering whether the judicial actions taken on behalf of the people have precluded the people from finally speaking for themselves. Under this standard, both the individualist and group positions are inadequate, for they both sustain judicial power at too high a cost to democratic rule. A better alternative would focus explicitly on the relationship between popular sovereignty and judicial authority. Such an alternative exists and should be adopted. Specifically, the Court should employ a deliberative understanding of political identity, using its power to bolster the democratic pursuit of common interests.

Although appeals to political deliberation are fairly common within contemporary political theory, few such appeals have grappled with the details of political practice. The failure to specify how deliberation is possible under concrete political conditions has stimulated a strong negative response, making the criticism of deliberation almost as common as its advocacy. I take these criticisms seriously and attempt to provide a realistic description of deliberation, anchored in an account of legislative learning. I outline judicial guidelines for the enforcement of deliberative procedures under the Voting Rights Act. These will not resolve every controversy involving minority representation; no single approach can hope to end the complex struggle over the meaning of political membership that has long characterized the act. Even so, the notion of a deliberative people does introduce a new set of terms in which better conceptions of representation can be advanced.

ASSESSING INDIVIDUALIST AND GROUP ALTERNATIVES

Thus far, my examination of political identity has illustrated the conceptual disagreements between prevailing views of minority representation. With the results of such conceptual analysis in place, a common problem can be discerned. For all the points of divergence between the individualist and group understandings of "the people," both approaches share an important feature: each takes political identity to be something formed prior to and apart from politics itself. Individualists like Abigail Thernstrom and Justice O'Connor argue that *because* political identity is fundamentally an amalgam of multiple affiliations, politics ought be to conducted without race-conscious rules. Similarly, group thinkers like Lani Guinier and Justice Marshall argue that

147

because political identity is fundamentally coextensive with discrete groups, politics ought to be conducted with racially sensitive rules.[5] In both cases, politics is treated instrumentally, as a passive medium configured to express political identities as they naturally are. Advocates of the individualist and group alternatives may promote distinct visions of representation, but they converge in their conviction that politics simply responds to the exigencies of a preset political identity.

The mutual effort to delimit "the people" independently of and prior to politics turns the debate between competing conceptions of political identity into a zero-sum exchange. Each side is committed to a fixed view of what political identity essentially is. There is little room here for half-measures or fresh alternatives; political identity is either a matter of individual or group attachments, period. In this context, to make concessions to the opposing side — to suggest that political identity is not entirely as one originally thought — is to lose the unwavering point of leverage on which all else depends.

The real difficulty with such intransigence is that it compromises the prospects for popular sovereignty. Relying on prepolitical conceptions, the Court gives a rigidly determinant identity to "the people" on whose behalf it claims to speak and, in doing so, sharply limits the range of identities that citizens themselves may ultimately choose to recognize. Such limitations on democratic sovereignty are problematic precisely because the foreclosed options have important political value.

To see this, consider the political possibilities that the individualist approach includes and those it does not. The individualist understanding begins with the claim that political identity can never be defined solely by membership in a single group. Multidimensional identities foster political action along market lines, with freewheeling bargaining

---

[5] It is true that Guinier has moved beyond the specific claims of racial minorities to call for the equal representation of all groups. Yet, since Guinier has essentially generalized her group understanding of the people (hypothesizing that the electorate is composed of discrete, unanimous constituencies), I continue to include her in the group camp, treating the difference between her and other "groupists" as a matter of degree. Guinier's advocacy of proportional representation would permit groups to organize themselves behind candidates, thereby removing the need for government to give special recognition to specific groups in the redistricting process. Although such self-identification has its virtues (Phillips 1995, pp. 104–8), Guinier is willing to leave self-identification behind when she claims minority groups should be given legislative vetoes over the issues that concern them — a move that would require the government to say a great deal about the nature of group identity and group interest. See Guinier 1991a and 1991b. Thus, again, Guinier remains well within the boundaries of the group approach.

yielding an on-going series of shifting alliances. Such "politics as usual" is analogous to running water: only when some external barrier blocks its course does the easy flow of political bargaining cease. Reasoning along such lines, one would expect African Americans to become a powerful swing vote soon after the electoral hurdles thrown up in the South had been removed.[6] To the extent that multiracial coalitions did not emerge, it was because government strategies of minority compensation raised new barriers in place of old ones, creating the "political apartheid" excoriated by Justice O'Connor in *Shaw v. Reno*. In the absence of such governmentally imposed obstacles, champions of the individualist perspective are reluctant to speak of distinct group identities at all. The vast "galaxy" of diverse interests held by the electorate makes the whole idea of a fixed "political group" highly ambiguous.[7] In the individualist ocean of multiple political attachments, there are no islands.

Thus stated, the individualist position provides a clear warning against the dangers of proportional racial representation. In creating and enforcing strict racial quotas, the government runs the risk of emphasizing the differences between racial groups while obscuring important cleavages within such groups.[8] The deeper problem is that the consistent use of such categorical schemes finally subverts the American ideal of a whole people. The United States was founded on the notion that it could be ruled by a one sovereign people—a notion embedded in the Constitution's "We the People," as well as in the Great Seal's "e pluribus unum."[9] Indeed, it is the notion of one whole people that has furnished the basis of judicial authority, allowing the Supreme Court to justify its actions as representative in nature.[10] The "whole people" may of course be characterized in a number of ways. But the establishment of proportional racial representation does not promise such an alternative characterization; on the contrary, it threatens to undermine the notion of a whole people by reducing political membership to discrete

[6] Thernstrom 1987, p. 23.

[7] See Burger's opinion in *UJO* at 186–87 and Stewart's opinion in *Bolden* at 75 and 78, n. 26.

[8] See Phillips 1995, p. 98–99, and Glendon 1991. It is also worth noting that as amended in 1982, Section 2 of the Voting Rights Act expressly disavows the "right to have members of a protected class elected in numbers equal to their proportion in the population" (Grofman and Davidson 1992, p. 319).

[9] See Beer 1993.

[10] See chapter two.

racial blocs. The harder claims for fixed racial representation are pushed, the more the politics of minority representation becomes a struggle for preservation *apart* from the majority group rather than a struggle for meaningful membership *among* the people as a whole.[11] Thus, the more stringently that political voice is coded by race and fixed by law, the more difficult it becomes to understand how the people as a whole can be a coherent political actor. As Justice Douglas once wrote, and as individualists from Abigail Thernstrom to Justice O'Connor have reiterated: "Racial electoral registers, like religious ones, have no place in a society that honors the Lincoln tradition — 'of the people, by the people, for the people.' Here the individual is important, not his race, his creed, or his color."[12]

The individualist arguments against racial balkanization provide a partial foundation for judicial entrepreneurship. By preserving the basic idea of a whole people, the individualist perspective does much to ensure the capacity of the people to speak for themselves. Yet, when the Court acts in the name of a strictly individualistic people, it ultimately hobbles democratic sovereignty. This is so because even though it is important to acknowledge the tensions between group identity and the notion of a whole people, it is wrong to dismiss the demands of group identity altogether. In attempting to circumvent divisive group politics, individualists call into question the very existence of politically relevant racial identities. Individualists thus save the citizenry from racial categorization by presupposing that racial identity is politically significant *only* when the government makes it so. As Justice Kennedy suggests in *Miller v. Johnson*, "communities defined by actual shared interests" are not to be confused with "racial considerations": the former are worthy of legislative recognition, while the latter are illegitimately imposed

---

[11] It is on these grounds that the Canadian debate over multiculturalism may be distinguished from the politics of minority representation in the United States. Much of the Canadian controversy is about how to ensure self-government for indigenous peoples, while the American debate is about how to secure inclusion of minorities within an existing government. Racial minorities in the United States wish to rule *as part* of a sovereign people; the indigenous peoples in Canada often wish to rule *apart*, as separate sovereign authorities of their own (see Kymlicka 1989, pp. 4, 136, 140–42, 144–57). For a good introduction to the multiculturalist debate, see Taylor 1994.

[12] *Wright v. Rockefeller*, 376 U.S. 52, 66 (1964). I have noted, however, that the individualist appropriation of this quote departs in important ways from the original terms of Douglas's broader argument (see chapter five).

identities. The problem with such a claim is that minority groups have been and, in many instances, continue to be politically constituted on the basis of "racial considerations." As debates surrounding the Voting Rights Act have long indicated and as comprehensive studies continue to show, minority groups comprise distinct voting blocs in many regions of the country.[13] In these regions, the vision of political protean individuals identifying with a large range of groups is belied by the persistence of racial cleavage and minority exclusion. To stress the need for colorblindness in the face of such hierarchy and division is to prevent the government from helping the very groups that have been discriminated against on racial and ethnic grounds.[14] Indeed, to permit majority *white* districts to persist regardless of shape while holding majority-minority districts to strict scrutiny is to do more than deny minority groups a potential remedy.[15] It is to suggest that citizens and their representatives cannot grant minorities the same treatment already accorded to members of the majority.

All of this suggests that judicial action should facilitate rather than foreclose the recognition of group identities. This conclusion is, of course, precisely the one drawn by adherents of the group approach. According to the group view, "politics as usual" has more to do with interactions among discrete groups than with bargaining among protean individuals. Stable group identification has been the central fact of political life borne out in the behavior of politicians who, as Justice Stevens noted, "have always relied on assumptions that people *in particular groups* are likely to vote in a particular way."[16] The interaction between groups, moreover, has taken place on an uneven playing field marked by discrimination and exclusion.[17] Given this history, to insist on an individualistic political identity is simply to ignore the enduring matrix of group attachments that structure and confine political voice.[18] Political identities are constituted by the experience of specific groups; such identities cannot be bargained away on the open political market.

[13] Davidson and Grofman 1994; see also Phillips 1995 and Mansbridge 1996.

[14] Strauss 1996, pp. 13–14, makes the same argument with regard to affirmative action.

[15] In this vein, recall that Justice O'Connor was reluctant to recognize "white" as a racial category in *Shaw v. Reno* (see chapter five).

[16] *Shaw* at 678, emphasis added.

[17] For a general argument in this vein, see Smith 1993.

[18] For more general criticisms of legal views that neglect the importance of broader social and political contexts, see Freeman 1989 and Bumiller 1988.

151

The Voting Rights Act merely recognizes the nonfungibility of certain political identities, affirming Justice Marshall's claim that the historical experience of racial groups has differed "in kind, not just in degree."[19] From the group perspective, then, the individualist concern over balkanization erroneously presumes that members of the political community are already united by a common perspective.[20] In fact, political majorities have frequently coalesced by excluding minority groups. Where political unity has been achieved by sacrificing minority inclusion, the status quo is simply not worth preserving.[21] The recognition of new rights and the introduction of new political voices may well disaggregate existing coalitions; but if properly practiced, "rights talk" promises new forms of coordination and connection.[22] A suitably reconstituted legislature will operate like a jury, seeking consensus among all representatives.[23] In this way, genuine fairness will be achieved, offsetting any losses in stability with gains in political legitimacy.

The group approach thus compensates for the shortcomings of individualism, supplying the Court with a notion of "the people" that permits claims of group identity to be expressed. Unfortunately, the insistence upon the essential group dimensions of identity ultimately compromises democratic sovereignty in its own way. Arguing against the dilution of minority votes, champions of the group approach too often rely on proportional representation as the implicit measure of the "undiluted" vote.[24] After all, if racial group identities are nonfungible, what else besides proportional representation can ensure that each racial minority possesses a meaningful political voice? Following the logic of the group approach, it is a short step to Lani Guinier's ideal of proportionate interest representation: to the extent that *all* political identities are nonfungible, the Court should ensure that *all* groups are able to articulate their interests through their own representatives, with legislative bodies configured so that each representative may have her interests satisfied a fair proportion of the time.[25] While those in the group camp are optimistic about the possibility of consensual, jury-like deliberations within the fully proportional legislature, it is difficult to see how the

---

[19] *Bolden* at 138, n. 37, internal quotation marks omitted.

[20] See Guinier 1991b, pp. 1489–93.

[21] See Justice Marshall in *Bolden* at 112–21. For an extended argument, see Bell 1987.

[22] For a general argument along these lines, see Minow 1987b.

[23] Guinier 1991b, 1485–87.

[24] See O'Connor in *Shaw* and Thomas in *Holder v. Hall*.

[25] Guinier 1993b.

analogy between juries and legislatures can be sustained on groupist terms. Jury deliberations operate on the premise that individual jurors *transcend* their own biases in a collective search for justice.[26] Selected as a cross-section of the community, jurors ideally bring different perspectives to bear without being bound to the interests of any group or constituency. By contrast, the group approach views legislators as the loyal agents of distinct interests; the whole point of proportional group representation is to generate representatives closely tied to the electoral mosaic of discrete interests. In this context of group advocacy, conflict and stasis, rather than discussion and consensus, are the likely outcomes. Without allowing legislators a significant degree of independence, an increase in the number of groups that must be represented merely multiplies the opportunities for dissension and strife.[27] Ultimately, the entrenchment of such a divisive group politics threatens to undermine the notion of a whole people, placing the Court in the paradoxical position of undercutting the democratic sovereign on whose behalf judicial power is claimed.

How then should one choose between the individualist and group alternatives? In an important sense, both of these positions are partially right. Advocates of the group alternative are surely correct to stress the historical and social factors that have wedded individual political identities to specific groups. America's past and present are punctuated by political exclusion engineered on the basis of race. In the face of such history, it is perverse to deploy colorblindness as a barrier to helping those very groups that have been marginalized on color-conscious grounds. Nonetheless, advocates of the individualist alternative are clearly right to insist that political identities cannot be limited always and everywhere to the boundaries of discrete groups. Individuals do identify with a range of groups, and political interests can be shared by members of groups with different historical experiences. Bargaining is an essential part of the political process, made possible in part by the overlapping group memberships and heterogeneous political identities that individual citizens possess. To obstruct this political flow with a rigid scheme of racial quotas is to undercut the possibility of government by the whole people, for the whole people.

Yet, neither of these alternatives alone provides an adequate founda-

---

[26] Abramson 1994, pp. 99–141.

[27] See O'Connor's opinion in *Shaw* at 656–58. For a general argument about the costs of unanimity, see Buchanan and Tullock 1962.

tion for the exercise of the Court's political entrepreneurship. Each approach fosters claims of judicial power that illegitimately impair democratic sovereignty, either by preventing the recognition of viable group identities or by undermining the idea of the whole people as a coherent political actor. Moreover, since both the individualist and group camp are wedded to fixed understandings of political identity, neither is able to incorporate the insights the other possesses. The choice between individualist and group alternatives is, in the end, no real choice at all.

THE POSSIBILITIES OF LEGISLATIVE LEARNING

When a debate proves to be irresolvable in the terms that it has been posed, the appropriate response is to seek different terms. The prevailing views of minority representation grant the Court power to speak for the people in a way that undermines the ultimate ability of the people to speak for themselves. Rather than continuing to explore the prevailing views, I will defend a different approach that explicitly works to preserve democratic capacities in the context of claims about judicial power. In particular, I will argue that there is more to legislative politics than the instrumental pursuit of fixed interests. Legislatures can be a site of deliberation about the interests that all hold in common as well as the policies best suited to serve those interests. Whatever might be said about what political identity fundamentally is, political deliberation itself alters identity by constituting "the people" in a certain way: a people that deliberates is a people which learns. Working from a deliberative conception of "the people," the Court can claim authority while permitting citizens to develop their own views of how the political community should be constructed.

The elements of such a position were initially asserted by Chief Justice Warren (chapter four). Warren described the original Voting Rights Act as a vivid example of political deliberation. He argued that members of Congress had held extensive hearings and engaged in lengthy debate during the passage of the act. As a result, Congress had learned that voting discrimination against African Americans was deeply entrenched and resistant to simple remedies. The decision to bring minority groups into the political community through court-supervised, race-conscious reform carried clear risks, but it was a decision supported by comprehensive information and arguments.

Warren appeared to push the point even further. He implicitly took congressional deliberation as a model for the sort of politics the Voting Rights Act was meant to ensure in the nation's legislatures. He recognized that the act's preclearance provisions would prohibit selected jurisdictions from unilaterally determining the fundamental rules of political organization. The act compelled political subdivisions to deliberate on behalf of the entire people without discriminating on the basis of race or color. This was, of course, exactly the task that Congress had performed in its passage of the act. Thus, in order to pass preclearance, covered subdivisions were required to justify new rules of the political game in a Congress-like fashion, demonstrating that a diversity of voices had been heard and common interests had been served.

On the whole, one could say that Warren viewed the Voting Rights Act as a mechanism for reviewing and reinforcing the deliberative basis of the political community, empowering the Court to promote the process of legislative learning. Although he clearly wished to remedy the political exclusion of racial minorities, his ultimate objective was not to construct a scheme of racial representation for its own sake. Racial redistricting was justified not because it reflected the most salient cleavage among competing interest groups but because Congress had learned that racial districting was necessary to help move the entire polity toward the goal of effective political deliberation. Warren kept his eye less on what "the people" were than on what they could make themselves into. The Court was to enforce the act's provisions in an effort to help legislatures work through racial divisions, producing the conditions in which representatives might seek and serve common interests.[28]

Warren's approach had a brief and undistinguished career on the bench. In the initial articulation of his views, Warren left the connection between the act and the political deliberation largely implicit. Failing to develop the notion of a deliberative people, Warren simply cleared space for rival judicial interpretations with distinct conceptions of political identity. Justice Brennan picked up the thread of Warren's argument nearly a decade later, but he too stopped short of indicating how deliberation worked and might be enforced. Where Warren had left his aim ambiguous, Brennan linked his account of congressional deliberation to the protection of particularistic racial concerns, neglecting to explain how the pursuit of such narrow concerns could possibly lead to the satisfaction of broadly shared interests. Brennan consequently fell

---

[28] Relying on Warren's arguments, Brennan made just this claim in *UJO v. Carey* (see chapter five).

victim to the very criticism that he had rightly leveled against Justice White's totality-of-circumstances approach: when racial divisions become the ground and goal of the Voting Rights Act, judicial action simply fosters a fragmentary politics of racial partition and threatens the very idea of a whole people.

Can Warren's argument be salvaged? Is it possible to develop a sharper understanding of how political deliberation works and how it might be judicially enforced? Warren's voice is hardly the only one that has been raised in support of political deliberation. James Madison believed that federal politics might *positively transform* the people by engendering a process of rational deliberation (chapter two). The people were passionate and prone to wicked projects but that was not all they were or ever could be. In the diverse American republic, Madison thought it unlikely that a majority of citizens bent on invading minority rights could coalesce and carry out its plans. Where passion was unable to convulse the community, the concerted action of a majority would almost of necessity have to depend upon principles of "justice and the general good."[29] Moreover, Madison argued that the division of power among the government's branches, allowing each to check and balance the other, would further loosen the grip of passion on representatives, reconfiguring the private interest of each into a "sentinel" over the rights of all.[30] Deploying representational structures to disable factional passions, the Constitution aimed at the creation of a political entity in which representatives could exercise their reason coolly. Thus, government was *neither* strictly instrumental, confined to reflecting a natural political identity, *nor* strictly negative, limited to imposing restrictions on what the citizenry might do. In Madison's view, government played an important generative role, actively molding "the people" into a deliberative sovereign capable of reasoning about the public interest.[31]

Madison lends some credence to Warren's approach, but his model of deliberation has problems of its own. Madison claimed that great diversity was necessary to drive the governmental engines of political deliberation. Even as he concentrated on the task of containing factions within a scheme of institutional checks, however, he simply stipulated that a sufficient diversity of factional interests would enter government in the first place. If some interests were systematically excluded, the Madiso-

---

[29] Hamilton, Madison, and Jay 1961, No. 51, p. 325.
[30] Ibid., p. 322.
[31] See Beer 1993, pp. 244–78.

nian legislature merely proceeded without them.[32] In addition to assuming the realization of sufficient diversity, Madison also failed to foresee the rise of modern political parties. Parties coordinate activity within and across political institutions, lessening the collective action problems that Madison counted on to stimulate deliberation. The aim of deliberation is to establish discussion in place of force as the primary means of political action. With interests organized and coordinated, however, opportunities for government by discussion may well be displaced by the will of the majority party.[33]

Madison's errors are his own, of course, and there is reason to believe that subsequent advocates of deliberation have developed better arguments. After all, many contemporary political theorists, including Jurgen Habermas, have celebrated political deliberation as the best mode of democratic governance.[34] The difficulty with many such arguments, however, is that they pay little attention to how political deliberation could be achieved under actual conditions.[35] The evasion of concrete conditions is fatal for defenses of deliberation. In principle, political deliberation foresees legislation in the common interest emerging from a reasoned exchange between conflicting views. Unfortunately, there is no guarantee that rational debate will in fact lead to anything like agreement or consensus.[36] Actual political conflict may be irreducible and resistant to change; to the extent this is true, reasoned argument may simply deepen disagreement, with political actors learning precisely how far apart they really are. Alternatively, an inflexible belief in consensus may be manipulated to paper over enduring conflicts. Appeals to deliberation may then be used to screen a reality of coercive domination.

In any event, whether it derails discussion or fosters a false assertion of agreement, the threat of conflict looms particularly large in the redistricting process. Redistricting efforts are frequently characterized by gerrymandering, as legislators manipulate district lines to maximize the number of seats the majority party can win. Gerrymandering itself is a highly uncertain and contentious enterprise. The electoral consequences

[32] For a more extended critique of Madison along such lines, see Goodin 1996.

[33] See Schmitt 1985. If the majority party has sufficient internal diversity, then it might produce Madisonian deliberation within its own ranks. Yet, since cleavages often get frozen in party structures, it is likely that a deliberative scheme that relied solely on parties would tend to neglect emerging interests (see Goodin 1996).

[34] Habermas 1989, 1992, and 1996.

[35] See Phillips 1995, pp. 154–55, and Sanders 1997.

[36] Mouffe 1994.

of any given district are predictable only to the degree that voters are predictably partisan. As partisan loyalty has declined in the United States, so too has the predictability of district elections.[37] Beyond this underlying voter volatility, the majority party is often riddled with conflicting goals (e.g., party interests in maximizing overall partisan advantage often cut across incumbent interests in enhancing individual chances for reelection) and competing demands (e.g., legal requirements of compactness, equal population, and, of course, fair minority representation).[38] The practice of gerrymandering thus spawns an enormous diversity of views about what constitutes the most fair redistricting plan. Indeed, as Bruce Cain has noted, the process of drawing district lines is so perforated with conflicting claims that a finished reapportionment plan "cannot pretend to be the 'best' plan. It is simply the one that enjoyed the broadest consensus, for *whatever reasons.*"[39] When it comes to redistricting, conflict is king and the deliberative ideal seems far-fetched.

All of the problems posed by conflict signal a deeper concern, for the deliberative commitments to diversity and reasoned agreement ultimately pull in different directions.[40] On the one hand, deliberation is driven by the diversity of political views and thus requires free and equal access to the political process. On the other hand, the greater the diversity of viewpoints, the less chance there is that any kind of consensus can be achieved—even if "consensus" is understood minimally as a shared understanding of the dimensions of disagreement. The essential difficulty is that while diversity threatens to consume the possibility of reasoned mutual understanding, there is no standard *within deliberative theory itself* that indicates how the appropriate range of diversity might be achieved. Deliberation seems doomed to subvert itself, as its own prerequisites encourage discussion to spiral aimlessly without producing decisions.

Taken together, then, these objections question the fundamental feasibility of political deliberation. How can reasoned discussion ever lead to legislation in the common interest when the very diversity that deliberation requires continually challenges the idea of common or shared interests?

An answer to such a basic criticism requires a focus on concrete con-

---

[37] Jacobson 1990, pp. 5–23, 94–96.
[38] Gelman and King 1994.
[39] Cain 1984, p. 6, emphasis added.
[40] Knight and Johnson 1994.

ditions, specifying how meaningful political deliberation is actually possible. But first, it is important to note that the presence of political deliberation does not presuppose the absence of conflict or of nondeliberative decision making.[41] To argue that political deliberation occurs is not to insist that every legislative decision is ultimately grounded in reasoned discussion and an understanding of the public interest. Many issues may be amenable only to adversarial processes governed by minimal wining coalitions, assembled so that individual members of the majority can satisfy their particularistic interests. Moreover, when political deliberation does occur, it need not arrive at broad consensus in every instance. Deliberative procedures aim at consensus through the reasoned exchange of arguments, but discussion may nonetheless end in a vote.[42] Log-rolling and deliberation are both compatible with majority rule, but only the latter is premised on the belief that political preferences can be altered within the political process, permitting new understandings of shared interests to emerge.[43] The important difference here is not the size of the governing coalition, but *the means* by which the governing coalition is formed. As John Dewey noted, majority rule need not be understood simply as method of tallying votes or aggregating preferences. "[W]hat is more significant is that the counting of heads compels prior recourse to methods of discussion, consultation, and persuasion. . . . Majority rule, just as majority rule, is as foolish as its critics charge it with being. But it never is *merely* majority rule."[44]

The basic point is that political deliberation does not require an ideal context of harmony and unanimity in order to occur. The very same legislatures that crank out pork-barrel policies keyed to particularistic interests are also capable of operating along different lines. Within American representative chambers, interests are neither merely orchestrated along strict party lines nor are all coalitions formed simply out of mutual (and fleeting) convenience. There is substantial empirical evidence that legislators discuss and deliberate on certain issues.[45] Such legislative activity is surprising if one assumes that representatives enter the legislature with a fully formed set of policy preferences matched by complete knowledge of how to realize their aims. But if one begins with the assumption that political decision making occurs under conditions

[41] Mansbridge 1980, 1981, and 1992.
[42] Cohen 1989.
[43] Reich 1988.
[44] Dewey 1927, p. 207, emphasis original.
[45] Maass 1983; Bessette 1994; and Krehbiel 1991.

of uncertainty, where legislators have only inchoate views of political ends and means, then the presence of deliberation is less surprising—for deliberation provides a mechanism for legislative learning.[46] The conflicting interests and disparate skills of representatives furnish the raw material for such deliberation.[47] Staffed with policy specialists from both ends of the political spectrum, legislative committees provide a means of eliciting information from conflicting sources.[48] Representatives may use the clash of argument and counterargument in committee to develop a more precise notion of what their ends actually are, as well as to amass information about the best means toward their preferred ends.[49] It is this development of views that creates opportunities for influence and exhortation, permitting legislators to persuade one another that a particular understanding of an issue is in the interests of all.[50] Indeed, insofar as conflict and uncertainty stimulate legislative learning, redistricting may present significant deliberative opportunities. Redistricting occurs under conditions of sharp conflict and tremendous uncertainty, without a clear sense of the best strategies or even a set of mutually consistent aims. The levels of conflict are certainly enough to preclude an idealized process of harmonious deliberation. Yet, the levels of uncertainty are such that some form of legislative learning may be a desirable and feasible option. Political deliberation, as a means of developing policy through conflict and argument, may well have a place in redistricting.

The foregoing remarks help dispel the notion that political delibera-

[46] Manin 1987; Kingdon 1993. The group view of deliberation misses this point.

[47] Krehbiel 1991, p. 78; Maass 1983, p. 12.

[48] Bessette 1994, pp. 150–81; Maass 1983, pp. 32–44.

[49] Committees also provide good information for the legislature as a whole because the check of bipartisanship prevents committees from using their informational advantage to secure policy outcomes that the median legislator would not prefer. In addition to bipartisanship, the United States Congress actually relies on a number of mechanisms designed to keep committees in check (see Krehbiel 1991, 79–101). Together these mechanisms help ensure that a committee cannot get the legislature to agree to a policy that is not in the latter's interest. Instead, the committee is limited to using its informational advantage to help enact policies in the interest of *both* the committee and the legislature.

[50] Political interaction among legislators can thus resemble Richard Neustadt's classic description of presidential power. "When one man shares authority with another, but does not gain or lose his job upon the other's whim, his willingness to act upon the urging of others turns on whether he conceives the action right for him. The essence of a President's persuasive task is to convince such men that what the White House wants of them is what they ought to do to for their sake and on their authority" (Nuestadt 1980, p. 27). This resemblance is noted by Krehbiel 1991.

tion is impossible, but they stop well short of demonstrating how deliberation can serve as a guide for action or reform. It is one thing to argue that legislators actually rely on deliberation as a vehicle of discovery and influence, but it is altogether another thing to formulate standards that indicate what counts as good or bad deliberation. With nothing more than empirical confirmation of deliberation's existence, there are no grounds on which to deal with the conceptual tensions of deliberative theory or to judge the quality of an actual deliberative process. Thus, the observation that legislators may exchange arguments to develop and expand their views tells us little about how widely the net of argumentation ought to be cast. Given an instance of deliberation, how would one know if the effort to persuade has been sufficiently broad? If one suspects that the deliberative process has not taken into account enough views, how many additional claims and arguments ought to be introduced?

There are no theoretical answers to such questions—a fact that is enough to make one skeptical of the claim that deliberative procedures can be established and enforced in representative legislatures.[51] The difficulty of formulating answers in the abstract should not, however, be allowed to overshadow answers developed through concrete political practice. Political ideals can be fleshed out within the political process, allowing political actors to work out the terms of the government which they operate. More specifically, deliberation *itself* may be used as a means of determining the grounds on which future deliberations ought to occur.[52] Legislators engaged in deliberation may unravel the conundrums that defy theorists working in abstraction and isolation.

The reliance on past deliberation to guide future deliberation is not without risks. The first is the possibility of selecting the wrong starting point. If one is to defer to deliberative cues for guidance about deliberation, it is critical that the initial set of cues be clearly identified. Assuming the first risk can be successfully run, a second risk is that the lessons of past political practice may be enforced at the expense of continuing deliberation. Amy Gutmann and Dennis Thompson, for example, scour specific instances of political deliberation in order to articulate the basic conditions necessary for deliberative practices to proliferate. Among other factors, Gutmann and Thompson stress the importance of reciprocity, requiring deliberators "to appeal to reasons that are shared or

---

[51] See Knight and Johnson 1994.
[52] See Williams 1995, and Miller 1992.

161

could come to be shared by our fellow citizens."[53] On this basis, Gutmann and Thompson work through a number of thorny political issues by eliminating arguments as unacceptable violations of reciprocity. The restrictions of reciprocity clearly facilitate reasoned political exchange, but it is hard to see how the external judgment of an argument's validity does not remove deliberation from the hands of the putative deliberators.[54] In any event, a robust standard of reciprocity is hardly appropriate in the judicial context, where the central concern is to ensure that claims of judicial power do not prevent the people from finally speaking for themselves.

With these risks in mind, can the Voting Rights Act be said to provide guidance for the judicial enforcement of political deliberation? Warren described the act as deliberative in its origins; it has also been deliberative in its broad development. Congress has revised and renewed the act four times over the past thirty years. On each occasion, the actions of a largely Democratic Congress were signed into law by Republican presidents, making the act truly bipartisan.[55] The national concern for the diversity of political voices has thus been stimulated and sustained by comprehensive argument and debate, suggesting that the struggle for meaningful political membership has been addressed through an extraordinary process of political deliberation.

Of course, to say that the act has been repeatedly reforged in the crucible of political deliberation is not to prove that political deliberation is the obvious goal of the act. At no point does the act discuss theories of deliberation — that was the work of Supreme Court majorities led by Chief Justice Warren. By the same token, however, the act endorses neither individualist nor group conceptions of political identity — those too were the work of justices attempting to make sense of equal political opportunity. While Congress and the president have established the broad framework of the act, it has fallen to the judiciary to determine what counts as fair minority representation within the confines of this framework.

The judiciary has retained this function even as the political branches

---

[53] Gutmann and Thompson 1996, p. 14.

[54] For an extended critique in this vein, see Berkowitz 1996.

[55] Indeed, the most far-reaching revisions to the act occurred in 1982, when Republicans held the Senate as well as the presidency. It is also worth noting that, unlike the Voting Rights Act, affirmative action policies have been developed largely through administrative directive and judicial decisions. It is only recently that broad deliberation on affirmative action within Congress and across branches is likely to occur.

have rebuked the Court.[56] In 1982, for example, Congress amended Section 2 of the Voting Rights Act, prohibiting all voting rules and procedures that had the effect of leaving minority groups with diminished political opportunity. Even though the 1982 amendments specifically rejected a judicially developed intent standard, Congress did not relieve the courts of their interpretative responsibilities. Congress fleshed out the "effects test" by offering various indicators of minority vote dilution, but nonetheless left it to the courts' "overall judgment" to determine exactly when a minority group suffered from unequal political opportunity. In exercising its "overall judgment" after 1982, the Supreme Court assessed the concrete effects of different electoral conditions—yet its interpretations were not confined solely to questions of electoral structure, nor could they be. The question of how electoral effects ought to be measured hinged on the selection of representational baselines against which equal political opportunity could be gauged. While the path of voting rights jurisprudence had been redirected by Congress, members of the Court continued to argue over the selection of representational baselines just as they had since minority representation first became an object of judicial concern.

The bottom line is that the Voting Rights Act, like other statutes, is always interpreted in the context of background principles expressing a particular vision of how politics ought to be organized and conducted.[57] The choice between different background principles depends on the relative merit of the political visions that they articulate. I have already described the alternative political visions generated by individualist and group approaches, indicating how they undermine popular sovereignty either by ignoring important group identities or by threatening the no-

---

[56] See chapters one, three, and five for my extended discussion of the points in this paragraph.

[57] Indeed, the Voting Rights Act admits a broader choice of background principles than some other programs deploying racial preferences. Consider affirmative action. Affirmative-action programs are sometimes taken to be strictly compensatory in design, circumventing conventional merit criteria in order to reward specific groups that have suffered past discrimination. (For a critical discussion of affirmative action as a backward-looking compensatory measure, see Sullivan, 1986.) The Voting Rights Act differs from such affirmative-action programs because there is neither mandatory criteria for designing electoral districts nor any right to be situated in a specific district—thus there is no obvious picture of the status quo *ex ante* that representational reform can restore. In this vein, it should also be noted that after 1982 the emphasis on discriminatory results explicitly moved the act away from compensatory rationales by sidelining the search for specific actors guilty of discrimination.

tion of a whole people. The critical question is whether political deliberation provides a baseline against which the judicial interpretation of the Voting Rights Act is better understood.

I believe that political deliberation is indeed the better option. Without demanding unrealistic consensus, the deliberative view takes redistricting to be a positive process, actively shaping and framing the political community. The emphasis on the active construction of political voice situates the deliberative view outside the zero-sum cycle of individualist and group claims. Against the individualist claim that racial redistricting inevitably balkanizes American politics, the deliberative approach allows room for the recognition of group claims. The Voting Rights Act singles out particular groups for protection — groups whose history of discrimination has been illuminated by congressional deliberations. Deliberation thrives on diversity, and the Voting Rights Act provides a means of ensuring the requisite cacophony of voices, calling into question electoral structures that have prevented racial and language minorities from electing candidates of their choice. Following the deliberative interpretation of the act, the judiciary should be committed to removing such electoral impediments.

Against the group inclination toward proportional racial representation, the deliberative view does not pursue the recognition of discrete racial identities as an end in itself. The aim of representative government here is not simply to mirror the electorate, but to resolve conflicting claims on the basis of argument and counterargument. The deliberative assembly provides an arena in which a shared democratic politics can be established — a domain in which the people and their representatives may finally speak for themselves. Where diversity is pursued for its own sake, legislatures do not promise to unite a fragmented people so much as make it impossible for a fragmented people to unite. The deliberative ideal calls for a different approach, seeking the creative transformation of conflict into ideas about common interests. This is not a guarantee of perfect consensus nor of continuous deliberation, for legislative learning does not occur on every issue nor does it necessarily yield harmonious agreement. The deliberative approach simply expects debates over fundamental political rules to be conducted with an eye toward shared interests. Interpreting the Voting Rights Act from this perspective, the judiciary should keep the locus of political learning within the legislature itself, requiring the kind of broad-based debate over basic rules undertaken by Congress in its initial consideration of the act.

In sum, then, the deliberative view of the Voting Rights Act requires the Court to be concerned (i) with the achievement of sufficient diversity inside legislatures and (ii) with the realization of deliberative procedures in the legislative determination of fundamental political rules. Political deliberation thus serves as both a means of justifying the act's passage and as model for the act's goals—a model to be realized in political assemblies subject to judicial overview. Unlike either the individualist or the group view of minority representation, the deliberative approach provides a way of exercising judicial authority while preserving the ultimate power of the sovereign people.

POLITICAL DELIBERATION AS A JUDICIAL STANDARD

As an engine of political deliberation, the Voting Rights Act has an obvious limitation. The act is broadly concerned with how legislative bodies produce electoral rules—a concern that directs attention toward the possibility of deliberation within the legislature rather than among the citizenry at large. Although it is neglected in the debate over minority representation, citizen deliberation has nonetheless been celebrated elsewhere.[58] Indeed, several commentators have located the mainsprings of political deliberation outside governmental institutions in the domain of civil society and social mores.[59] Even Madison, a strong advocate of political institutions, had a healthy appreciation of their limits. He claimed not only that representative institutions transmuted popular passion into reasonable government but also that this work required the prior cultivation of some political virtue. While American institutions did not presuppose that citizens were angels, they did suppose that citizens were fit for self-rule. "Were the pictures which have been drawn by the political jealousy of some among us faithful likenesses of the human character," Madison wrote, "the inference would be that there is not sufficient virtue among men for self-government; and that nothing less than the chains of despotism can restrain them from destroying and devouring one another."[60]

To the extent extra-institutional practices advance political deliberation, the Voting Rights Act can only be one part of the larger effort to

[58] For general analyses of citizen deliberation, see Fishkin 1991; Habermas 1989 and 1992; Kinder and Herzog 1993; and Barber 1984.

[59] This argument was most famously made by Tocqueville 1966 and more recently by Putnam 1993.

[60] Hamilton, Madison, and Jay 1961, No. 55, p. 346.

165

improve American government.[61] Even though a recognition of the act's limitations may spur additional reform, however, it should not prevent us from making the best use of the reforms already in place. The deliberative approach requires the Court to be concerned about legislative diversity and legislative learning. The final question is how the terms of this two-tiered judicial concern can be fleshed out.

First, the appropriate standard for legislative diversity can be drawn from *Thornburg v. Gingles*. In that decision, Justice Brennan took a cue from Congress and rightly focused his analysis on the concrete operation of electoral politics. He ruled that an at-large electoral system diluted votes only where a minority group was (i) politically cohesive, (ii) sufficiently large and geographically compact to form a majority in a single-member district, and (iii) opposed by a white-majority voting bloc often enough that the minority-preferred candidate usually lost. The emphasis on a few factual conditions streamlined voting rights litigation under Section 2, making it much easier for minority groups to gain the political voice that multi-member districts had previously denied them. Brennan called his approach "functionalist," claiming that only the interaction between voter behavior and electoral structures mattered, regardless of any broader account of what minority failure to win elections might mean. Unfortunately, functionalism did not serve Brennan well: it left him without a substantial justification either for using single-member districts as the vote dilution baseline or for ever continuing judicial inquiry where minorities had achieved sustained electoral success.

Relying on an understanding of political deliberation, the *Gingles* test can be reformulated in less restrictive terms. Historically, Americans introduced the single-member district as a mechanism for increasing the range of legislative voices.[62] In comparison to at-large elections, single-member districts permitted smaller majorities to elect candidates and expanded the pool of represented interests. Thus, single-member districts can be seen as the basic means of ensuring representational diversity; and, in turn, representational diversity can be seen as the raw material for legislative learning. As a result, the *Gingles*' measurement of minority voting strength against a baseline of single-member districts is

---

[61] For example, while the Voting Rights Act removes some of the obstacles facing language minorities, the act is silent on issues of citizenship. Without some effort to address the low citizenship levels among groups like Latinos, equal political opportunity will remain an elusive goal (see de la Garza and DeSipio 1993).

[62] Zagarri 1987, pp. 105–24.

racial classifications were hardly an accept-
political flow, the liberal exchange of informa-
the consideration of racial factors legitimate
ce. In the words of Justice Brennan, the length
ssional deliberations demonstrated that "[w]hat-
ect and undesirable counter-educational costs of
eaching racial devices, Congress . . . confront[ed]
before opting for an activist race-conscious reme-
by federal officials."[64] Following this example, the
re race-conscious redistricting to be conducted in the
ess-like deliberations. The most easily administrable
g this requirement is for the Court to push legislatures
n redistricting.

s of bipartisan redistricting are already employed in some
, Washington, and New York require a supermajority of
to ratify redistricting plans and, in doing so, essentially
participation of both parties. Several states, including Con-
v Jersey, Montana, and Hawaii, rely on balanced bipartisan
s either to recommend districting plans to the legislature or to
stricting plans in instances of legislative gridlock. As a matter of
ractice, bipartisan redistricting is somewhat more common than
l requirements would suggest. Whenever control of state gov-
is split between different parties, bipartisanship is generally nec-
o translate redistricting bills into law.

rtisan procedures move the politics of redistricting in a delibera-
irection by multiplying the viewpoints represented as well as in-
ing the amount of information gathered and arguments exchanged.[66]
uiring the consent of all major parties, bipartisan redistricting pre-
ts any party from enacting one-sided proposals. The only plans that
pass are those that serve the interests of all. Of course, critics of
partisan redistricting would paint a darker picture.[67] In their view, the
nly interests served by bipartisan redistricting are those of the incumbents. Bipartisan redistricting plans simply insulate incumbents from
electoral competition, creating a dense network of safe seats and con-
demning dissenters to the political margins.

[64] *UJO* at 176.
[65] Butler and Cain 1992, pp. 151–53.
[66] Dixon 1968, 1970, and 1982.
[67] Wells 1982. Members of the Court have made similar arguments. See Justice O'Connor's concurrence in *Davis v. Bandemer*, 478 U.S. 109, 154–55 (1986).

hardly arbi~
politic~^
vot~
pola~
the su~
political~
group's in~
is because p~
judicial inqui~
where minorit~
should retain res~
damental rules of ~

This brings us to~
deliberative approach~
point of the latest Cou~
tween the *Gingles* vote ~
tively unobjectionable, for~
around Section 2. *Shaw v. k*~
test as a legitimate mechanism~
tricts. The central issue in these ~
minority districts in the absence ~
In this context, a narrow Court m~
harms occur wherever "race for its o~
principles, [is] the legislature's domin~
drawing its district lines."[63] As I have ~
sense given an individualistic understandin~
erative approach rejects this understanding~
as the judicial standard that follows from it. ~
liberative approach directs judicial attention to~
fundamental political rules, with the purpose of ~
versity of voices are actually brought to bear on~
than attempting to discern whether race has been a ~
in redistricting, the goal is to ensure that redistricting~
deliberative fashion.

What does this mean in terms of an enforceable judi~
The one concrete example of legislative learning identified ~
involved the passage of the Voting Rights Act. Here delibe~
defined as a matter of extensive fact-finding, prolonged hear~

lengthy debate. Although~
able part of the ordinary~
tion and arguments ma~
in this particular insta~
and breadth of congre~
ever may be the indi~
employing such far-~
these considerations~
dial role supervised~
Court should requ~
context of Congr~
means of enforci~
toward bipartis~
Various form~
states.[65] Maine~
the legislature~
guarantee th~
necticut, Ne~
commission~
produce di~
political p~
the form~
ernment~
essary ~
Bip~
tive ~
creas~
Req~
ver~
ca~
b~
c~

---

[63] *Miller* at 2486.

1~

The most comprehensive studies of redistricting deflate such objections.[68] In practice, successful two-party gerrymanders are substantially more difficult to engineer than successful one-party gerrymanders. This is so because competition for constituencies heightens the conflict and uncertainty of redistricting, making the design of safe seats more problematic. Under bipartisan conditions, where both parties are forced to agree on a single plan, the competition among representatives is the sharpest and the consequences of redistricting are the least predictable. The result is that bipartisan redistricting plans not only exhibit a lower degree of partisan bias than single-party alternatives but also produce a district scheme that is more sensitive to vote swings within the electorate. Thus, bipartisan redistricting does not simply amount to an incumbent protection plan; on the contrary, by pitting parties against one another, bipartisan redistricting loosens incumbents' grip on their constituencies and keeps the legislature responsive to the electorate as a whole. Through conflict and counterargument, policy is made in the common interests of all.

One may agree that bipartisan redistricting is preferable to single-party redistricting yet argue that redistricting according to neutral criteria is superior to both.[69] The difficulty with this argument is that there are no truly neutral criteria in redistricting. Every district boundary, whether drawn by the interested legislator or randomly assigned by computer, shapes the opportunities for political mobilization and power. Robert Dixon, Jr., captured this insight thirty years ago with the dictum "all districting is gerrymandering."[70] The insistence that district lines be drawn according to mathematical definitions of compactness does not negate the political consequences of redistricting so much as remove these consequences from conscious control. Political voice is made, not found. The question of how political voice should be made cannot be answered by denying that an act of construction is necessary in the first place.

Finally, one might reject bipartisan redistricting as a recipe for political deadlock, preventing legislatures from reaching agreement and forcing the courts to shoulder all redistricting responsibilities. This objection is similar to those questioning the possibility of political deliberation and is similarly overdrawn. The goal of bipartisan redistricting is not to

[68] Gelman and King 1994.
[69] Wells 1982.
[70] Dixon 1968, p. 462.

guarantee perfect consensus (which would be a practical impossibility) but to facilitate legislative learning, ensuring that representatives develop their views in the context of conflicting arguments. It is true that bipartisan redistricting calls for greater coordination than the single-party process. Yet bipartisan procedures can be designed to encourage coordination.[71] Moreover, consistent pressure applied by a judiciary committed to bipartisan redistricting would most likely lessen incentives to blockade the legislative process. If the courts respond to legislative recalcitrance by advocating more bipartisanship, the frequency of such recalcitrance may well decline.[72]

IMPLICATIONS

Together, then, the general requirements of legislative diversity and legislative learning translate into the specific enforcement of the *Gingles* test and bipartisan redistricting. These requirements are interdependent. Bipartisan redistricting plans are free to recognize a plethora of political identities, provided that they do not dilute minority voting power as defined by the *Gingles* test. The *Gingles* test, as well as the Voting Rights Act itself, may in turn be altered by deliberation as Congress reconsiders the prerequisites of successful legislative learning.

In articulating these judicial standards, I have merely outlined the deliberative approach to minority representation, leaving unexplored

---

[71] For example, if its ten-member bipartisan redistricting committee failed to produce a plan, New Jersey required a tie-breaking, eleventh member (appointed by the Chief Justice of the New Jersey Supreme Court) to be added to the committee (Dixon 1968, pp. 380–85). Where the legislature itself undertakes bipartisan redistricting, agreement may be encouraged by denying representatives certain privileges of office unless a plan is passed (see Cain 1992, p. 139).

[72] Inevitably, the courts will be called upon to do some redistricting, just as they are called upon today. The deliberative approach would still make a difference. In the context of minority representation, the individualist Court majority currently requires court-ordered redistricting plans to be guided by legislative policies underlying the existing redistricting plan, *provided* that racial considerations were not the predominant factor in designing the existing plan (*Abrams v. Johnson*, 65 U.S.L.W. 4478 [1997]). The deliberative approach dispenses with the individualist baseline and, instead, would have courts defer to the policies underlying existing plans, provided that these plans do not dilute voting power (as measured by the *Gingles* test) and granting special consideration to legislative choices made in a bipartisan process.

questions of scope and detail.[73] I have done so because the precise reso-
lutions to legal controversies are necessarily dependent on the partic-
ularities of the case at hand. There is little point in specifying a comprehensive blueprint for judicial practice when the dynamics of that
practice continually work to change the blueprint. Instead, my goal has
been to describe a general mode of judicial entrepreneurship that permits the Court to address minority representation in the name of the
people without finally preventing the people from speaking for themselves. Unlike the individualist and group views that currently prevail,
the deliberative approach neither precludes the recognition of important
group identities nor undermines the notion of the whole people as a
coherent political actor. Political deliberation simply does not depend
on an essentialized, prepolitical understanding of "the people." Instead,
deliberation is based on the notion that the political identity develops
during the process of debate and discussion, making it possible for decisions to be made in the common interest. The deliberative approach
enlists the judiciary to uphold the legislative preconditions for such debate and discussion, ensuring that the politics of minority representation unfolds in the context of legislative learning.

Working toward the realization of political deliberation, the Court
would take a different path than the one it has followed since *Shaw v.
Reno*. Contrary to the individualist majority, the Court would not sift
through redistricting records in order to root out the political recognition of racial identities. And, contrary to the group dissenters, the Court
would not simply accept any legislative recognition of racial identity
that did not lead to vote dilution. A deliberative Court would remain
sensitive to the iniquities of vote dilution while scrutinizing the actual
process of redistricting for traces of political deliberation.[74] For exam-

---

[73] For example, I leave open the question of how rigorously bipartisan procedures
should be enforced outside the context of redistricting and minority representation. Extensions of the deliberative approach would lead to very different outcomes in cases like
Presley v. Etowah County Commission, 502 U.S. 491 (1992). See chapter five for my
discussion of this case. For more general arguments about how the judiciary may help to
ensure political deliberation, see Sunstein 1984 and 1993. For an account of how the
Court might pursue the same goal in the specific context of affirmative action, see Strauss
1996.

[74] In scrutinizing the redistricting process, the Court would assign positive value to the
Department of Justice's involvement in redistricting where it feeds into the deliberative
goals of bipartisanship. As Justice Brennan pointed out in *UJO*, the preclearance process

ple, in considering the North Carolina district that was the subject of *Shaw*, a deliberative Court would pay particular attention to the fact that redistricting had been dominated by a single party.[75] From this perspective, the problem would not be that the legislature drew districts that granted racial groups political recognition but that the drawing of such districts occurred without the degrees of conflict, debate, and coordination that bipartisan procedures would engender.

Pursuing this approach, the Court may provide few across-the-board rulings about race-conscious districts. The central question will always be whether the recognition of racial identities is legitimate in any given process of redistricting. While the answers to these question will inevitably vary according to local context, all such answers will be related to the end of achieving political deliberation rather than to the end of expressing an inherently problematic view of what political identity must be. And in our government, where the people should remain sovereign even as the Court speaks in their name, political deliberation is an end well worth pursuing.

---

transforms the attorney general into a "champion" of minority interests — a role that enables him to invalidate any discriminatory electoral rules that covered subdivisions might attempt to pass (*UJO* at 175). Active involvement by the Department of Justice should thus be taken as affirmative (though not conclusive) evidence of deliberation. Such an approach would contrast sharply with the judicial criticism the Department of Justice has received in recent cases like *Miller*.

[75] See Justice Stevens's dissent in *Shaw v. Hunt*, 116 S.Ct. 1894 (1996), for an account of North Carolina redistricting politics.

TABLE OF CASES

Note: This is a list of cases cited in text, followed by the page numbers on which they appear.

Reference List

Abraham, Henry J. 1993. *The Judicial Process*. 6th ed. New York: Oxford University Press.

Abrams, Kathryn. 1988. "'Raising Politics Up': Minority Political Participation and Section 2 of the Voting Rights Act." *New York University Law Review* 63:449–531.

———. 1993. "Relationships of Representation in Voting Rights Act Jurisprudence." *Texas Law Review* 71:1409–35.

Abramson, Jeffrey. 1994. *We, the Jury*. New York: Basic Books.

Ackerman, Bruce. 1991. *We the People: I Foundations*. Cambridge: Belknap Press of Harvard University Press.

Alexander, Larry. 1989. "Lost in the Political Thicket." *Florida Law Review* 41:563–79.

Bailyn, Bernard. 1967. *The Ideological Origins of the American Revolution*. Cambridge: Belknap Press of Harvard University Press.

Barber, Benjamin. 1984. *Strong Democracy*. Berkeley and Los Angeles: University of California Press.

———. 1993. "Book Review: American Citizenship." *Political Theory* 21:146–53.

Barber, Sotorios. 1989. "Normative Theory, the 'New Institutionalism,' and the Future of Public Law." In *Studies in American Political Development*, ed. Karen Orren and Stephen Skowronek. vol. 3. New Haven: Yale University Press.

Baum, Lawrence. 1988. "Measuring Policy Change in the U.S. Supreme Court." *American Political Science Review* 82:905–12.

———. 1992a. *The Supreme Court*. 4th ed. Washington, D.C: Congressional Quarterly Press.

———. 1992b. "Membership Change and Collective Voting Change in the United States Supreme Court." *Journal of Politics* 54:3–24.

Beard, Charles. 1949. *An Economic Interpretation of the Constitution of the United States*. New York: Macmillan.

Beer, Samuel. 1993. *To Make a Nation: The Rediscovery of American Federalism*. Cambridge: Harvard University Press.

Beitz, Charles. 1989. *Political Equality*. Princeton: Princeton University Press.

Bell, Derrick. 1987. *And We Are Not Saved: The Elusive Quest For Racial Justice*. New York: Basic Books.

Berkowitz, Peter. 1993. "Book Review: *We the People*." *Eighteenth Century Studies* 26:692–97.

———. 1996. "The Debating Society." *New Republic*, Nov. 25, pp. 36–42.

Bessette, Joseph, M. 1994. *The Mild Voice of Reason*. Chicago: University of Chicago Press.

Bickel, Alexander. 1962. *The Least Dangerous Branch: The Supreme Court at the Bar of Politics*. Indianapolis: Bobbs-Merrill.

———. 1971. "The Supreme Court and Re-apportionment." In *Reapportionment in the 1970s*, ed. Nelson Polsby. Berkeley and Los Angeles: University of California Press.

———. 1975. *The Morality of Consent*. New Haven: Yale University Press.

Blacksher, James U. 1993. "Non-majoritarian Representation in American Politics: For Whites Only?" Paper presented at the Annual Meeting of the American Political Science Association, Washington, D.C., Sept. pp. 2–5.

Bositis, David A. 1994. *The Congressional Black Caucus in the 103rd Congress*. Washington, D.C.: Joint Center for Economic and Political Studies.

Brigham, John. 1978. *Constitutional Language: An Interpretation of Judicial Decision*. Westport, Conn.: Greenwood Press.

———. 1987. *The Cult of the Court*. Philadephia: Temple University Press.

Browning, Rufus, Dale Marshall, and David Tabb. 1984. *Protest Is Not Enough: The Struggle of Blacks and Hispanics for Equality in Urban Politics*. Berkeley and Los Angeles: University of California Press.

Buchanan, James M., and Gordon Tullock. 1962. *The Calculus of Consent*. Ann Arbor: University of Michigan Press.

Bullock, Charles S. 1995. "Affirmative Action Districts: In Whose Faces Will They Blow Up?" *Campaigns and Elections*, April, pp. 22–23.

Bumiller, Kristin. 1988. *The Civil Rights Society*. Baltimore: Johns Hopkins University Press.

Butler, David, and Bruce Cain. 1992. *Congressional Redistricting*. New York: Macmillan.

Butler, Katherine. 1985. "Denial or Abridgement of the Right to Vote: What Does It Mean?" In *The Voting Rights Act: Consequences and Implications*, ed. Lorn Foster. New York: Praeger.

Cain, Bruce. 1984. *The Reapportionment Puzzle*. Berkeley and Los Angeles: University of California Press.

———. 1990. "Perspectives on Davis v. Bandemer: Views of the Practitioner, Theorist, and Reformer." In *Political Gerrymandering and the Courts*, ed. Bernard Grofman. New York: Agathon.

———. 1991. "The Contemporary Context of Ethnic and Racial Politics in California." In *Racial and Ethnic Politics in California*, ed. Michael C. Preston and Byran O. Jackson. Berkeley: IGS Press.

———. 1992. "Voting Rights and Democratic Theory—Where Do We Go from Here?" In *Controversies in Minority Voting*, ed. Bernard Grofman and Chandler Davidson. Washington, D.C.: Brookings.

Cain, Bruce, and Kenneth Miller. 1996. "The Fragile Logic of Voting Rights: Extending the VRA to 'Other Minorities.'" Paper presented at the Annual

Meeting of the American Political Science Association, San Francisco, Aug. 29–Sept. 1.

Caldeira, Gregory. 1992. "Litigation, Lobbying, and the Voting Rights Law." In *Controversies in Minority Voting*, ed. Bernard Grofman and Chandler Davidson. Washington, D.C.: Brookings.

Calhoun, John C. 1953. *A Disquisition on Government and Selections from the Discourses*. Ed. C. Gordon Post. Indianapolis: Bobbs-Merrill.

Cameron, Charles, David Epstein, and Sharon O'Halloran. 1996. "Do Majority-Minority Districts Maximize Substantive Black Representation in Congress?" *American Political Science Review* 90:794–812.

Canon, David T., Matthew M. Schousen, and Patrick J. Sellers. 1996. "The Supply Side of Congressional Redistricting: Race and Strategic Politicians, 1972–1992." *Journal of Politics* 58:846–62.

Carter, Leif H. 1985. *Contemporary Constitutional Lawmaking*. New York: Pergamon Press.

Cohen, Joshua. 1989. "Deliberation and Democratic Legitimacy." In *The Good Polity: Normative Analyses of the State*, ed. Alan Hamlin and Philip Pettit. New York: Basil Blackwell.

Connolly, William E. 1983. *The Terms of Political Discourse*. 2d ed. Princeton: Princeton University Press.

Constable, Marianne. 1994. *The Law of the Other: The Mixed Jury and Changing Conceptions of Citizenship, Law, and Knowledge*. Chicago: University of Chicago Press.

Corwin, Edward S. 1928. "The 'Higher Law' Background of American Constitutional Law." *Harvard Law Review* 42:149–85, 365–409.

Dahl, Robert. 1956. *A Preface to Democratic Theory*. Chicago: University of Chicago Press.

———. 1957. "Decision-Making in a Democracy: The Supreme Court as a National Policy-Maker." *Journal of Public Law* 6:279–95.

———. 1961. *Who Governs?* New Haven: Yale University Press.

Davidson, Chandler. 1984. "Minority Vote Dilution: An Overview." In *Minority Vote Dilution*, ed. Chandler Davidson. Washington, D.C.: Howard University Press.

———. 1992. "The Voting Rights Act: A Brief History." In *Controversies in Minority Voting*, ed. Bernard Grofman and Chandler Davidson. Washington, D.C.: Brookings.

Davidson, Chandler, and Bernard Grofman. 1994. *Quiet Revolution in the South*. Princeton: Princeton University Press.

Days, Drew S., III. 1992. "Section 5 and the Role of the Justice Department." In *Controversies in Minority Voting*, ed. Bernard Grofman and Chandler Davidson. Washington, D.C.: Brookings.

de la Garza, Rodolfo O., and Louis DeSipio. 1993. "Save the Baby, Change the Bathwater, and Scrub the Tub: Latino Electoral Participation after Seven-

177

teen Years of Voting Rights Coverage." *Texas Law Review* 71:1479–1539.

Delgado, Richard. 1989. "Storytelling for Oppositionists and Others: A Plea for Narrative." *Michigan Law Review* 87:2411–41.

———. 1993. "Words that Wound: A Tort Action for Racial Insults, Epithets, and Name Calling." In *Words that Wound*, ed. Mari J. Matsuda, Charles R. Lawrence III, Richard Delgado, and Kimberle Williams Crenshaw. San Francisco: Westview Press.

D'Entreves, Allesandro Passerin. 1970. *Natural Law*. 2d rev. ed. London: Hutchinson University Library.

Dewey, John. 1927. *The Public and Its Problems*. Athens: Ohio University Press.

Diamond, Raymond. 1989. "No Call to Glory: Thurgood Marshall's Thesis on the Intent of a Pro-slavery Constitution." *Vanderbilt Law Review* 42:93–131.

Dixon, Robert G., Jr. 1968. *Democratic Representation: Reapportionment in Law and Politics*. New York: Oxford University Press.

———. 1970. "The Warren Court Crusade for the Holy Grail of 'One Man–One Vote.'" *Supreme Court Review 1969*, pp. 219–70.

———. 1971. "The Court, the People and 'One Man, One Vote.'" In *Reapportionment in the 1970s*, ed. Nelson Polsby. Berkeley and Los Angeles: University of California Press.

———. 1982. "Fair Criteria and Procedures for Establishing Legislative Districts." In *Representation and Redistricting Issues*, ed. Bernard Grofman, Arend Lijphart, Robert McCay, and Howard Scarrow. Lexington, Mass.: D.C. Heath.

Dworkin, Ronald. 1977. *Taking Rights Seriously*. Cambridge: Harvard University Press.

———. 1985. *A Matter of Principle*. Cambridge: Harvard University Press.

Easterbrook, Frank H. 1983. "Statutes' Domains." *University of Chicago Law Review* 50:533–52.

Edley, Christopher, Jr. 1986. "Affirmative Action and the Rights Rhetoric Trap." In *The Moral Foundations of Civil Rights*, ed. Robert K. Fullinwider and Claudia Mills. Totowa, N.J.: Rowman and Littlefield.

Elliot, Ward E. Y. 1974. *The Rise of Guardian Democracy*. Cambridge: Harvard University Press.

Ely, John Hart. 1980. *Democracy and Distrust*. Cambridge: Harvard University Press.

Engstrom, Richard L. 1995. "Voting Rights Districts: Debunking Myths." *Campaigns and Elections*, April, pp. 24, 46.

Epstein, Lee, and Joseph F. Kobylka. 1992. *The Supreme Court and Legal Change*. Chapel Hill: University of North Carolina Press.

Eskridge, William M., Jr. 1988. "Politics without Romance: Implications of Public Choice Theory for Statutory Interpretation." *Virginia Law Review* 74:275–338.

———. 1991. "Overriding Supreme Court Statutory Interpretation Decisions." *Yale Law Journal* 101:331–455.

———. 1992. "Cycling Legislative Intent." *International Review of Law and Economics* 12:260–62.

Farber, Daniel A., and Philip P. Frickey. 1988. "Legislative Intent and Public Choice." *Virginia Law Review* 74:423–69.

Fish, Stanley. 1994. *There's No Such Thing as Free Speech*. New York: Oxford University Press.

Fishkin, James S. 1991. *Democracy and Deliberation*. New Haven: Yale University Press.

Fiss, Owen M. 1976. "Groups and the Equal Protection Clause." *Philosophy and Public Affairs* 5:107–77.

Foner, Eric. 1988. "Rights and the Consitution in Black Life during the Civil War and Reconstruction." In *The Constitution and American Life*, ed. David Thelen. Ithaca: Cornell University Press.

Fraga, Luis. 1992. "Latino Political Incorporation and the Voting Rights Act." In *Controversies in Minority Voting*, ed. Bernard Grofman and Chandler Davidson. Washington, D.C.: Brookings.

Fraga, Luis, and Bari Anhalt. 1993. "Ethnic Politics, Public Policy, and the Public Interest." Paper presented at the Annual Meeting of the American Political Science Association, Washington, D.C., Sept. 2–5.

Frankfurter, Felix. 1956. "The Reading of Statutes." In *Of Law and Men: Papers and Addresses of Felix Frankfurter*, ed. Philip Elman. Hamden, Conn.: Archon Books.

Freeman, Alan. 1989. "Legitimizing Racial Discrimination through Antidiscrimination Law: A Critical Review of Supreme Court Doctrine." In *Critical Legal Studies*, ed. Alan Hutchinson. Totowa, N.J.: Rowman and Littlefield.

Fuller, Lon. 1967. *Legal Fictions*. Stanford: Stanford University Press.

Garvey, Gerald. 1971. *Constitutional Bricolage*. Princeton: Princeton University Press.

Geertz, Clifford. 1973. *The Interpretation of Cultures*. New York: Basic Books.

———. 1983. *Local Knowledge*. New York: Basic Books.

Gelfand, David M., and Terry E. Allbritton. 1989. "Conflict and Congruence in One-person, One-vote and Racial Vote Dilution Litigation: Issues Resolved and Unresolved by Board of Estimate v. Morris." *Journal of Law and Politics* 6:93–123.

Gelman, Andrew, and Gary King. 1994. "Enhancing Democracy through Legislative Redistricting." *American Political Science Review* 88:541–59.

George, Tracey, and Lee Epstein. 1992. "On the Nature of Supreme Court Decisionmaking." *American Political Science Review* 86:323–37.

Gillman, Howard. 1993. *The Constitution Beseiged: The Rise and Demise of Lochner Era Police Powers Jurisprudence*. Durham: Duke University Press.

Glendon, Mary Ann. 1991. *Rights Talk: The Impoverishment of Political Discourse*. New York: Free Press.

Goodin, Robert E. 1996. "Institutionalizing the Public Interest: The Defense of Deadlock and Beyond." *American Political Science Review* 90:331–43.

Graham, Hugh Davis. 1992. "Voting Rights and the American Regulatory State." In *Controversies in Minority Voting*, ed. Bernard Grofman and Chandler Davidson. Washington, D.C.: Brookings.

Grofman, Bernard, ed. 1990. *Political Gerrymandering and the Courts*. New York: Agathon.

———. 1992. "Expert Witness Testimony and the Evolution of Voting Rights Case Law." In *Controversies in Minority Voting*, ed. Bernard Grofman and Chandler Davidson. Washington, D.C.: Brookings.

———. 1993. "Would Vince Lomabardi Have Been Right If He Had Said, 'When It Comes to Redistricting, Race Isn't Everything, It's the Only Thing'?" *Cardozo Law Review* 14:1237–76.

Grofman, Bernard, and Chandler Davidson, eds. 1992. *Controversies in Minority Voting*. Washington, D.C.: Brookings.

Grofman, Bernard, Lisa Handley, and Richard Niemi. 1992. *Minority Representation and the Quest for Voting Equality*. New York: Cambridge University Press.

Guinier, C. Lani. 1991a. "The Triumph of Tokenism: The Voting Rights Act and the Theory of Black Electoral Success." *Michigan Law Review* 89:1077–1154.

———. 1991b. "No Two Seats: The Elusive Quest for Political Equality." *Virginia Law Review* 77:1413–1514.

———. 1992a. "Voting Rights and Democratic Theory: Where Do We Go from Here?" In *Controversies in Minority Voting*, ed. Bernard Grofman and Chandler Davidson. Washington, D.C.: Brookings.

———. 1992b. "Development of the Franchise: 1982 Voting Rights Amendments." In *Voting Rights in America*, ed. Karen McGill Arrington and William Taylor. Washington, D.C.: Leadership Conference Fund.

———. 1993a. "The Representation of Minority Interests: The Question of Single-Member Districts." *Cardozo Law Review* 14:1135–74.

———. 1993b. "Groups, Representation, and Race-conscious Districting: A Case of the Emperor's Clothes." *Texas Law Review* 71:1589–1642.

———. 1994. "[E]racing Democracy: The Voting Rights Cases." *Harvard Law Review* 108:109–37.

Gutmann, Amy, and Dennis Thompson. 1996. *Democracy and Disagreement*. Cambridge: Belknap Press of Harvard University Press.

Habermas, Jurgen. 1989. *The Structural Transformation of the Public Sphere*. Trans. Thomas Burger with the assistance of Fredrick Lawrence. Cambridge: MIT Press.

———. 1992. "Further Reflections on the Public Sphere." In *Habermas and the Public Sphere*, ed. Craig Calhoun. Cambridge: MIT Press.

——. 1996. "Three Normative Models of Democracy." In *Democracy and Difference*, ed. Seyla Benhabib. Princeton: Princeton University Press.

Hacker, Andrew. 1992. *Two Nations: Black and White, Separate, Hostile, Unequal*. New York: Charles Scribner's Sons.

Hamilton, Alexander, James Madison, and John Jay. 1961. *The Federalist Papers*. New York: Mentor.

Hartz, Louis. 1955. *The Liberal Tradition in America*. New York: Harcourt Brace Jovanovich.

Hill, Kevin A. 1995. "Does the Creation of Majority Black Districts Aid Republicans?" *Journal of Politics* 75:384–401.

Hirsch, H. N. 1992. *A Theory of Liberty: The Constitution and Minorities*. New York: Routledge.

Horwitz, Morton J. 1985. "Santa Clara Revisted: The Development of Corporate Theory." *West Virginia Law Review* 88:173–224.

——. 1992. *The Transformation of American Law, 1870–1960*. New York: Oxford University Press.

Issacharoff, Samuel. 1992. "Polarized Voting and the Political Process: The Transformation of Voting Rights Jurisprudence." *Michigan Law Review* 90:1833–91.

——. 1996. "The Constitutional Contours of Race and Politics." *Supreme Court Review 1995*, pp. 45–70.

Jacobson, Gary C. 1990. *The Electoral Origins of Divided Government*. Boulder, Colo.: Westview Press.

Jacobson, Norman. 1963. "Political Science and Political Education." *American Political Science Review* 57:561–69.

Jones, Mack. 1985. "The Voting Rights Act as an Interventionist Strategy for Social Change: Symbolism or Substance?" In *The Voting Rights Act: Consequences and Implications*, ed. Lorn Foster. New York: Praeger.

Judd, Dennis, and Todd Swanstrom. 1994. *City Politics*. New York: HarperCollins.

Kalman, Laura. 1986. *Legal Realsim at Yale, 1927–1960*. Chapel Hill: University of North Carolina Press.

Karlan, Pamela. 1989. "Maps and Misreadings: The Role of Geographic Compactness in Racial Vote Dilution Litigation." *Harvard Civil Rights–Civil Liberties Review* 24:173–248.

——. 1991. "Undoing the Right Thing: Single-Member Offices and the Voting Rights Act." *Virginia Law Review* 77:1–45.

——. 1993. "The Rights to Vote: Some Pessimism about Formalism." *Texas Law Review* 71:1705–40.

——. 1994. "All over the Map: The Supreme Court's Voting Rights Triology." *Supreme Court Review 1993*, pp. 245–87.

Karlan, Pamela, and Peyton McCrary. 1988. "Without Fear and Without Research: Abigail Thernstrom on the Voting Rights Act." *Journal of Law and Politics* 4:751–77.

181

Kelly, Michael. 1995. "Segregation Anxeity." *New Yorker*, Nov. 20, pp. 43–54.

Kennedy, Duncan. 1980. "Toward an Historical Understanding of Legal Consciousness: The Case of Classical Legal Thought in America, 1850–1940." In *Research in Law and Sociology*, ed. Steven Sptizer, vol. 3. Greewich, Conn.: JJAI Press.

Kenyon, Cecelia, ed. 1966. *The Antifederalists*. Indianapolis: Bobbs-Merrill.

Kettner, James. 1978. *The Development of American Citizenship, 1608–1870*. Chapel Hill: University of North Carolina Press.

Kinder, Donald R., and Don Herzog. 1993. "Democratic Discussion." In *Reconsidering the Democratic Public*, ed. George E. Marcus and Russell Hanson. University Park, Pa.: Penn State University Press.

King, Gary, John Bruce, and Andrew Gelman. 1993. "Standards of Racial Fairness in Legislative Redistricting." Occasional Paper 92-11, Center for American Political Studies, Harvard University.

Kingdon, John W. 1993. "Politicians, Self-Interest, and Ideas." In *Reconsidering the Democratic Public*, ed. George E. Marcus and Russell Hanson. University Park, Pa.: Penn State University Press.

Klare, Karl E. 1978. "Judicial Deradicalization of the Wagner Act and the Origins of Modern Legal Consciousness, 1937–1941." *Minnesota Law Review* 62:265–339.

Knight, Jack, and James Johnson. 1994. "Aggregation and Deliberation: On the Possibility of Democratic Legitimacy." *Political Theory* 22:277–96.

Kousser, J. Morgan. 1984. "The Undermining of the First Reconstruction: Lessons for the Second." In *Minority Vote Dilution*, ed. Chandler Davidson. Washington, D.C.: Howard University Press.

———. 1992. "The Voting Rights Act and the Two Reconstructions." In *Controversies in Minority Voting*, ed. Bernard Grofman and Chandler Davidson. Washington, D.C.: Brookings.

Krehbiel, Keith. 1991. *Information and Legislative Organization*. Ann Arbor: University of Michigan Press.

Kymlicka, Will. 1989. *Liberalism, Community and Culture*. New York: Oxford University Press.

Lakoff, George, and Mark Johnson. 1980. *Metaphors We Live By*. Chicago: University of Chicago Press.

Lane, Charles. 1991. "Ghetto Chic: New York's Redistricting Mess." *New Republic*, Aug. 8, pp. 14–16.

Lasser, William. 1988. *The Limits of Judicial Power*. Chapel Hill: University of North Carolina Press.

Lawrence, Charles R., III, Mari J. Matsuda, Richard Delgado, and Kimberle Williams Crenshaw. 1993. Introduction to *Words That Wound*, ed. Mari J. Matsuda, Charles R. Lawrence, III, Richard Delgado, and Kimberle Williams Crenshaw. San Francisco: Westview Press.

Levi, Edward. 1949. *An Introduction to Legal Reasoning*. Chicago: University of Chicago Press.

Levinson, Sanford. 1985. "Gerrymandering and the Brooding Omnipresence of Proportional Representation: Why Won't It Go Away?" *UCLA Law Review* 33:257–81.

Llewellyn, Karl N. 1950. "Remarks on the Theory of Appellate Decision and the Rules or Cannons about How Statutes Are to Be Construed." *Vanderbilt Law Review* 3:395–406.

Lloyd, Randall. 1995. "Separating Partisanship from Party in Judicial Research: Reapportionment in the U.S. District Courts." *American Political Science Review* 89: 413–20.

Lowenstein, David, and Jonathan Steinberg. 1985. "The Quest for Legislative Districting in the Public Interest: Elusive or Illusory?" *UCLA Law Review* 33:1–76.

Lowi, Theodore. 1979. *The End of Liberalism*. 2d ed. New York: W. W. Norton.

Lublin, David Ian. 1995. "Race, Representation, and Redistricting." In *Classifying by Race*, ed. Paul E. Peterson. Princeton: Princeton University Press.

Lynd, Staughton. 1967. *Class Conflict, Slavery and the United States Constitution*. Indianapolis: Bobbs-Merrill.

Maass, Arthur. 1983. *Congress and the Common Good*. New York: Basic Books.

Manin, Bernard. 1987. "On Legitimacy and Political Deliberation." *Political Theory* 15:338–68.

Mansbridge, Jane. 1980. *Beyond Adversary Democracy*. New York: Basic Books.

———. 1981. "Living with Conflict: Representation in the Theory of Adversary Democracy." *Ethics* 91:466–76.

———. 1992. "A Deliberative Theory of Interest Representation." In *The Politics of Interests*, ed. Mark Petraca. Boulder, Colo.: Westview Press.

———. 1996. "In Defense of 'Descriptive' Representation." Paper presented at the Annual Meeting of the American Political Science Association, San Francisco, Aug. 29–Sept. 1.

Marks, Brian A. 1989. "A Model of Judicial Influence on Congressional Policymaking: Grove City College v. Bell (1984)." Ph.D. diss., Washington University.

Massaro, Toni M. 1989. "Empathy, Legal Storytelling, and the Rule of Law: New Words, Old Wounds." *Michigan Law Review* 87:2099–2127.

Matsuda, Mari J. 1993. "Public Response to Racist Speech: Considering the Victim's Story." In *Words that Wound*, ed. Mari J. Matsuda, Charles R. Lawrence, III, Richard Delgado, and Kimberle Williams Crenshaw. San Francisco: Westview Press.

Maveety, Nancy. 1991. *Representation Rights and the Burger Years*. Ann Arbor: University of Michigan Press.

McCloskey, Robert G. 1960. *The American Supreme Court.* Chicago: University of Chicago Press.

McCubbins, Mathew D., and Thomas Schwartz. 1988. "Congress, the Courts, and Public Policy: Consequences of the One Man, One Vote Rule." *American Journal of Political Science* 32:388–415.

McDonald, Laughlin. 1992. "The 1982 Amendments to Section 2 and Minority Representation." In *Controversies in Minority Voting,* ed. Bernard Grofman and Chandler Davidson. Washington, D.C.: Brookings.

Melnick, R. Shep. 1994. *Between the Lines: Interpreting Welfare Rights.* Washington, D.C.: Brookings.

Mensch, Elizabeth. 1982. "The History of Mainstream Legal Thought." In *The Politics of Law,* ed. David Kairys. New York: Pantheon Press.

Miller, David. 1992. "Deliberative Democracy and Social Choice." *Political Studies* 40:54–67.

Minow, Martha. 1987a. "Foreword: Justice Engendered." *Harvard Law Review* 101:10–95.

———. 1987b. "Interpreting Rights: An Essay for Robert Cover." *Yale Law Review* 96:1860–1915.

Moore, Wayne D. 1996. *Constitutional Rights and Powers of the People.* Princeton: Princeton University Press.

Mouffe, Chantal. 1994. "Political Liberalism, Neutrality and the Political." *Ratio Juris* 7:314–24.

Murphy, Walter. 1964. *Elements of Judicial Strategy.* Chicago: University of Chicago Press.

NAACP Legal Defense & Educational Fund. 1994. "The Effect of Section 2 of the Voting Rights Act on the 1994 Congressional Elections." NAACP Legal Defense & Educational Fund, New York.

Nedelsky, Jennifer. 1990a. *Private Property and the Limits of American Constitutionalism.* Chicago: University of Chicago Press.

———. 1990b. "Law, Boundaries, and the Bounded Self." *Representations* 30:162–89.

Neustadt, Richard E. 1980. *Presidential Power: The Politics of Leadership from FDR to Carter.* New York: Macmillan.

Newmyer, R. Kent. 1988. "Harvard Law School, New England Legal Culture, and the Antebellum Origins of American Jurisprudence." In *The Constitution and American Life,* ed. David Thelen. Ithaca: Cornell University Press.

Noonan, John T., Jr. 1976. *Persons & Masks of the Law.* New York: Farrar, Straus & Giroux.

O'Brien, David M. 1983. "Reconsidering Whence and Whither Political Jurisprudence." *Western Political Quarterly* 36:558–63.

O'Neill, Timothy J. 1981. "The Language of Equality in a Constitutional Order." *American Political Science Review* 75:626–35.

O'Rourke, Timothy G. 1992. "The 1982 Amendments and the Voting Rights

Paradox." In *Controversies in Minority Voting*, ed. Bernard Grofman and Chandler Davidson. Washington, D.C.: Brookings.

Parker, Frank. 1990. *Black Votes Count*. Chapel Hill: University of North Carolina Press.

Perry, Barbara. 1991. *A "Representative" Supreme Court?: The Impact of Race, Religion, and Gender on Appointments*. New York: Greenwood Press.

Perry, H. W. 1991. *Deciding to Decide*. Cambridge: Harvard University Press.

Perry, Michael J. 1982. *The Constituiton, the Courts, and Human Rights*. New Haven: Yale University Press.

Pertschuk, Michael. 1986. *Giant Killers*. New York: W. W. Norton.

Peterson, Paul E. 1995. "A Politically Correct Solution to Racial Classification." In *Classifying by Race*, ed. Paul E. Peterson. Princeton: Princeton University Press.

Phillips, Anne. 1995. *The Politics of Presence*. New York: The Clarendon Press, Oxford.

Pildes, Richard, and Richard Niemi. 1993. "Expressive Harms, 'Bizarre Districts,' and Voting Rights: Evaluating Election-district Appearances after Shaw." *Michigan Law Review* 92:483–587.

Pildes, Richard, Jamin Raskin, and Carol Swain. 1996. "Controversy." *American Prospect* 24 (Winter): 15–18.

Pitkin, Hanna. 1967. *The Concept of Representation*. Berkeley and Los Angeles: University of California Press.

Pocock, J. G. A. 1971. *Politics, Language, and Time*. New York: Atheneum.

———. 1975. *The Machiavellian Moment*. Princeton: Princeton University Press.

———. 1985. *Virtue, Commerce, and History*. New York: Cambridge University Press.

Polsby, Nelson, ed. 1971. *Reapportionment in the 1970s*. Berkeley and Los Angeles: University of California Press.

Purcell, Edward. 1973. *The Crisis of Democratic Theory*. Lexington: University Press of Kentucky.

Putnam, Robert, with Robert Leonardi and Raffaella Nanetti. 1993. *Making Democracy Work: Civic Traditions in Modern Italy*. Princeton: Princeton University Press.

Quinn, Naomi. 1991. "The Cultural Basis of Metaphor." In *Beyond Metaphor*, ed. James W. Fernandez. Stanford: Stanford University Press.

Quinn, Naomi, and Dorothy Holland. 1987. "Culture and Cognition." In *Cultural Models in Language and Thought*, ed. Naomi Quinn and Dorothy Holland. New York: Cambridge University Press.

Reich, Robert B. 1988. "Policy Making in a Democracy." In *The Power of Public Ideas*, ed. Robert B. Reich. Cambridge: Harvard University Press.

Reid, John Phillip. 1989. *The Concept of Representation in the Age of American Revolution*. Chicago: University of Chicago Press.

185

Rogers, Daniel T. 1987. *Contested Truths: Keywords in American Politics since Independence*. New York: Basic Books.

Rosen, Jeffery. 1996. "Southern Comfort." *New Republic*, Jan. 8, pp. 4, 49.

Rosenberg, Gerald. 1991. *The Hollow Hope: Can Courts Bring About Social Change?* Chicago: University of Chicago Press.

———. 1992. "Judicial Independence and the Reality of Political Power." *Review of Politics* 54:369–98.

Rush, Mark E. 1994. "In Search of a Coherent Theory of Voting Rights: Challenges to the Supreme Court's Vision of Fair and Effective Representation." *Review of Politics* 56:503–23.

Sanders, Lynn M. 1997. "Against Deliberation." *Political Theory* 25:347–76.

Scheppele, Kim Lane. 1988. *Legal Secrets*. Chicago: University of Chicago Press.

———. 1990. "Facing Facts in Legal Interpretation." *Representations* 30:42–77.

Schmitt, Carl. 1985. *The Crisis of Parliamentary Democracy*. Trans. Ellen Kennedy. Boston: MIT Press.

Schwartz, Nancy. 1988. *The Blue Guitar: Political Representation and Community*. Chicago: University of Chicago Press.

Segal, Jeffrey. 1984. "Predicting Supreme Court Cases Probabilistically: The Search and Seizure Cases, 1962–1981." *American Political Science Review*. 78:891–900.

Segal, Jeffrey A., and Harold J. Spaeth. 1993. *The Supreme Court and the Attitudinal Model*. New York: Cambridge University Press.

Shapiro, Ian. 1990. "Three Fallacies Concerning Majorities, Minorities, and Democratic Politics." In *Majorities and Minorities*, ed. John W. Chapman and Alan Wertheimer. New York: New York University Press.

Shapiro, Martin. 1964. *Law and Politics in the Supreme Court*. New York: Free Press.

———. 1981. *Courts: A Comparative and Political Analysis*. Chicago: University of Chicago Press.

———. 1983. "Recent Developments in Political Jurisprudence." *Western Political Quarterly* 36:541–48.

———. 1985. "Gerrymandering, Unfairness, and the Supreme Court." *UCLA Law Review* 33:227–56.

———. 1988. *Who Guards the Guardians?* Athens: University of Georgia Press.

———. 1989. "Political Jurisprudence, Public Law, and Post-consequentialist Ethics: Comments on Professors Barber and Smith." In *Studies in American Political Development*, ed. Karen Orren and Stephen Skowronek, vol. 3. New Haven: Yale University Press.

Shepsle, Kenneth A. 1992. "Congress Is a 'They' Not an 'It': Legislative Intent as an Oxymoron." *International Journal of Law and Economics* 12:239–56.

Shklar, Judith. 1991. *American Citizenship: The Quest for Inclusion*. Cambridge: Harvard University Press.

Silverstein, Gordon. 1994. "Statutory Interpretation and the Balance of Institutional Power." *Review of Politics* 56:475–500.

Skerry, Peter. 1993. *Mexican Americans: The Ambivalent Minority.* New York: Free Press.

Smith, Rogers M. 1985. *Liberalism and American Constitutional Law.* Cambridge: Harvard University Press.

———. 1988a. "The 'American Creed' and American Identity: The Limits of Liberal Citizenship in the United States." *Western Political Quarterly* 41: 225–51.

———. 1988b. "Political Jurisprudence, the 'New Institutionalism,' and the Future of Public Law." *American Political Science Review* 82:89–108.

———. 1989. "'One United People': Second-class Female Citizenship and the American Quest for Community." *Yale Journal of Law & the Humanities* 1:229–93.

———. 1993. "Beyond Tocqueville, Myrdal, and Hartz: The Multiple Traditions in America." *American Political Science Review* 87:549–66.

Still, Edward. 1991. "Voluntary Constituencies: Modified At-large Voting as a Remedy for Minority Vote Dilution in Judicial Elections." *Yale Law and Policy Review* 9:354–69.

Stimson, Shannon. 1990. *The American Revolution in the Law.* Princeton: Princeton University Press.

Strauss, David. 1996. "Affirmative Action and the Public Interest." *Supreme Court Review 1995*, pp. 1–44.

Strong, Tracy B. 1990. *The Idea of Political Theory.* Notre Dame: University of Notre Dame Press.

Stumpf, Harry. 1983. "The Recent Past." *Western Political Quarterly* 36:534–41.

Sullivan, Kathleen. 1986. "Sins of Discrimination: Last Term's Affirmative Action Cases." *Harvard Law Review* 100:78–98.

Sunstein, Cass. 1984. "Naked Preferences and the Constitution." *Columbia Law Review* 84:1689–1732.

———. 1987. "Lochner's Legacy." *Columbia Law Review* 87:873–919.

———. 1988. "Constitutions and Democracies." In *Constitutionalism and Democracy*, ed. Jon Elster and Rune Slagstad. New York: Cambridge University Press.

———. 1989. "Interpreting Statutes in the Regulatory State." *Harvard Law Review* 103:405–508.

———. 1990. "Political Self-Interest in Constitutional Law." In *Beyond Self-Interest*, ed. Jane Mansbridge. Chicago: University of Chicago Press.

———. 1993. *The Partial Constitution.* Cambridge: Harvard University Press.

———. 1994. "Voting Rites." *New Republic*, April 25, pp. 34–38.

———. 1996. *Legal Reasoning and Political Conflict.* New York: Oxford University Press.

187

Swain, Carol. 1992. "Some Consequences of the Voting Rights Act." In *Controversies in Minority Voting*, ed. Bernard Grofman and Chandler Davidson. Washington, D.C.: Brookings.

———. 1993. *Black Faces, Black Interests*. Cambridge: Harvard University Press.

———. 1995. "The Future of Black Representation." *American Prospect* 23 (Fall): 78–83.

Taylor, Charles. 1994. *Multiculturalism and "The Politics of Recognition."* Expanded paperback ed. Princeton: Princeton University Press.

Thernstrom, Abigail. 1987. *Whose Votes Count?* New York: Twentieth Century Fund.

Tocqueville, Alexis de. 1966. *Democracy in America*. Trans. George Lawrence. Ed. J. P. Mayer. New York: Harper & Row.

Tribe, Laurence. 1988. *American Constitutional Law*. 2d ed. Mineola, New York: The Foundation Press.

Truman, David. 1971. *The Governmental Process*. 2d ed. New York: Knopf.

Turner, James. 1992. "A Case-specific Approach to Implementing the Voting Rights Act." In *Controversies in Minority Voting*, ed. Bernard Grofman and Chandler Davidson. Washington, D.C.: Brookings.

Tushnet, Mark. 1988. "The Politics of Equality in Constitutional Law: The Equal Protection Clause, Dr. Du Bois, and Charles Hamilton Houston." In *The Constitution and American Life*, ed. David Thelen. Ithaca: Cornell University Press.

———. 1989. "Following the Rules Laid Down: A Critique of Interpretivism and Nuetral Principles." In *Critical Legal Studies*, ed. Alan C. Hutchinson. Totowa, N.J.: Rowman and Littlefield.

United States. 1937–. *United States Statutes at Large*. Washington, D.C.: GPO.

U.S. Commission on Civil Rights. 1965. *The Voting Rights Act . . . The First Months*. Washington, D.C.: GPO.

———. 1975. *The Voting Rights Act: Ten Years After*. Washington, D.C.: GPO.

———. 1981. *The Voting Rights Act: Unfulfilled Goals*. Washington, D.C.: GPO.

U.S. House of Representatives. 1992. *Voting Rights Language Assistance Act of 1992*. House Report 102-665, 102d Cong., 1st sess. Washington, D.C.: GPO.

U.S. Senate. 1982a. *Voting Rights Act Extension*. Report of the Committee on the Judiciary. No. J-97–92, 97th Cong., 2d sess. GPO.

———. 1982b. *Voting Rights Act*. Report of the Subcommittee on the Constitution. 97th Cong., 2d sess. GPO.

Walzer, Michael. 1983. *Spheres of Justice*. New York: Basic Books.

Wells, David. 1982. "Against Affirmative Gerrymandering." In *Representation and Redistricting Issues*, ed. Bernard Grofman, Arend Lijphart, Robert McCay, and Howard Scarrow. Lexington, Mass.: D. C. Heath.

White, James Boyd. 1973. *The Legal Imagination*. Boston: Little, Brown.

———. 1984. *When Words Lose Their Meaning*. Chicago: University of Chicago Press.

———. 1985. *Heracles' Bow*. Madison: University of Wisconsin Press.

———. 1990. *Justice as Translation*. Chicago: University of Chicago Press.

Williams, Melissa. 1992. "Memory, History, and Membership: The Moral Claims of Marginalized Groups in American Political Representation." Paper presented at the Annual Meeting of the American Political Science Association, Chicago, Sept. 3–6.

———. 1995. "Justice Toward Groups: Political Not Juridical." *Political Theory* 23:67–91.

Wolin, Sheldon. 1989. *The Presence of the Past*. Baltimore: Johns Hopkins University Press.

———. 1993. "Democracy, Difference, and Re-Cognition." *Political Theory* 21:464–83.

Wood, Gordon. 1969. *The Creation of the American Republic, 1776–1787*. Chapel Hill: University of North Carolina Press.

Woodward, Vann C. 1974. *The Strange Career of Jim Crow*. 3d revised ed. New York: Oxford University Press.

Young, Iris Marion. 1989. "Polity and Group Difference: A Critique of the Ideal of Universal Citizenship." *Ethics* 99:250–74.

———. 1990. *Justice and the Politics of Difference*. Princeton: Princeton University Press.

Zagarri, Rosemarie. 1987. *The Politics of Size: Representation in the United States, 1776–1850*. Ithaca: Cornell University Press.

Index

ABOUT THE AUTHOR

Keith J. Bybee is Assistant Professor of Government at Harvard University.